ROBERT A. LEWIS has published many articles and chapters in books on male sex role socialization and on fathers and children. He was coordinator of the Second National Conference on Men and Masculinity in 1976.

Robert A. Lewis, editor

MEN IN DIFFICULT TIMES

Masculinity Today and Tomorrow

A SPECTRUM BOOK

Prentice-Hall, Inc., Englewood Cliffs, New Jersey 07632

Library of Congress Cataloging in Publication Data
Main entry under title:

Men in difficult times.

    (A Spectrum Book)
    Includes bibliographies and index.
    1. Men—Psychology—Addresses, essays, lectures.
2. Sex role—Addresses, essays, lectures.
3. Social role—Addresses, essays, lectures.

I. Lewis, Robert A., 1932–
HQ1090.M43   305.3   80-27760
ISBN 0-13-547718-0
ISBN 0-13-574400-8 (pbk.)

Special thanks to the following photographers for photographs depicting men in difficult times: Phillip I. Danzig for "Men's Conference, New Jersey, 1975," "Getting the Message Across in Song," and "Sharing"; to David P. Lewis for "Into Oblivion," "Self Suppression," "Ending It All," "Dressing for Sexual Identity II," "A Question of Custody," "Demonstration," "Motivating," "Imitation," "Explanation," "One Egg or Two?," "Housespouse," "Even Daddies Get Sick," "What's Good for the Gander . . . ", "Helping," "An Opportunity to Share," "You've Got the Hang of It Now," "This Wire Must Go Here," "Dad, I Didn't Know Work Can Be Fun," "If We Both Lift Together . . . "; and to William Lloyd Bennett for "Dressing for Sexual Identity I," "Hugging," "Caring," and "A Men's Support Group, State College, Pennsylvania, 1976."

© 1981 by Prentice-Hall, Inc., Englewood Cliffs, New Jersey 07632

A SPECTRUM BOOK

10   9   8   7   6   5   4   3   2   1

Printed in the United States of America

Editorial/Production supervision by Suse Cioffi and Frank Moorman
Interior design by Suse Cioffi
Cover design by Honi Werner
Manufacturing buyer: Cathie Lenard

PRENTICE-HALL INTERNATIONAL, INC., *London*
PRENTICE-HALL OF AUSTRALIA PTY. LIMITED, *Sydney*
PRENTICE-HALL OF CANADA, LTD., *Toronto*
PRENTICE-HALL OF INDIA PRIVATE LIMITED, *New Delhi*
PRENTICE-HALL OF JAPAN, INC., *Tokyo*
PRENTICE-HALL OF SOUTHEAST ASIA PTE. LTD., *Singapore*
WHITEHALL BOOKS LIMITED, *Wellington, New Zealand*

Contents

RESOURCES FOR CHANGE IN MALES

Foreword

JESSIE BERNARD

In the last chapter of this important book, Donald Bell traces the history of the sex-role models that have characterized industrial society since the end of the eighteenth century, a history that is essential for understanding what this book is all about. At that time industrialization began to separate the worlds of men and women, consigning men to the increasingly harsh world of the new industrial order, whose brutality came to be intensified with the rugged individualism rationalized by Darwinian social theory. The male world was a dog-eat-dog one in which, as Robert Ringer to this day teaches, you won by intimidation, you looked after Number One. Winning was the name-of-the-game. It was a world in which every man's hand was against every other man. It was tolerable only because there were women in the home to supply the needed emotional support for survival in that outside world. The home was the sphere of women, and "heart" was its function. Women endowed men with the self-image their life outside kept tearing down. The new industrial order may have been congenial to the robber barons and the industrial tycoons, but millions of men suffered. In more ways than one.

Not until the last third of the twentieth century when, as Bell reminds us, the old industrial society was giving way before the new service-oriented society, did the emotional support women had supplied men until then become problematic. Only then did men begin to become acutely aware of the barrenness of their lives without it. Some men began to blame women for loss of potency. Not the men represented in this book: They began to see that in the new order they could no longer expect as a matter of course to receive emotional support from women without reciprocity. They began to see, as women had in the nineteenth century, that they would have to look to one another in the way of such emotional support. Schooled almost from infancy in the machismo role—so vividly reported in this book—they would have to learn how to overcome its damaging constrictions. They would have to resocialize one another. This book describes how they have tried to do this, the roadblocks they have had to overcome, the "worlds of pain" they have had to endure.

They do not ask women to do this for them. In the past it was taken for granted that, of course, women could be counted on to drop whatever they were doing and serve men in dealing with whatever problems they were confronting. Abolition, reform, war, whatever movement men were engaged in, women were expected in one form or another to help them. The men represented in this book do not expect such help. They seem to recognize that this is a do-it-youself effort, that not until both sexes have freed themselves from artificial dependencies—economic on one side and exploitative on the other—can they achieve the creative mutual inter-dependence which rests on true equality. I honor their efforts and wish them well.

Introduction

We are all around you.

We often touch the periphery of your life . . . and sometimes the core. And yet you may never recognize fully who we are.

One of us is a businessman, impeccably dressed, seated next to you on the train, the plane, or the subway. He makes no sound. There is no nod or smile. You do not know his pain. You do not know his fears of growing older, of death, even of living each day.

One of us is your buddy, nineteen years on the job next to you. The two of you have often spoken together, sharing bits and pieces about your lives—the wife, the kids, your bike, his camper—but never acknowledging the long silences between you.

Another of us is your lover or spouse who lies beside you at night and yet to you is a stranger still in so many ways.

We surround you, yet you may not really know us, because we are men in difficult times.

We are unemployed men, too proud to take just anything, and afraid of not taking something, soon. We are men who have just gone through the last retchings of a divorce or a separation from someone who became a sudden stranger to us. We are men boxed into a job, a career, from which there seems to be no way out, except into the sameness of each morning, and each afternoon, until we could scream.

These are difficult times for us, since men too are experiencing major transitions in their lives. Some of these men have written recently about their critical transitions. Jerry Rubin, who as a youth once led the Yippies, is now a "rebel without a cause" and *Growing (Up) at 37*. He documents the grief he has found in life changes, and we know that he too is a man in difficult times. Charles Reich in *The Sorcerer of Bolinas Reef* has recently charted the three stages of his life and the transitions between. We know him too, since many of the pieces of his life we have lived ourselves, in another body, another time, another place.

You ask, what do these men have in common? Not all of them, but many, are questioning the traditional values of our society which say a real man must be ... super cool, a stud, a leader of men and a seducer of women. And yet, most of us have never quite measured up to all these ideals. We have fallen short somewhere. Besides, we no longer believe in all these things. The world about us is changing. Our women have been changing ahead of us. And we are changing too, mostly in reaction as the shadow follows the player. We have been socialized into believing that there are only a few ways to be a man. But these old ways do not always work. New ways are needed to solve our problems. New integrations. Syntheses.

Some of us are learning how to break out of traditional molds laid out for men at a time when life was less complex, when few questioned tradition. Now our roles hurt us and those about us. We are, therefore, slowly learning how to build different types of relationships with women, other men and children. And we feel good about these changes.

I, myself, have been married 24 years to a loving and strong woman, who has helped me to evolve gradually over the years. She herself has changed greatly, from a wife and mother of two sons to a professional woman with a Ph.D. I, too, have changed—from a predictable chauvinist to a less predictable, more sensitive, questioning and whole person. I, too, have gone through many transitions in my life; the last one occurred only four years ago. Our first son left home. From that time I began to question the value of "all work and no play," the role constraints which keep me and other men from caring for children and ourselves, and the societal structures which thwart my humanness.

This book was conceived nearly three years ago in the minds of some men and women who participated in the Second National Conference on Men and Masculinity at State College, Pennsylvania. The development and labor pains, however, have continued until this day, on which many of my colleagues, sisters, brothers and I have finally brought these pages to full term.

This quest has driven me to take a leave of absence from work, to cross this continental USA numerous times and the Atlantic twice, so that I could talk with ordinary as well as prominent members of the silent majority of men who are in difficult times. I therefore have talked with bellboys, mill workers, artists, cowboys, teachers, and high court judges. From them I have learned the sources of their personal anguish, their perplexities and their confusions. Many of them have written their own stories and thoughts in these pages. Some of them have helped me dream about another world which could be, a world of brotherhood and sister-hood . . . of personhood. Some of the articles in this book convey these dreams and visions.

To me, one thing is very clear. Men *are* in difficult times and they *must* change. But to what? Women can tell us men what *they* want from us, and some of them do. Yet none of them can tell us what *we* should want in ourselves and our relationships. Women have the right today to remind us about what unfair and unloving automatons we men have become. How-ever, few of us are going to change because of this. More of us will change, if we are challenged to give up our sexist ways, if we are reinforced for the things we do inwardly to grow, and if we are supported for the positive efforts we make to change our environment in more egalitarian ways.

ACKNOWLEDGMENTS

My profound gratitude is directed to all those men and women who had such concerns for men (and women) that they have written the essays, papers, poems, and autobiographical accounts which make up this book. Many of these writers are those most responsible for my own personal growth and awareness. Therefore, it is to them that I dedicate this book.

I owe this book, however, to James Nelson, our informal editor, who went beyond the ordinary tasks which fall to such persons. He not only has maintained a continual correspondence which I had begun with the authors and edited most of the copy, but he also located new sources of persons and materials and thereby kept alive the pulse of these pages, when I was necessarily separated from them.

I consecrate this book to my wife, Kathy, from whom many years ago I took away some of her personhood by taking away her name. Without her constant support and encouragement, however, I would never have found my way through life or to the pages of this book. To our two sons, Craig and David, I bequeath this book. Not all of its words and phrases will now mean as much as it may mean someday in their lives. However, I hope that their reading of this book may prevent them from having to make some of the same errors in their lives that I did in mine. To my father, Laurence, and mother, Lois, who this year celebrated their fiftieth anniversary, I extend my thanks for their nurturing me through my lifetime. To my brother, Dick, and my sisters, Diane and Shari, I promise in the next years of my life to continue the development we have experienced as adult friends. To my mentor in men's issues, Joe Pleck, my friends, and my loved ones, I offer this book as a small but real part of my life. Through the reading of these pages I hope they may come to know me even better. Finally, a word of deep appreciation for those who typed many of the pages of this manuscript: Patricia Maas, Dottie DeWitt, Patricia Bruchman, John Darling, Sylvia Pauley Nelson, and Teresa Griffis.

Robert A. Lewis

Men in Difficult Times

Joe went and played the heavy, left Judy at
  twenty-nine
"Who is she, is she younger?" he hears it all
  the time
He felt trapped and going nowhere, he tries to
  explain
But he's supposed to be free and have it all,
  no one believes his pain

Chorus:

Men in difficult times
Often trapped with nowhere to turn
Men in difficult times
When choosing not to play the parts they've
  learned

Steve was in construction, loved working with his
  hands
Satisfied not moving up, his boss couldn't under-
  stand
Steve, there's something wrong here, the world
  will pass you by
Think of your future, and Steve would only smile

Chuck is feeling lonely, Bill is out of town
They've been together just a year, but it's the
  best love that he's found
Straight friends smile and listen, when he talks
  of his plans
They're tolerantly waiting till he's like them again

Paul went into court, sure the times have changed
But would he get joint custody, depended on two
  things
The court still had the power, a judge might not
  understand
Susan was still the mother, and he was just a
  man

GEOF MORGAN

part one

THE HIGH COSTS OF TRADITIONAL MALE ROLES

Dressing for Sexual Identity:
Two Styles

Into Oblivion . . .

A Question of Custody

THE HIGH COSTS OF TRADITIONAL MALE ROLES

Ending It All

Self Suppression

The burgeoning interest recently in male and female sex roles has again revitalized the drawing of comparisons between the life expectancy of males and females in the United States and possible reasons for the 7.8 years by which women now outlive men. This 17 percent shorter life expectancy for men is due in part to higher rates of strokes, heart attacks and lung cancer among males, to a higher rate of suicide (three times more), and to a greater proclivity to alcoholism (five times more) and mental illnesses (except for depression). According to Harrison (1978), "a higher perinatal and early childhood death rate, a higher rate of congenital birth defects, a greater vulnerability to recessive sex-linked disorders, a higher accident rate for males during childhood and all subsequent ages, a higher incidence of behavioral and learning disorders, a higher suicide rate, and a higher metabolism rate . . . [may be partly explained by] the psychosocial perspective that sex-role *socialization* accounts for the larger part of men's shorter life expectancy" (p. 65).

The intent of these contrasts and the articles which follow in Part One of this book, however, is not to argue that men have a worse lot in life than women, since one can also make a case that men as a group are still a "privileged class." The purpose of this section is rather to probe some of the ways in which men have "difficult times," due in large part to the pressures and constraints of traditional male roles.

Verser, for instance, in "Strokes and Strokes: Men and Competition" provides an analysis of the ways in which men are socialized into being competitive and how competing to always win is intricately wrapped up in men wanting to be seen as masculine. The central thrust of this article is the thesis that learning to be competitive eventually drives men into emotional alienation from each other. Therefore, instead of teaching men to always compete until they get a stroke or heart attack, men could be trained to give positive "strokes" to themselves and others. This theme is carried also through the second half of the article by means of a description of a workshop on "stroking exercises" which the author has conducted for various groups of men.

Liss-Levinson in an article on playfulness argues that traditional sex-role stereotypes have brought men to the "pits" of the work-ethic. That is, sex as work drives men to less creativity, less intimacy, and less personal sex. Sports as work fosters violence on and off the field. Parenting as work causes children to see that fathers should not be fun or nurturant. Employment as work condemns less fortunate men into seeing themselves as failures in life, as, for example, unemployed men. Liss-Levinson's indictment is brutal: Most American men are in difficult times because they are unable to be playful.

Most males are not only unable to play or have many meaningful relationships, but they also stand to lose some of those vital relationships which they have built. One case in point is the fact that the legal system in the United States outrightly rejects joint custody of children in most cases of divorce, and concomitantly fathers usually lose the legal custody of their children. One article in this section is an account of the personal experiences of a father who lost the legal custody of his two children. Dworkin's autobiographical account of his custody battle, his loss, loneliness, depression and financial pressures is not only a reminder of the difficult times that some divorced fathers experience in our society but also of the inequalities in a legal system which prevent some men from being evaluated as individuals.

Mental illnesses occur among males with greater frequency than among females. Yet, according to Ettkin, the greatest "madness of men" is their inability to ask for and to receive psychotherapy. "Men experience their share of pain," writes Ettkin, "if mental illness is defined as 'the stunting and crippling of full humanness.'" What is to blame for this invidious situation? Traditional ideals of masculinity, Ettkin writes, result in the inability of most males to relate to other persons in intense closeness. As a result, men become even more captives of the rigid male stereotypes which lead men to illness, physically and mentally.

In another article within this section, Rosenberg and Farrell address some of the outcomes for middle-aged men of our societal emphasis upon youthful strength and toughness. Somewhere between one third to one half of all men these authors have studied experienced depression, despair and confusion about themselves somewhere between the ages of 39 and 43. The mid-life crisis (or male menopause) is experienced as changes in feelings, behavior changes, unsubstantiated concerns about illness, death and disability, and emotional withdrawal from friends, family and work. These symptoms of distress are rigidly denied by many of the men, except for working-class men, who project their distress upon their work situation or other persons. The prognosis for effective recovery from this syndrome is not optimistic, since most of the middle-aged men will probably languish in their difficult times for much of their lives, as they "resort to denial, interpersonal withdrawal and manic activity as modes of ego defense."

Strokes and Strokes: Men and Competition

JAMES VERSER

Floating around is a quote from Vince Lombardi, acknowledged as one of the greatest coaches of all time, "Winning isn't everything. It's the only thing." The idea of competing to win is intricately wrapped up in being "masculine." Men are perceived both by themselves and by women as being competitive. Some men and most women complain that this competitiveness is destructive to human relationships. But how do men become competitive? This essay will explore the nature of competition, competitiveness in men and how we were socialized to become competitive. An underlying idea of this paper is that training in competitiveness helps men behave in superficially connected, intimate ways (male bonding) while it actually drives them to relate in emotionally separated, alienated ways.

THE NATURE OF COMPETITION

Competition is based on a scarcity of resources. Since there is an insufficient supply, tangible or perceived, of the resources necessary to meet my needs, I must fight to survive. In order to achieve my needs I must achieve a superior position, thereby dominating them and getting my needs met. To be inferior is intolerable, so I must be constantly on guard to maintain my superior position (Steiner, 1973:7). My success thwarts the success of others (Social Science Research Council, 1937:14).

What are some of the consequences of competition? As long as we live in a society where scarcity exists, then competition may be an essential mode for survival. But when scarcity is no longer real (as in the United States), then competition actually creates scarcity.

The hoarding behavior which goes along with competitiveness causes certain people to have a great deal more than they truly need while large numbers of others, who could be satisfied with the surplus of those few who have, go without. Competitive, hoarding behavior is based on unrealistic anxiety based on fears of scarcity. Oppressive as he is to others, the hoarder is himself oppressed by it (Steiner, 1973:7).

The hoax of the whole process is that we are taught that competitiveness will free us and get us the resources to meet our needs.

Another consequence of competition is the feeling of being superior or inferior, and the resulting feeling of separateness.

Whatever the form of competition—whether the rivalries of the stock market or a contest for political leadership—the emotional consequences of winning and losing remain the same. The winner experiences an immediate rise in ego level, a thrill of elation which he inevitably communicates to others through an increase in assertiveness and self-confidence. The loser is overcome with despondency. His social behavior becomes more than usually inhibited and he may withdraw altogether from social relationships (Maclay and Knipe, 1972:61–62).

This separateness is especially encouraged in athletic competitiveness, where the opponent is often dehumanized and stereotyped (Bach and Goldberg, 1974:132). Just recall the many coaches and/or television commentators who talk of killing, mauling or trouncing the opponent.

One of the primary ways men are taught to be competitive is through athletics. Ideally athletic competition does not emphasize winning but finding an opponent of equal ability against which to test one's own ability. *Compete* comes from "com - petere" which means to strive together (Social Science Research Council, 1937:14). To compete, then, should be a mutual striving in order to possibly learn more about oneself. "The claim of competitive athletics to importance rests squarely on their providing for us opportunities for self-discovery which might otherwise have been missed. . . . To stress victory to the point of overlooking quality of performance is to improvise our sense of success in competitive athletics" (Delattre, 1975:135, 138). This kind of competition can promote connectedness, but in reality most athletic competition emphasizes winning and separateness.

COMPETITIVENESS IN MEN

One does not have to look very far to find the emphasis on competition and winning in men, especially in athletics. The goal, of course, is the winner's trophy (Havemann, 1973:42–49). Sports fans throw coins, cans, bottles, chairs and other objects at losing players and umpires (*Newsweek,* June 17, 1974:93–94). College coaches cheat in recruiting, trying to get the best players so they can win (Starnes, 1974). Parents help young boys cheat so they can win the Soap Box Derby (*Newsweek,* Sept. 3, 1973:59–60). When Gerald Ford was Vice-President, he wrote an article in which he said, "It is not enough just to compete. Winning is very important. Maybe more important than ever" (1974:17).

In our culture successful athletes (winners) are folk heroes. They get their pictures on bubble gum cards, and any boy worth his salt will have a fine collection of such cards. It was always very frustrating to have fifteen "Moose" Skowrons (who?) and no Mickey Mantles.

In the last three years, I have conducted a number of male awareness workshops for men (and sometimes women, too). I often have the participants make a list of the characteristics of what it means to be male. From 14 to 70, they always include and emphasize "competitive," "winners," "strong," "athletic," "better than women."

SOCIALIZATION INTO COMPETITION

I would now like to turn to the question of how men are taught to compete, to win. Therefore, I will present three related ideas which have some support and then present the theory of *stroking* (from transactional analysis theory) and indicate how it offers an understanding of competition.

First Idea: Winning a Fight

The first idea comes from George Bach and his work with aggression and anger (Bach and Goldberg, 1974). Bach says that most people do not know how to fight fair and to constructively rid themselves of their angry, aggressive feelings. We have the misconception that interpersonal arguments must be won, that nothing is settled unless one person comes out the winner. Children observe their parents fighting and quickly learn that one of them always wins; therefore, it becomes important in life to win, to be superior. Rather than allowing for a full release of the anger with no desire to win, we often harness our emotional power to annihilate the partner.

Second Idea: Indirect Socialization

Another idea is that boys are taught indirectly, rather than directly, to be masculine. This usually occurs when boys are told what *not* to do or be rather than what to do or be. For example, boys are told not to be "sissy," not to be feminine, not to cry like a girl, not to lose. Only if they actually get into athletics are they exhorted to be men and win. In addition, the absence of a boy's father forces him to learn male behavior on a trial-and-error basis, from his peers and from cultural heroes, often bubble-gum-card athletes (Hartley, 1959:457–468, athletic emphasis mine; see also Bigner, 1970:357–362, on the absence of the father).

Third Idea: Winning in Relationships

While boys learn to compete to win overtly in athletics, they do not also learn that the desire to win should remain in athletic endeavors. In other words, the desire to win bleeds over into relationships, inhibiting the ability to relate equally and honestly.

Since competition depends upon some vague comprehension of the other person's wants, and a desire to get ahead of him, the pattern of its growth is determined to a large degree by forces making for general social awareness; and affection or hostility towards the competitor profoundly affects the whole development.

Habits of competing are, nevertheless, carried over from one situation to another, often rather blindly; and in some individuals the competitive habits are so deeply ingrained that they may manifest themselves even to the detriment of the individual who could obtain his ends better by other means (Social Science Research Council, 1937:3–4).

At the basis of competitive programming is fear, particularly fear of scarcity. . . . The result is that men often think that they are protecting themselves, or taking care of themselves, by competing. This is particularly clear in terms of men not expressing their ideas or feelings. Men are taught to watch out for everyone, especially other men, because if "someone gets to know something on you, it will be used against you." The idea is not to trust anyone and not to show feelings because if a person trusts or shows his feelings, then he is (1) weak, and (2) the means through which people get manipulated (DeGolia, 1973:16).

Strokes

These are some examples of the kinds of pressures that men are under as they grow up. What dynamics in child rearing make us vulnerable to giving in to these pressures, and do these dynamics reinforce these pressures in later life? The concept of stroking is a great help in understanding these dynamics.

Every human being has certain basic human needs which must be met if he or she is to survive in this world. The ones most commonly mentioned are food, shelter and water. But there is another one which is just as basic, and its absence can cause death—that need is human interaction, human recognition, love. Lack of human interaction can produce a person with a poor sense of self and tragic outlook on life that can lead to suicide. Studies of foundling homes, where only the minimum basic necessities are provided, indicate that most of the children are withdrawn and have extreme difficulty in relating to the world. This is primarily because they were raised in a "recognition-hunger" environment, a place where strokes were passed out only sparingly. Therefore, a basic need for all people is to be recognized.

. . . "stroking" may be employed colloquially to denote any act implying recognition of another's presence. Hence, a stroke may be used as a fundamental unit of social action. An exchange of strokes constitutes a transaction, which is the unit of social intercourse (Berne, 1964:15).

Strokes are the means by which we satisfy human psychological needs. Positive strokes are healthy and life giving; they help us to know that we are acceptable people. Negative strokes are unhealthy and force us to conclude that we are bad and unworthy. Nonetheless, negative strokes are preferred over no strokes, over non-recognition as a human being. For example, if my daughter comes up to me and says, "Daddy, let me tell you what I did in school today," she is asking me to recognize her existence in the world. If I do not respond, she might go away or she might start yelling, which then might prompt me to give her a negative stroke by scolding her. But for her it is better to be scolded than to be ignored. Or, if I had told her to go away because I was reading (and assuming that I did that frequently), she might kick the dog, call her sister a name or engage in some other form of misbehavior designed to get strokes, any kind, from me. In other words, if I refuse to give her positive strokes, she will do her best to get negative strokes. A beating is emotionally more reassuring than non-recognition; a beating at least says, "I know you exist."

Claude Steiner (1974:131–140) has observed what he calls *stroke economy*. As we grow, we learn from our parents certain stroking patterns, certain ways in which our psychological needs can be met. These patterns are most often based upon the assumption that there are only a limited number of strokes available. Rather than being taught that each of us has the capacity to stroke and love endlessly, we are taught to stroke and love very selectively. In other words, I did not learn to be loving toward everybody, but only to special people—parents, siblings, spouses, children, and a few friends. Not only that, even with these few people I learned not to give and receive strokes openly; rather, I learned to compete and manipulate based on the assumption that since there are not enough strokes to go around, I have to be sneaky to get any at all.

Steiner has observed five rules in this stroke economy; using these rules we set up an artificial scarcity of stroking and loving. Rather than summarize, I will quote at length.

1. Don't give strokes *if you have them to give. This injunction . . . simply means that people are enjoined against freely giving of their loving feelings.*

2. Don't ask for strokes *when you need them. Again, this injunction is . . . probably the one that is most thoroughly taught to people.*

3. Don't accept strokes *if you want them. This injunction is not as common as the two above. When present it prevents people from accepting the strokes that are given them even when they are wanted.*

4. Don't reject strokes *when you don't want them. Frequently people are given strokes which, for one reason or another, don't feel good or are not wanted. As an example, women who are "media" beauties . . . have the experience of being constantly stroked for their "beauty." It is common for such women, especially after many years of receiving these strokes, to begin to resent them. . . . Women who have these feelings rarely, if ever, have permission to reject those strokes. . . .*

5. Don't give yourself strokes. *Self-Stroking, or . . . "Bragging," is enjoined against. Children are taught that "modesty is the best policy" and that self-praise and self-love are in some way sinful, shameful, and wrong (Steiner, 1974:137–140).*

These five rules are the enforcers of the stroke economy which everybody learns and carries around in his head. The free exchange of strokes is severely limited by these rules, guaranteeing that people will be stroke-starved. The end result is that the capacity to love is thwarted, leaving people vulnerable and weak.

With this basic training in sneaky stroking, it becomes clear why men are so vulnerable to competitive training. The stroke economy is based on the creation of scarcity, namely the lie that there are not enough strokes to go around. Because I must compete for strokes, because I am afraid that I will not get any (leading to my death), I am constantly fighting to be in a superior position so I will be sure to get my strokes. The insidious thing is that the stroke economy ensures that I will never get enough so that I will be forced to continue to strive and compete for my superior position, hoping that it will ensure my stroking needs. In addition, we have created within our culture a glut of artificial scarcities—grades, TVs, first in class, first in the league, championships, presidents—which keeps us competing.

Since a main form of winning is exploiting the opponent's weaknesses, men close themselves off from each other so that we do not expose any vulnerabilities. We are raised on the stroke economy, and then we are exposed to athletic, competitive winning. We men wind up losing all the way around. In terms of separateness and connectedness, we can come together on the field of competition (ballfield, boardroom, classroom), but in our striving to win, we eliminate the possibility of really being connected, of really caring, of stroking and being stroked, of loving and being loved.

CONNECTING BY STROKING: THE SENSUOUSNESS OF THE MALE BODY

The foregoing discussion focused on psychological stroking, but that is not the only kind of stroking that is necessary for human existence. Physical stroking—touching—is just as necessary. Studies have shown that babies who do not receive sufficient physical attention develop a deformity called *marasmus,* which is a slow wasting away, sometimes accompanied by a shriveling of the spine. Therefore, it seems that physical touching is a primary biological need.

Men, in their tendency to isolate themselves from others, cut themselves off from a large amount of touching, especially from other men; therefore, we reduce the possible sources of obtaining a basic necessity. In addition, we become unaware of the joys and pleasures that come from hugging a male friend or feeling free to reach out and touch him in a gesture of closeness. The reasons for this "uptightness" are legion, but they lie mainly in fear—the fear of what it means to be close to another man.

Overcoming this fear is important if we are able to learn noncompetitive ways of relating and if we are to allow ourselves to get closer to other men. I have found that group experiences are often very beneficial in assisting people in facing their fears and working through them. What follows is a detailed description of a workshop experience that I first designed for the Second National Conference on Men and Masculinity at State College, Pennsylvania, in August of 1976, and have conducted several times since. It is a group experience that allows and encourages feelings to be expressed and touching to occur. The purpose is to explore the sensuousness (that is, the physically pleasurable but not necessarily sexual) aspects of the male body, to deal with our fears and blocks about touching and to achieve a higher degree of comfort with our own bodies as well as those of other men. I believe it is in a form that can be easily used and adapted by other men.

INTRODUCTION (5 minutes) Make an opening statement about the purpose of the workshop.

I shared some of the thoughts that are contained in the above paragraphs, plus some comments that were pertinent to the men who were present.

CONCENTRIC CIRCLES (15 minutes)

Two concentric circles are formed so that each man has a partner. It is important to allow a few seconds for the partners to say hello and to discover names. The exercise works as follows: A question is asked or a statement is read, and the partners respond to each other for approximately 30 seconds each. At the end of the minute, the men in the outside (or inside) circle move one man to the left so that each man has a new partner. This procedure continues until all the questions and statements have been read and responded to. This exercise is excellent to use at the beginning because it has a low threat level, and it allows everyone to be involved. Following are the questions I used, although any that seem better or more appropriate can be substituted.

1. The activity that I most often engage in with men is . . .

2. The characteristics of the man I am closest to are . . .

3. What kind of physical attention that is not sexual do you like to receive and from whom?

4. List four things you like about your body.

5. What standards of beauty do you look for in other men?

6. What standards of beauty do you look for in yourself?

7. (This last question is purely for fun.) Take a step back from your partner. You now have about one minute to look at your partner. (Give various kinds of instructions to encourage them to look over their partner well.) Now, take a step back toward your partner and tell him . . . (slowly and with dramatic emphasis) . . . exactly . . . what your favorite . . . flavor of ice cream is. (The laughter and disbelief that normally follows this question releases a lot of tension.)

RANDOM SELECTION (5 minutes)

In some random manner, divide the men into groups with four members each. One method of random selection follows: Count the number of men and divide by four. This will give you the number of groups. Then have the men count off by that number and then find the other men with that number. For example, if there were forty men, there would be ten groups. After counting off by tens, the ones find each other, the twos find each other, and so on. The confusion accompanying the locating of one's group uses up even more nervous energy and further relaxes the men. Take a minute or two for the men to learn something about their group members.

SELF-EXPLORATION (10 minutes)

This exercise is designed to help each man get in touch with his own body. The men are asked to remove their shirts and shoes and socks (if there is sufficient privacy and willingness, this exercise could be done nude). After finding their own space, the men are instructed to do this exercise non-verbally. With eyes closed, and using his hands, each man slowly explores as much of his body as he can, making mental notes of things he had never noticed before. Three or four minutes are allowed for this exploration, ending with each man sitting motionless and meditating upon the experience for a minute.

The exercise is then repeated with the eyes open, and again ends with meditation.

SMALL-GROUP DISCUSSION (15 minutes)

The men return to their small groups and share their feelings and responses to their own bodies. Questions can be asked to stimulate discussion. For example: What hindered or helped you in touching yourself? How do you feel about touching yourself? What internal messages could you hear while doing the exercise?

PARTNER EXPLORATION (20 to 30 minutes)

Each man gets a partner who is *not* in his small group. After greeting each other, the men take some time to slowly look at their partner. This exercise is also done non-verbally. After the visual exploration is completed, the men close their eyes and simultaneously explore each other's hands. After a minute they open their eyes and explore hands. Next, they close their eyes and explore each other's heads, faces and shoulders, followed by the same exploration with their eyes open. If the group has been together for some time and a high trust level is present, further exploration of the partner's body could be attempted.

Now comes the best part. Continuing non-verbal communication, have one partner be receiver and the other the giver. Supply copious amounts of baby oil and paper towels and have the men do foot massages. After about five minutes, have the partners switch. Give whatever instructions seem appropriate, such as cover the whole foot; press firmly, even hard; use plenty of oil; pull the toes; use the heel of your hand and your thumbs on the arch. The foot massage is incredibly relaxing.

When the foot massage is over, have the partners sit facing each other so that their knees touch. Give each man time to contemplate himself so that he can get in touch with his own feelings and thoughts. Then give the men time to share their experience.

SMALL GROUPS (15 minutes)

The men return to their small groups to share their experience. Discussion can be assisted, if needed, by repeating the questions asked in the other small group.

GOODBYE CIRCLE (3 to 5 minutes)

Have all the men form one big circle. In order to get in touch with vocal sensuality, choose a word for the men to say very softly and then slowly increase in volume until everyone is yelling at the top of his voice. Since I like affirmations, we used the word *yes*. When the men are yelling yes the loudest, yell out for everyone to try to get into the center of the circle. The resulting hustle, bumping, shoving, loving confusion is the final sensual experience of the exercise. After a few minutes everyone gets tired, so the group breaks up and men wander off talking with new friends and putting their clothes back on.

Since I was leading and not experiencing, somewhere toward the end I asked for a foot massage. Later, I received my foot massage and floated through the rest of the day. Oh, the joys of the male body!

CONCLUSION

Most of us have had a coach in our lives who made us winners, and we have been competing ever since. Yet in our constant striving for success and victory, we have shut others out of our lives. Understanding who we are and the whys and hows of our competing will not automatically change us into loving, non-competitive men. But perhaps a little understanding of who we have been will help us to take the risk of reaching out to our brothers (and sisters, too), of touching one another where we are vulnerable, where we hurt, and to find the closeness of non-competitive relationships. Writing this has been more than an intellectual exercise for me, and I hope you will make it more than an intellectual exercise for you by conducting your own touching experience with some of your male friends. Stroke one another and be friends.

References

BACH, GEORGE R., and HERB GOLDBERG
   1974 *Creative Aggression.* New York: Avon Books.
BERNE, ERIC
   1964 *Games People Play: The Psychology of Human Relationships.* New York: Grove Press, Inc.
BIGNER, JERRY J.
   1970 "Fathering: Research and Practice." *The Family Coordinator* 19 (Oct.): 357–362.
DEGOLIA, RICK
   1973 "Thoughts on Men's Oppression." *Issues in Radical Therapy* 1 (Sum): 14–17.
DELATTRE, EDWIN J.
   1975 "Some Reflections on Success and Failure in Competitive Athletics." *Journal of the Philosophy of Sport* 2 (Sept.): 133–139.
FORD, GERALD R., WITH JOHN UNDERWOOD
   1974 "In Defense of the Competitive Urge." *Sports Illustrated,* July 8: 16–23.
HARTLEY, RUTH E.
   1959 "Sex Role Pressures in the Socialization of the Male Child." *Psychological Reports* 5: 457–468. Reprinted in Joseph H. Pleck and Jack Sawyer. *Men and Masculinity.* Englewood Cliffs, N.J.: Prentice-Hall, 1974: 7–13.
HAVEMANN, ERNEST
   1973 "Down Will Come Baby, Cycle and All." *Sports Illustrated* 39 (Aug. 13): 42–49.
MACLAY, GEORGE, AND HUMPHREY KNIPE
   1972 *The Dominant Man: The Pecking Order in Human Society.* New York: Delacorte Press.
NEWSWEEK
   1973 "99 and 44/100% Pure?" *Newsweek,* Sept. 3: 59–60.

———
1974 "The Ugly Sports Fan." *Newsweek,* June 17: 93–94.
STARNES, RICHARD
1973 "Coaches Become More Outspoken." *The Chronicle of Higher Education,* Nov. 19. Reprinted in the Iowa State Daily, date unknown.
SOCIAL SCIENCE RESEARCH COUNCIL
1937 "Memorandum on Research in Competition and Cooperation." New York: Social Science Research Council.
STEINER, CLAUDE
1973 "Cooperation." *Issues in Radical Therapy* 1 (Sum): 7–9.

———
1974 *Scripts People Live: Transactional Analysis of Life Scripts.* New York: Bantam Books.

The Matador

The matador enters the ring
The hot desert sun is pouring down
Approaching the life he will take
He holds out his cape, he stands tall and proud
His passes are daring, the time it is nearing
His eyes hold the breath of the crowd
The thrust, the legs crumble
He throws up his hand
The shouts and the roses come down

Chorus:

Hail the matador, he's our champion
He alone stands in the light
Hail the matador, hail the champion
He's our hero, tonight

The front line is quiet, in a trench and alone,
He watches the stars in the sky
The snap of a twig, and he's back in the war
Where he sweats and prays that he won't die
He fixes his bayonet and follows the shadow
That's soon to feel his cold reply
He jumps, and it's over, and one won't grow older,
In silence he stares at the sky.

The baby is crying, the dinner is burning
He yells he wants another beer
She opens the oven but she can save nothing
She cries, "just a minute, dear"
But that's not the answer tonight he can take from her
"I'm the boss, is that clear"
He pushes, she falls, too hard against the wall
But the crowd just stands up and cheers

GEOF MORGAN

Men Without Playfulness

WILLIAM LISS-LEVINSON

In American society there is a negative value placed on play for adults, and for adult males in particular. The Calvinistic influence on American culture and its concomitant attitude toward work is directly related to the negative attitude toward play. Work is seen as virtuous and productive; play is shameful and a waste of time for the mature, responsible adult. Traditional sex-role stereotypes have cast the male as the central character in this work-ethic—Man the Breadwinner, Man the Provider. The emphasis on work in American society is so great that many men define themselves and base their masculine self-concept on their work role (Feigen Fasteau, 1974; Gronseth, 1972, in Howe, 1972; Nichols, 1975; Pleck and Sawyer, 1974).

An examination of some of the definitions of play reflects the negative bias that exists in our society toward adults at play. Michelman (1971) says that "play, as the purposeful activity of childhood, is that instrument that facilitates growth and well-balanced development" (p. 285). Haun, noted author in the field of leisure and mental health, simply states that play is "the business of childhood" (1973, p. 20). Bettleheim (1972) also defines play as "the activities of the young child" (p. 4). It is apparent that adults do not—and implicitly, *should not*—play.

Bettleheim (1972) succinctly summarizes the prevalent adult feelings toward play: "Adults are uncomfortable with and anxious about play" (p. 1). These definitions are inadequate because they restrict play to a particular age group.

There is another school of thought which says that "play is undefinable." These authors focus on "playfulness" as a pervasive attitude (Otto and Mann, 1968, p. 23). It is a concept which is reflected in the attitudes and behaviors of an individual. Playfulness is then not restricted to one sex or age group.

Levinson (1976) has developed a new theoretical conceptualization of the attitudinal and behavioral components of playfulness. He views playfulness as situation specific (Mischel, 1968, in Bem, 1972), and *not* as an underlying personality trait (Liberman, 1964). The components have been identified and are listed below along with a brief explanation and some sources of supporting research.

1. *Non-competitiveness*—The attitudes and behaviors of the person are not motivated by a desire to "win" or to do better than another person. (Greenwald, in Otto and Mann, 1968; Ogilvie and Tutko, 1971; Nichols, 1974; Talamini and Page, 1973).

2. *Non-violence*—Simply stated, there is no violent behavior exhibited, either verbal or non-verbal. (Meggyesy, 1970; Nichols, 1975).

3. *Emotional and physical spontaniety*—The individual expresses his/her emotions, freely and spontaneously, both through verbal and non-verbal means (Bettleheim, 1972; Greenwald, in Otto and Mann, 1968; Jourard, 1964; Lieberman, 1964, 1965, 1976a, 1967b).

4. *Creativity*—The individual feels free to cognitively explore, fantasize, and imagine. (Maslow, 1962, in Feldhusen and Hobson, 1972; Michelman, 1971; Sadler, 1969; Winnicott, 1971).

5. *Non-goal or task orientation*—There is no particular goal or task to be achieved. Being playful is both a means and an end. (Bettleheim, 1972; Nichols, 1975; Pleck and Sawyer, 1974; Stone, in Talamini and Page, 1974).

6. *De-emphasis on external control and evaluation*—The behaviors and attitudes are neither subject to external controls and regulations, nor to evaluation. (Bettleheim, 1972; Lefcourt and Sardoni, 1973; Nichols, 1975; Talamini and Page, 1973).

7. *Self-acceptance*—The individual positively values and accepts

himself or herself as a person, as opposed to making self-acceptance contingent on his or her behaviors. (Jourard, 1964; Nichols, 1975; Sadler, 1969).

8. *Joy, fun, and pleasure*—The individual enjoys what he or she does and feels (Brightbill, 1960; Greenwald, in Otto and Mann, 1968; Lieberman, 1964, 1965, 1967a, 1967b; Murphy, in Piers, 1972).

Writers in the new field of Men's Liberation (Farrell, 1975; Feigen Fasteau, 1974; Nichols, 1975; Pleck and Sawyer, 1974) have all expressed concern over the effects of traditional sex-role stereotyping on American males. The overemphasis on intellect, power and work have led men to be what Farrell terms "emotionally constipated." It may follow that most American males are "playfully constipated." They don't know how to be playful; at best they work hard at playing certain activities (while following rules and social conventions). However,

Playfulness must—by definition—cut through social conventions to find its life. Demarcation lines determining how far it may go keep it from blooming. . . . Today's attempts at playfulness are stymied by a trustless pall of regulations. . . . A spritely and imaginative bounce to life is effectively squelched (Nichols, 1975, p. 85).

Four life areas must be examined in regards to playfulness and American males in relation to self and others. They are

1. *Sexuality* (relations with women)*

2. *Sports* (relations with other men)

3. *Parenting* (relations with children)

4. *Work* (relation with self and society)

Sexuality

Much of male sexuality is penis and orgasm centered. Even the term *foreplay* signifies those activities to be performed before the "main bout," that is, the real goal, penile intercourse and orgasm. Precisely because sexuality is an arena for men, there is a tremendous pressure to do well, to

---

*Note: While male sexuality is certainly not limited to heterosexual relations, this paper is focusing solely on male-female sexual relations. See Levinson (1976) for a more complete discussion of male sexuality.

be a good lover. The experience of sexual joy and pleasure is minimized if the man must constantly be concerned whether his performance was okay—whether he "came" too soon, too late, too little or too much. How can a man feel free to explore new aspects of sexuality, to be "creative," if that means risking vulnerability and possible failure? So much of male sexuality is controlled by performance standards as expounded in traditional scripts of the male sex role. The notion that a man is also expected to perform "indefatigably as a cocksman" (Money and Tucker, 1975, p. 200) pressures men into "performing" in sexual situations they may not really be desirous of.

Burton has found in his clinical experience that the chief complaint of women clients about their husbands is that the males are unable to be emotionally expressive and intimate in their sexuality.

Sports

Nearly all sports that are played in America are competitive to varying degrees. The object of these activities is to win, to score more than your opponent. (Note the commonly used term *opponent*, which connotes antagonism.) Contrary to the popular belief that the competitive spirit in sports builds character, Ogilvie and Tutko (1971) have found that "there is evidence that athletic competition limits growth in some areas" (p. 61). Professionalization and commercialization of sports have increased by leaps and bounds, thereby increasing the incentives and pressures to win, to be number one.

With such a heavy emphasis on a goal of winning, "the feeling that success in athletics is a sine qua non of manhood is learned early" (Feign Fasteau, 1974, p. 104). The covert goal becomes proving one's manhood. The structure (rules), as well as the judgment placed on the participant's worth as team member, reflects the external control and evaluation present in sports. Meggyesy (1970) shares his personal experiences as a football player, where players are often dehumanizingly ridiculed for failure to achieve. In Consciousness-Raising (CR) groups, many men have related similar experiences from their youth, the ultimate insult-evaluation from their peers having been "You sissy, you played like a girl!" Self-acceptance becomes difficult when personal worth is made contingent upon performance in a sports activity. Also, these aforementioned factors would make it very difficult to introduce the element of creativity into a sports activity.

Violence varies in the different sports activities, occurring most often in the so-called contact sports. Football, the most popular American spectator sport, is a prime example of violence under the guise of being a sport. One need only read newspaper articles describing football players, such as "Bill Gray, the Silent Killer" (Schaefer, 1975), to get a feel for the extent of violence that is acceptable as part of the game. Dave Meggyesy (1970) vividly describes some of the violent aspects of football and its players. While many American males are not active participants in various sports, it would seem that much of the competitiveness and violence is experienced by them vicariously through their roles as spectators.

Interestingly, sports is one of the few areas where men—both as participants and spectators—feel free to be emotional. They express anger at losing, joy about winning, and little else. I wonder about this "joy and fun" upon examination of its origins: the grueling training men go through (both for professional and non-professional sports); the pain and injuries often incurred; and the fact that the joy is contingent upon winning, or beating the opponent.

It is a sad reflection on American society that in the one area of men's lives where the word *play* is most common—sports—so little playfulness is to be found.

Parenting

The archetypal figure of playfulness in our society is the child. The child is permitted to be carefree, spontaneous and fun-loving. One might assume, therefore, that as parents, men are playful. There is, however, a basic problem inherent in male involvement in parenting. While the role of father is certainly part of the traditional male image, the notion of parenting, or the actual caring for the child, is not part of this image (Feigen Fasteau, 1974). In fact, studies have shown that many American males have had little or no contact with infants during their own childhood and early manhood (Fein, 1974, in Pleck and Sawyer, 1974). Parenting, learning how to relate to and with children, how to play and be playful with them, is just not part of the socialization curriculum for American males.

The traditional male sex role places a high value on external control and evaluation of behavior. Parenting simply is not reinforced by these means. True, many men may *help* their wives with *some* of the responsibilities for child care. However, they aren't assuming an equal responsibility for the whole process. As Farrell (1975) points out, imagine the external reactions to a male with a resume that read "1973–1974—Stayed home and raised my children!"

Studies of children's and young adults' perceptions of their parents are particularly revealing of the traditional role fathers play. Walters and Stinnett (1971), in a review of a decade of research on parent-child relationships, found that fathers are consistently perceived as being more fear arousing, punitive, restrictive, cold, and less understanding than mothers. Males often feel the pressure to raise their children in a certain way, to impart their values to them (Nichols, 1975). The pressure for a male with a son is to raise the child to be manly (Benson, 1968). The fear that otherwise the child would be feminine or not fully masculine places a burden on both the child and the father. Too many overt and covert goals would seem to impair the potential playfulness a male could experience in the fathering/parenting process. These goals translate themselves into a competitiveness, trying to raise the child to be the man or woman he or she should be. Probably for many fathers, parenting a male child is also a means of attempting to vicariously experience unfulfilled traditional male activities.

While it is true that the majority of males are not violent with their children, fathers are generally not perceived by their children as warm or nurturant (Benson, 1968; Walters and Stinnett, 1971). In CR groups, men of varying ages and backgrounds have revealed that few of their fathers were, or are, emotionally and/or physically expressive with their sons. Granted, low-level joy and anger are expressed, both verbally and nonverbally. However, the less traditionally masculine emotions, such as tenderness, hurt, fear, or outward signs of affection, such as kissing, are sadly missing, especially between father and son. Few fathers are able to take the risk of being vulnerable by sharing a wide range of emotions, fantasies and playing with their children.

Work

Work may be the area in which it is most difficult for a male to be playful in our society. Most people would see the two concepts as being antithetical, at opposite ends of a continuum. As was stated in the beginning of this paper, work has been traditionally seen as virtuous, worthwhile endeavor in contradistinction to play. The emphasis on work as the basis for a masculine identity is so strong that "in American society it is well-nigh impossible to be a man without having an occupation, and how much of a man and what kind of man one is are measured largely by the nature of the occupation and the success with which it is pursued" (Turner, 1970, p. 225).

The cultural value that is placed on money as a symbol of success puts pressure on males and affects their self-worth and acceptance. As Gould (in Pleck and Sawyer, 1974, p. 98) says, money is a "pretty insecure peg on which to hang a masculine image." The success ethic places a tremendous responsibility on males; and coupled with the notion of the male as the breadwinner, competition becomes an integral part of the male's working life. There is competition to prove oneself better than co-workers, as well as competition to prove oneself a better worker this week than last week. The goal of one's work is rarely permitted to be enjoyment or pleasure. As Braude (1975) points out, " . . . the most heinous sin that could be committed by an American (and the least forgivable) is the admission of failure to achieve, with the concomitant renunciation of the success orientation altogether" (p. 128). A neon sign, flashing *SUCCESS*, hangs over the heads (and beds) of American males.

Because there is this constant competition, any sign of weakness or playfulness is considered taboo, unmasculine, and eventually will doom one to failure (Bartolome, in Pleck and Sawyer, 1974). Admittedly, there are jobs which require constant creativity; but there, too, there is the pressure to produce and achieve success, such as in the advertising industry. Overall, with all the constant pressure to succeed, to do better, to be strong, independent and self-sufficient, one wonders: How many American males can say they enjoy their jobs, or get pleasure from an activity that consumes so much of their time?

Discussion

Where do we go from here? Admittedly, the picture I have just painted is somewhat gloomy. The paucity of research on men and playfulness reflects the degree to which it is considered (or *not* considered) a subject worthy of investigation. Yet, I feel quite hopeful. I have spoken in generalities when referring to males. Fortunately, not all males are "playfully constipated." Many men are reexamining the roles they play, the molds they've been cast into, and are beginning to question. The process is slow and the effects of prior socialization and present pressures are great. Still, the beginnings of changes can be seen.

Many of the writers both on Women's Liberation and Men's Liberation have discussed the area of male sexuality and the performance ethic that exists. No doubt they have had an impact on American males. Women are becoming sexually more assertive and thus assuming more of an active and initiating role in sexual activities. While this does ostensibly take some of the pressure off men, undoubtedly many men are frightened by the change. Males will first have to learn how to give up some of their control and power in sexual activities and allow themselves to fully experience themselves and their partners. It is time for males to recognize that the old equation—lack of power or control = impotency = you're not a real man—is simply not true.

In the area of sports, there are a number of people who are involved in trying to develop new activities that will allow men to be more playful. George Leonard, in his book *The Ultimate Athlete,* offers some possible new games and sports activities that involve considerably less competition. Bob Kriegel, at the Easalen Sports Center in California, is also involved in the development of new activities and games. Some recent articles that have been written on the pressures put on male children from early years to participate in sports (for example, Little League baseball) reflect an increasing awareness and sensitivity to some of the issues that have been discussed.

Regarding parenting, Pleck and Sawyer (1974) point out that men are beginning to reexamine the role that they play as fathers and their relationships with their children. These changes will be most rewarding, for they will enable men to reclaim "the spontaneous emotional awareness that our masculine training drove into hiding so long ago!" (Pleck and Sawyer, 1974, p. 53).

Finally, there is the area of work. The shortened work-week and high unemployment rate are forcing men to reexamine their work role and its importance in their lives. People are beginning to ask themselves, "Who am I, and what do I really want to do and get out of life?" This process and changes that may come about will admittedly be easier for people who are presently working in more flexible occupations.

Changes in attitudes and behaviors come slowly, especially if they are to be on a societal level. American males, one hopes, will learn how to be playful and will *be* playful. In the process, they may come to realize they are really reclaiming a part of themselves that may be, to paraphrase Sadler (1969, p. 61), a very basic form of human existence.

References

BEM, S.

Sex role adaptability: one consequence of psychological androgeny. *Journal of Personality and Social Psychology,* 1975.

BEM, S.

Psychology looks at sex roles: Where have all the androgynous people gone? Unpublished paper presented at UCLA symposium on women, May 1972.

BENSON, L.

Fatherhood: A Sociological Perspective. New York: Random House, 1968.

BERNARD, J.

Women, Wives, Mothers: Values and Options. Chicago: Aldine Publishing Co., 1975.

BETTLEHEIM, B.

Play and education. *School Review,* 1972, *81* (1), 1–13.

BRAUDE, L.

Work and Workers: A Sociological Analysis. Englewood Cliffs, N.J.: Prentice-Hall, 1960.

BRIGHTBILL, C.

The Challenge of Leisure. New York: Holt, Rinehart & Winston, 1975.

BRODERICK, C., AND BERNARD, J., EDS.

The Individual, Sex, and Society. Baltimore: The Johns Hopkins Press, 1969, 327–341.

BURTON, A.
Marriage without failure. *Psychology Reports,* 1973, *32,* 1199–1208.
ELLIS, M. J.
Why People Play. Englewood Cliffs, N.J.: Prentice-Hall, 1973.
FARRELL, W.
The Liberated Man. New York: Bantam, 1975.
FEIGEN FASTEAU, M.
The Male Machine. New York: McGraw-Hill, 1974.
FELDHUSEN, J., AND HOBSON, S.
Freedom and play: catalysts for creativity. *Elementary School Journal,* 1972, *73* (3), 149–155.
HAUN, P.
Recreation: A Medical Viewpoint. New York: Teachers College Press, 1973.
JOURARD, S.
The Transparent Self. New York: D. Van Nostrand, 1964, 46–55.
KURLAND, M.
Sexual difficulties due to stereotyped role playing. *Medical Aspects of Human Sexuality,* 1975, *9* (6), 8–22.
LEFCOURT, H., AND SARDONI, C.
Locus of control and the expression of humor. *Proceedings. Eighty-first Annual Convention A.P.A.,* 1973, *8* (1), 185.
LEONARD, G.
The Ultimate Athlete. New York: Viking, 1974.
LEVINSON, W.
Men and playfulness: an investigation of the concept and its implications for education. Unpublished Ph.D. dissertation, Southern Illinois University, June 1976.
LIEBERMAN, J. N.
A developmental analysis of playfulness as a clue to cognitive style. *Journal of Creative Behavior,* 1967(a), *1* (4), 391–397.
LIEBERMAN, J. N.
Personality traits in adolescents: an investigation of playfulness–nonplayfulness in the high school setting. City University of New York, 1967(b), ERIC #ED 032 584.
LIEBERMAN, J. N.
Playfulness and divergent thinking: an investigation of their relationship at the kindergarten level. Unpublished Ph.D. dissertation, Teachers College, Columbia University, 1964.
MEGGYESY, D.
Out of Their League. Berkeley: Ramparts Press, 1970.
MICHELMAN, S.
The importance of creative play. *American Journal of Occupational Therapy,* 1971, *25* (6), 285–290.

MONEY, J., AND TUCKER, P.
Sexual Signatures. Boston: Little, Brown, 1975.

NICHOLS, J.
Men's Liberation: A New Definition of Masculinity. New York: Penguin, 1975.

OGILVIE, B., AND TUTKO, T.
Sport: If you want to build character, try something else. *Psychology Today,* 1971, *5* (5), 61–63.

OTTO, H., AND MANN, J., EDS.
Ways of Growth: Approaches to Expanding Awareness. New York: Viking, 1968.

PIERS, M, ED.
Play and Development: A Symposium. New York: W. W. Norton & Co., 1972.

PLECK, J., AND SAYER, J., EDS.
Men and Masculinity. Englewood Cliffs, N.J.: Prentice-Hall, 1974.

POLATNICK, M.
Why men don't rear children: a power analysis. *Berkeley Journal of Sociology,* 1973, *18,* 45–86.

SADLER, W.
Creative existence: play as a pathway to personal freedom and community. *Humanities,* 1969, *5* (1), 57–79.

SCHAEFER, F.
C.S.U. Football: Rams should be winners in 1975. *Triangle Review,* 1975, *3* (17).

TALAMINI, J., AND PAGE, C., EDS.
Sports and Society: An Anthology. Boston: Little, Brown, 1973.

TURNER, R.
Family Interaction. New York: John Wiley, 1970.

WALSH, R., AND LEONARD, W.
Usage of terms for sexual intercourse by men and women. *Archives of Sexual Behavior,* 1974, *3* (4), 373–376.

WALTER, J., AND STINNETT, N.
Parent-child relationships: A decade review of research. *Journal of Marriage and Family,* 1971, *33,* 70–111.

WINNICOTT, D. W.
Playing and Reality. New York: Basic Books, 1971.

why don't salmon have to go to masters and johnson?

does the mighty lion
smoke marlboro cigarettes

does he have a hardon
for every lioness

does he swear
honor love and fidelity
before she says
yes

are there sex objects
in the oceans of the world

do female caribou
get raped

do arabian stallions
go to workshops
on male privilege

has the lumbering elephant
gotten in touch
with the question of foreplay

is the bull
a sensitive lover
who makes sure
that his sweetie always has an orgasm

are there whores and pimps
doing their thing
with the water buffalo
on the serengeti plains

forgive me
I forget these are the lower creatures

its only us lucky folks
who are having coitus
with sex manuals

and if you pays your money
you can get your guided missile guided
satisfaction guaranteed

like the woman says

"there may be a ghost in the machine"

SIDNEY MILLER

Two Homes or One?

STEPHEN L. DWORKIN

At the present time there are 2.7 million children from divorced families in the United States. Given the present divorce rate (30 to 50 percent, depending on the particular location in the country) the number of children experiencing parental separation and/or divorce will be increasing significantly over the next decade. In the majority of these cases, the mother is given legal custody and the children seldom maintain a close, loving relationship with the father. In these situations, children often suffer irreparable harm due to this loss. In effect, they lose a primary person in their lives. While parent surrogates or male replacements may frequently appear and play significant roles in the lives of these children, the genetic father has been lost. The effects of this loss are lasting and major; unconsciously, children without the experience of a close, intimate attachment with their father will at some time wonder about, fantasize, and perhaps search for the male model in their lives.

This article contains a description of my personal experience as a father who lost legal custody but who has maintained, successfully I believe, a second home for my children, ages ten and eight. In addition, it examines some of the common problems and adjustments affecting children and their fathers in the process of maintaining a second home.

While I realize that mothers are also affected by these living arrangements, that is not the focus of this paper. Finally, I address some possible solutions relating to building or maintaining two homes for children following a divorce in the family. I believe that both men and women may find my experiences useful in their own adjustments toward reaching a healthier and more personally satisfying life for themselves and their children. Also, I sincerely hope that professionals in the fields of social work, psychiatry and law will be open to considering my experiences through my work with divorced families.

I was legally divorced a little over four years ago after a long, bitter and painful custody battle which centered around the future lives of my two children, Scott and Rebecca, then aged seven and five. At the final divorce hearing, I lost sole legal custody and was awarded "generous visitation rights." This was based upon a regular and routine schedule developed through intense negotiations involving both attorneys, the judge and, of course, my ex-spouse and me. Originally, I had sought joint legal custody, which was rejected at the initial temporary court hearing.

Previously, while I was still married, I had begun to reevaluate my role as a husband, father and man in our society. My ex-wife's involvement and my own sympathies with the women's movement influenced me to make many changes in my life style, particularly in my role as a father. Initially, I was hesitant, but gradually, over a period of four years, I began to discover in myself an intense desire to be more directly involved with parenting my children. This transformation was, and still is, not easy, particularly in view of my fairly typical conservative Jewish background. At the time of the divorce proceedings, I realized I wanted custody of my children; but, due to existing societal attitudes still found in family courts, I lost. A factor in my case was that my ex-wife is a good mother and she also wanted custody of our two children. Thus, the stage was set for a prolonged court battle. As it is commonly known, if two good parents are involved, both of whom want to raise their children, the court usually gives them to the mother.

These past four years as a non-custodial parent have not been easy for me or the children. The easiest part of this adjustment has been to follow a regular schedule: The children are with me every other weekend and every Wednesday from five to eight in the evening. In addition, I have the children three weeks during the summer and on alternating Jewish and other holidays each year. In effect, this amounts to approximately 30 percent of my children's life! In general, this schedule has been maintained with few exceptions. Practically, problems have been few, since I live only five minutes away from my ex-wife. Usually, I pick up the children and drop them off.

While it has taken four years of considerable effort, I have a new family: myself and my children. One evening, as I was planning a lecture for a course I teach called "Men's Changing Roles," I asked the children how they feel about having two homes. Scott replied, "I like it because when things aren't going so well at Mommy's house, I have another place to go." "Well," I said, "don't you ever get tired of going back and forth?" Scott answered, "Yes, sometimes, but that's better than not having a mommy *and* a daddy." Rebecca interjected, "Besides, we're lucky, we have two daddies; most kids have only one!" My ex-spouse has remarried, while I have chosen to remain single.

As the conversation progressed, and I encouraged the kids to talk, what became clearer to me was that they finally learned to accept the situation as it is. Scott, for example, said at one point that he didn't like the situation at first, but he knew that he had to accept it, so he did. And so did I. Furthermore, he and Rebecca have shown an ability to do more than just adjust. They seem to make the best out of what's given to them. For example, both children now look forward to two birthdays, two holidays, and two vacations—certainly justifiable excessiveness. They know that they belong to two separate and distinct families with separate rules, expectations and disciplines. It is not perfect, it is not imperfect. It is what it is, with different options, different opportunities and, of course, very different role models in two different familial environments.

In the beginning of this arrangement, the children were confused, angry and sometimes uncontrollable. They had every right to be. One positive factor was that they felt comfortable at my house, since they had grown up there (I kept the house—my ex-wife got the kids). However, for a period of time, especially before the custody battle ended, the children were in the middle of the conflict between me and my ex-wife. This a problem: Although we both tried to keep our conflicts separate from the children, this was not always possible.

A second stage then seemed to evolve. The children seemed more relaxed. They became more positive and even took on an attitude of helpfulness, particularly toward me, as I was still going through my own struggles centering around loneliness and grieving over my loss. Slowly but naturally, the children became more open about their feelings concerning the divorce and their living in two homes. They also began to be more assertive about their situation independent of mine.

Of course, as the children experienced different stages of adjustment, so did I. First I suffered painfully over the loss of my ex-wife and especially the children. I was and continue to be under severe financial pressure. I experienced loneliness and a long period of depression while trying to become more self-reliant, especially at home doing domestic chores while trying to continue functioning professionally. At the center of this, I was constantly facing the struggle around "should I get remarried or at least be deeply involved with a woman to give me some support?" As a man in my late 30's, I have learned to accept how dependent I was on a woman for help with home and domestic activities. My single greatest accomplishment these past four years has been learning to care for and raise my children without a woman around to direct me. It's a very slow process, especially in a world that discourages and devalues male parenting.

My present life style with my children is not blissful, but it is what I want—a family consisting of me and the kids. The greatest joy is through intimacy with them, being able to share my life with two people to whom I feel deeply committed. In many ways, it would be easier if the children lived with me all of the time, though most people may believe the opposite. I realize now that my children are my good friends who helped me face loneliness and grief in my life.

There are several major problems I have faced these past four years. First is the extreme hardship the children must face while both parents are actively fighting with each other. It is not fair to the children, but it exists. Parents naturally use children against each other. No one escapes this temptation. A second problem is manipulation by the children. To make it worse, children are good at it, especially while the parents are feeling weak and vulnerable and questioning their roles as parents. It may last for years. Men, I believe, are particularly vulnerable because they are not usually comfortable setting limits with their children. It's compounded in situations in which control as a parent seems to have been removed. A third obstacle against two homes is a general lack of community or public support. Most books written about divorce and custody issues advocate one home for children that supposedly assures children of a sense of continuity and stability. The well-known book *Beyond the Best Interests of the Child** strongly advocates this position. In my opinion, though, it is based on traditional beliefs and assumptions about children which have never been adequately researched. One of these assumptions is the notion that children tend to develop psychological ties to only one parent, usually the mother. Another common belief, strongly supported by society, is that the healthiest family unit is triangular, consisting of a mother, father and the children. If this is true, unfortunately, there will be an increasingly significant number of children who are potentially unhealthy adults. It behooves us to reevaluate our ideas about family life, since we cannot deny the reality of split households. Whether we like it or not, family life is changing. My children and I know this. It seems to me that we can all become more accepting about the various family lifestyles which are emerging.

Men like myself have special problems that must be overcome. One is a natural feeling that we are not adequate to raise children. We may be are our own worst enemies and, unfortunately, we reinforce these feelings,

---

*Freud, A., Goldstein, J., and Solnit, A. J. *Beyond the Best Interests of the Child.* New York and London: Free Press, a division of Macmillan, 1973.

as we often run away from emotionally demanding situations before, during and after marriage. Traditionally, men are socialized to avoid asking for help. Yet, men experiencing divorce need help, and the need for help is exacerbated when children are around. Single men interested in maintaining second homes for their children have additional problems. We are faced with such questions as: How involved should my women friends become with my children? Should I involve my children in my intimate physical life with women? How do I discipline my children without more control as a parent? How do I handle the normal pressures of my work life while trying to maintain a primary parental role with my children? Should I stay in the same community with my ex-wife instead of starting a new life elsewhere? How do I learn to protect my own rights as a single man aside from my role as a parent?

Implicit in these questions are several other issues relating to maleness and masculinity. At the root of these dilemmas is one central question: Who am I as a man? Personally, as a father, professional social worker, friend or lover, I am still learning that growing up in today's world requires a sincere effort on my part to ask how I got this way before I can begin to make relatively free choices about where I would like to go. For my children's sake, I know it is worth it!

More and more, I am discovering that the most obvious solutions to most problems are often easily overlooked. My children taught me this one. It refers to our talking with our children as early as possible and letting them know about our troubles and confusions. They will let us know, in their unique way, what they want and need. Listen to them, then act. However, the talking has to be continuous and actively encouraged. Support groups for men can be extremely valuable and I still appreciate the benefits of a men's consciousness-raising group. Professional counseling can also be useful, though I realize how infrequently men use this source of support. Finally, education courses or workshops specifically designed to help people know and understand the processes of growing up are invaluable. Workshops pertaining to the social and legal aspects of custody and divorce are imperative. And let's not forget courses in men's changing roles. I never enrolled in one as a student, but I'm taking it now as an instructor. As my children proudly proclaim, "My dad teaches 'Men's Changing Rules.'" Revise, kids. It's "Men's Changing Roles."

Treating the Special Madness of Men

LARRY ETTKIN

Over the past ten years, a strong case for women as economic, sexual, and emotional victims and casualties of Western civilization has been persuasively and poignantly argued. In contrast, men are viewed as the designers, perpetrators and beneficiaries of this unjust system. More recently, and with increasing anger, men are renouncing the supposed beauty and benefits of the "privileged sex." If mental illness is as Maslow suggests "the stunting and crippling of full humanness," then men experience their share of pain. Beyond the classic symptoms of neurosis and psychosis, beyond the lack of intimate human contact, beyond the existential conditions of separation from body and soul, beyond the isolation from other members of the human species in a chaotic universe, there is a unique condition which I call the *madness of men*. This is the almost universal inability of men to ask for or receive help from psychotherapy, an institution created, designed and directed by males.

To begin to understand the roots of this madness and its pervasive effect requires examining what happens in the course of psychotherapy. The core experience in all psychotherapies is called the therapeutic relationship. At first emphasized by Freud, it was a brilliant elaboration on the simple notion that talking about and thereby being known to yourself and others positively affects one's mental health. Conversely, inability to talk about and thereby be known to yourself and others contributes to mental illness. Freud further described how maintaining rigid defenses against revealing yourself, particularly defenses against being known as sexual or angry, creates a state of tension which subtracts energy from healthy functioning.

This version of the therapeutic relationship has been developed and modified by both Freud's followers and critics. Thus, the principal architects of modern psychotherapy were those who developed relationship models based on the original work of Freud. In some models, the therapist is a distant, wise, powerful, knowing father while the client is a child and supplicant in search of identity. Other models emphasize an intensely personal and subjective encounter of equals in which feelings are explored that have previously been denied awareness. In other models, the helper serves as a guru or wise teacher who instructs through metaphors and parables which serve to frustrate the client into discovering his or her own answers. Also, there are models in which the helper can be seen as an engineer of behavioral changes and his client, a willing subject of systematic goal-directed reshaping. Within these diverse models, one common element is apparent—the necessity of relating to another person, usually a man, at a more or less intense level of closeness.

In *Some Lethal Aspects of the Male Role*, Jourard argues that men seem to "dread being known," and this creates a state of continual unhealthy tension over being found out. "Manliness, then, seems to carry with it a chronic burden of stress and energy expenditure which could be a factor in men's relatively shorter life-span." I would argue that the same dread of being known prevents men from entering into and becoming involved in the psycho-therapeutic process. So it seems that men, in spite of physical and mental suffering, are unable to use a system that they have designed purportedly to ameliorate their ills, and this is the special madness of men. What's more, this madness affects all of us (Jourard, Sidney M., 1971).

I have been a psychologist in private practice for three years. My clients are mostly women. I find them to be strong and courageous in considing change and in challenging life. I wonder where the men are. I admit that I often don't enjoy working with other males and that, in fact, I have difficulty connecting with most men. I decided that there is something missing from both my practice and my growth as a man, and I began to work on ways of inviting men into therapy and facilitating their change. From my experience, study and limited work with male clients, I decided that some degree of self-disclosure is most often the variable distinguishing therapy that facilitates change from therapy that goes nowhere.

I have come to believe that self-disclosure, that is, how and to whom one lets himself or herself be known, is central to understanding the developmental processes of men and, similarly, that self-disclosure is central to understanding male involvement in psychotherapy. At this point, I would like to examine some aspects of self-disclosure in relationship to the development of male identity.

I find it useful to define self-disclosure in its broadest sense as all of the ways, both verbal and non-verbal, that one becomes known to others.

Letting one's self be known is a selective act. That is, each of us makes choices at different levels of awareness about what, with whom, and how much we will disclose. Moreover, we decide when and under what conditions we will be known. From this, we each develop a characteristic style of disclosure which I believe is remarkably different for men than for women. Disclosing yourself to a "significant other," as Freud pointed out, is the principal way of getting to know yourself. If this is true, then restricted psychological growth in males can be attributed to a restricted male disclosure pattern.

It has been useful to my understanding of male identity to ask to whom do men and boys first let themselves be known? In exploring this question we begin with their mothers. It is clear that the male child is deeply dependent on his mother. As Goldberg (1977) states, "She is the one who holds, rocks, cleans, comforts and clothes him. She sets his limits, teaches him right from wrong, reinforces him with praise and controls him with punishment." It would seem to follow that the male child would disclose to the person closest to him, his mother; yet this is not the case because of the kind of issues most crucial to developing his sense of self. This is his need to deal with aggression, anger and sexuality. These issues as they emerge in the lives of male children are extremely threatening to women, particularly mothers. It is rare in our culture for a man to report talking about sex to his mother or feeling his mother understands and accepts his sexuality. It is also rare for a man to feel comfortable about having shown anger or aggression in the presence of his mother. So we conclude that boys fear showing important parts of their personality to their mother and this may later lead to restricted development (Hartley, Ruth E., 1959).

How about fathers as sources of, and models for, self-disclosure? Boys don't talk about themselves to their fathers. They typically report "I don't see him very often" or "Father hardly has time to talk to me." What's more, boys are taught to view their fathers as agents of punishment. "Wait till your father hears about this!" (Hartley, 1969). The opportunity for close contact with an adult male is further limited by the increasingly large numbers of male children raised in matriarchal households.

It is significant that there are very few recorded studies of the effects of fathering on male development. One might conclude either that researchers don't believe that fathers are important or they have difficulty locating fathers willing to be researched (Macoby and Jacklin, 1974). It is clear that for many male children, often there is no available adult to serve as a father figure. More important, boys often learn to view fathers as distant, uncaring, prone to punish and too busy to become involved.

If the development of a healthy male identity can be achieved by way of the male child allowing himself to become known to significant others, then finding persons and ways of disclosing becomes a necessity. I believe that this is so, and it is not whether this process takes place in males, but with whom and by what means. Further, if disclosing one's self is also a necessary part of the therapeutic process, it is essential for the therapist who wants to have impact on male clients to understand with whom and how males let themselves be known.

It would seem that in situations that discourage disclosure with either parent, secondary figures, particularly males—both real and imaginary—become more developmentally significant. Who are these figures? In the lives of most boys, they are his peers, his heroes, his coaches and his teachers. They provide both potential outlets for disclosure and models for learning how to let one's self be known. These secondary male figures become most important when male children don't have access to their mothers and fathers. They are particularly vital to the expression of male sexuality and aggressiveness because these areas are connected with much parental ambivalence. An understanding of male disclosure, then, must include consideration of the influence of peers, heroes, and mentors.

In regard to *peer-group* influence, observations of orphans from concentration camps offers compelling evidence of peer-group influence on children raised without close parental contact. These children deprived of parents formed intimate loyal attachments to one another so intense that it was hard for them later to form ties with sympathetic caretaking adults. It appears that the need for attachment is so much a necessity that when parents aren't available, children invest more in their peer grouping. Even in more typical development, as the child matures and as he moves from boyhood to adolescence, he increasingly turns to his peers for approval. The picture which emerges is that of a boy selecting and being selected by peer companions usually of similar ages, status and sex. While this group changes over time, it is often a salient factor in his development—the place where interesting activities are discovered, the place where skills are learned and the place where values are formed. In reviewing research on peer grouping, Maccoby and Jacklin provide strong evidence that "boys (more than girls) are highly oriented toward a peer group" (Maccoby and Jacklin, 1974).

It is within this group that some important aspects of what is considered male character are formed. Moreover, the nature of this group and the way members become known, one to another, reflect the way men disclose to each other. A primary noticeable characteristic of male peer grouping is the emphasis on activity rather than relationship. These groups form around a game. If there is a choice of players, they will be chosen on the basis of game skills rather than personal attractiveness or worth.

The male child lets himself be known by doing, that is, by participating in activities. Many times, the action is aggressive and his place in the group is determined by skills useful in the game. The male child's way of being known is often through his body as he tests his speed, strength and perseverance. And particularly relevant to therapy, a boy's emotional expression, the way he reveals anger, sadness, fear, joy and love, is tested and shaped by his group. Years later, after leaving his companions, they are still a part of his awareness, an invisible jury he carries within, who continue to review and judge his performance.

Another major factor in shaping the male disclosure pattern is the *hero*. In the absence of a close male parenting figure, boys strongly identify with hero figures. These heroes are most often extreme exaggerations of stereotypical cultural norms. The hero is powerful, keeps his own counsel, solves his own problems and holds a tight rein on emotional expression. He is decisive, certain and almost never wrong. I would suggest that these influences are most pervasive in the lives of men who have no close male model to positively identify with. The hero is also a potent source of original insight into male development and relationships. The hero looks for and accepts challenges, and develops through experiencing life. He is not all-powerful, but rather has a well-disguised vulnerability often connected with his greatest strength. The hero, while endowed with amazing potential, often goes through a period of tenaciously and painfully lonely skill development. He has to learn to ride, to fight, to reason, to struggle for the solution to problems. Most important, the hero is a man of action and he discloses himself through what he does, rather than through what he says. He is concrete, goal oriented and direct. He is, in fact, an enlarged reflection of what is considered manly in the culture and therefore an undeniable part of each of us.

A final indication of the patterning of male disclosure is relationships with *coaches, teachers* and other male *mentors*. Through these relationships the young male has opportunity to reach out and let himself be known by older men in relationships that are clearly defined, more limited and perhaps less threatening than father-to-son. Here, he has a chance to incorporate and test out his fantasy relationships with heroes in the context of a personal relationship.

The effective mentor is a trusted guide; he attempts to bring out the best in his pupils, to fully develop the pupils' potential skills. Running Coach Percy Wells Carutty was such a person. He coached both John Landy and Herb Elliott to run four-minute miles. He began by coaching himself from a sickly 43-year-old into an outstanding long-distance runner and athlete. Carutty urged his students to integrate all their mental, spiritual and physical powers into their sport. The morning before a big race, even when he was over 60 years old, he would run along with his athletes to exhaustion, at which point he is quoted as saying, "You may run faster today, but you will not run harder" (Spino, 1976).

As I write this, I remember wanting desperately to be recognized, appreciated, known by various teachers and coaches, and the fear of rejection that kept me at a distance, alone and disconnected. At conferences and workshops in the presence of esteemed colleagues, as my breathing constricts and my body stiffens, I begin to reexperience this old fear. Male biographical reports repeatedly indicate the fear and disappointment men experience as they attempt to contact their spiritual and emotional "fathers."

In this review of male development I have become increasingly aware that by the time a boy becomes a man, he has learned to allow others to know him only infrequently and very selectively. Some of the directions these paths of male disclosure lead in therapy are beginning to become more apparent.

I see the ghost of the absent, punishing father haunting the therapeutic encounter—the mythical, silent, cool and controlled distant father. He looks down critically at any weakness in his offspring. His presence provides a formidable, but not unsurmountable, obstacle to the therapeutic relationship. Clearly, to treat the madness of men requires that a different and more equal balance between therapist and client must be established, for the man coming into therapy is entering foreign and potentially dangerous territory. He is not ready to engage in a close verbal relationship, particularly with another man. He needs to be able to establish himself and gain some understanding of what will happen in this new and fear-evoking situation. More likely than not he comes to therapy because someone, his wife, lover or boss, is putting pressure on him to change. He is often pretty well into an agitated, anxious and/or depressed state. He may carry a heavy burden of anger or guilt after holding back expressing himself for so long. He typically feels responsible for the unsatisfactory situations that led him to therapy, inadequate because he cannot solve his own problems and resentful and afraid of the therapist who offers him help. He is a difficult, challenging client who is often written off by the mainstream clinician as "not motivated."

In approaching such a client, I want to give him every opportunity to establish himself with me as a powerful, adequate individual—to let me know his strengths. I encourage him to tell me about the triumphs and high points of his life, as well as the downers. I find that men whom I work with generally need to test and prove their adequacy, particularly as they enter therapy. I encourage them to let me know how skillful they are or have been in work and play, how sexual they are or have been, how clever and how responsible. Perhaps I am also tapping into my need as a man to develop respect for the individual strengths of other men, and I too need to experience these strengths to relate to deeper levels.

Men disclose to other men most easily on the basis of mutual recognition of power and adequacy. So, each man must be given every opportunity to establish himself on his own terms. For some men this may involve telling war stories, "throwing the key block," "winning the scholarship," "making the homecoming queen," "writing the big order." Some men experience a need to show me that they are intellectually equal or superior, and some need to prove that they are or have been sexually more proficient. This is generally a lot of teasing and checking of limits as male clients become involved in relating to me. I find that men often are most comfortable establishing relationships in much the same ways as they enter and gain acceptance in peer groups. Thus, the therapeutic relationship evolves out of recognition of mutual competencies and skills. This relationship is punctuated by banter and humor, a process of give and take.

In examining past and present peer interaction I am interested in how my client sees himself in these situations. I find that only after establishing himself as a "strong normal male" in a way that is developmentally familiar to him, through peer relationships, is he able to define himself as a person with a problem. More important, he begins to see himself as a person who has the power to affect what is happening in his unique life situation. Paradoxically, his problem often involves an overwhelming need to establish and continually prove himself to be a "strong normal male." I have suggested that the male disclosure pattern requires that "man-to-man" interaction begins with a recognition of strengths and that this recognition sets the stage for mutual respect and the possibility of change.

Another aspect of counseling men which deserves particular attention is motivation. If the client has been pressured into coming to therapy by a wife, lover, or boss, as is typically the case, then at some point he needs to recognize that he has something to gain from being there. For as a man he has been taught from birth to look out for himself. He needs to see what's in it for him, what he gets out of it, how this experience serves his best interest.

Too often the therapist mistakenly approaches the male client with an abstract proposal to help him better understand, express or get in touch with "deep feelings." The opportunity to express feelings may not be a strong motivation, and in fact it may trigger panic in clients who are struggling to maintain emotional control. The freer expression of feelings is an exciting and important part of therapy with men, but for most men the expression of feelings must arise from within the context of the life or therapy situation—feelings flow from life issues, and the idea that the expression of feelings has value in itself is contrary to the male developmental experience. It appears that men have little understanding of the expression of feelings as a goal in itself. When a man is confronted by his angry wife complaining, "You never tell me how you feel," he is generally sincerely confused and will respond with, "Feel? About what?" It is easier for most men to begin by talking about a proposed vacation, a sexual encounter, an event participated in, and then learn how to express feelings about the experience.

Another misguided yet frequently used approach to motivating men in therapy is through an appeal to responsibility or fair play. This is usually attempted by the well-intentioned therapist who has listened sympathetically and warmly to the woman partner's long tale of her mate's uncaring and non-communicative chauvinism. At this point the therapist admonishes the male client with, "You know, Joe, maybe Sally has a point and you ought to look at some of your other family responsibilities besides bringing home a good paycheck." The key word *responsibility* evokes very strong and deep resentment in many men. For men from early childhood have been told how irresponsible they are. So, while the male client can recognize his partner's pain, he is also in touch with his own mute resentment, guilt and anger at being told again and again that he has fallen short.

It is my experience as a therapist that appeals to responsibility, fair play and guilt don't work. Statements that I make as a therapist which evoke guilt in clients signal that it is I who is stuck, frustrated and blocked.

If the male has no overwhelming interest in "getting in touch with deep feeling," "fair play" or "being responsible," how can he maintain enough motivation to survive the painful process of getting help? I find that male clients are motivated only when they are firmly convinced that therapy is serving their self-interest, that is, their present wants and needs. We live in a "*me* society" and, for better or worse, therapy produces change only when it is understood by client and therapist to be a powerful aid to achieving self-interest. So rather than telling Joe, "It seems that your wife is reasonable in asking for more sexual foreplay," the therapist can suggest, "Joe, if you are willing to work on spending more time in foreplay, you might experience deeper, more pleasurable orgasms." Or instead of, "These kids seem to want more time from you as a father," one can say, "Playing with the kids might give you some relief from the pressures of these long hard hours of tax work." If society teaches me to be selfish, then the therapeutic motivation must begin with self-interest, and the therapeutic process must periodically refocus on how the client's wants and needs are being served. In the words of McClelland (1978), an eminent motivational researcher, "When everyone involved correctly understands the motivational aspects of the situation in a concrete behavioral way, then and only then are we likely to bring about change."

After the situation is defined and goals are set, a further aspect of motivation is creating a plan by which goals can be reached. This process is best understood as the negotiation of a contract. The contract outlines the relationship between therapist and client, the goals of therapy and the steps to be taken toward reaching those goals. I find that contracting with male clients is a particularly effective methodology because it avoids some of the unnecessary ritualistic mystification that turns men away from therapy. Moreover, contracts that spell out tasks leading to skill development appeal to the usually problematic male client. He learns in action by doing, that is, by behaving differently and by developing a different sense of world and of self. He experiences through activity and shares the process with his therapist. This sharing of experience intensifies the therapeutic relationship in much the same way as male-to-male relationships are intensified developmentally. The therapist, after forming a sharing relationship through contracting, can offer his client a large body of effective change technology. This technology can and has been used to facilitate better communication, exhance sexuality, reduce stress and encourage more creative problem solving.

This technology can provide tools that men can use to increase their own power to change troubling aspects of their lives. As therapists we can increase the efficacy of treatment by creating clear and precise contracts with male clients. If the client is to spend ten minutes a day involved in a relaxation exercise, then instructions as to how and why this exercise is to be performed must be precisely spelled out in terms that he can relate to. If he is asked to plan and carry out an ideal evening with his non-communicative son, the plan should be clearly reviewed and the possible benefits of the plan emphasized.

A separate therapeutic consideration which underlines the process is the importance of the body. It is through the body and its functioning that men become known and grow to know themselves. Often it is through the abandoning of their physical beings that men both signal and speed up emotional disaster.

Physically, boys establish themselves as able to run, throw, persevere, react to and, therefore, live through their bodies. They test their limits and become whole by means of an integrated mind and body. Emotional expression can occur and is often released in play; excitement, anger, joy and sorrow are most totally expressed by mind and body in play.

Eric Nesterenko is a 38-year-old ex-hockey player who remembers himself as a "skinny, runty kid with a bad case of acne who wanted to be someone. Once you learn how to play, you are accepted in the group, there is a rapport. . . . You learn to survive in a very tough world. It has its own reward." And he cogently expresses the excitement of becoming known in play: "People can see who we are. Our personality comes through in our bodies" (Studs Terkel, 1972).

Unfortunately, the body also becomes the reservoir of unacceptable and unexpressed feelings as the male learns to hide his being, often to the point of severely restricted movement, stifled breathing and chronic tension. The male often trades his birthright of a free, functioning body and mind for control, and control becomes a straitjacket which sacrifices his emotional expression and restricts and strangles his being.

It is absurd to ask such a man to express what he is feeling when he has actually overdeveloped aspects of his musculature to lock in expression. After years of rigid holding of body and breath, the motility of his body becomes severely reduced. For this client, the road to healthy functioning should include working with the body. Therapists and theoreticians such as Reich, Louen, Alexander and Feldenkrais have argued persuasively that the mind and body are one. They and others have developed systems aimed at restoring expressive functioning and movement capacity. This type of body work is particularly relevant to men because so much of the male's development and sense of being comes about through the functioning of his body. Further, for a good many men their problems are essentially body problems. Their development has incorporated strong conditioning to block the expression of feelings, and so they exist in a chronic state of emotional isolation which may lead to periodic agitation and depression. With other men, problems stem from deciding to give up the "foolish" early emphasis on physical development. They have given up the joy of an integrated mind and body for what they believe to be a higher goal—getting ahead.

As more effective approaches are designed to treat the madness of men, the most relevant and difficult issue that will emerge is the role of the therapist. For it is apparent that he too is faced with the apprehension and uncertainty of meeting another man in a situation requiring mutual disclosure. Does he force a close and intense, but one-sided, intimacy where the burden of disclosure is with the client? Does he hide his vulnerability behind a guise of professionalism? Does he play a cool master or other-worldly mystic to remove himself from being with his client? Does he distance himself by being the classic all-knowing father or the efficient technician? If so, then perhaps he too is a captive of the rigid male stereotype that has contributed so much to making men ill and prevented them from getting well. In any case, the therapist's role cannot be separated from his history, his personal relationships, his heroes, his teachers and coaches and, one hopes, his own clear understanding of himself as a man.

References

MASLOW, A. H. *The Furthest Reaches of Human Nature.* New York: Penguin Books, 1976, p. 30.

FREUD, S. *An Outline of Psychoanalysis.* New York: W. W. Norton & Co., Inc., 1949.

JOURARD, S. M. *The Transparent Self.* New York: D. Van Nostrand, 1971, p. 36.

GOLDBERG, HERB. *The Hazards of Being Male.* New York: Nash Publishing, 1976.

HARTLEY, RUTH E. "Sex-Role Pressures in the Socialization of the Male Child." *Psychological Reports,* 1959, 5, 457–68.

MACCOBY, E., and JACKLIN, C. *The Psychology of Sex Differences.* Stanford University Press, 1974.

PLECK, J., and SAWYER, J. *Men and Masculinity.* Englewood Cliffs, N.J.: Prentice-Hall, 1974.

GREEN, R. L. *Heroes of Greece and Troy.* New York: Henry Z. Walck, 1961.

SPINO, M. *The Innerspace of Running.* Millbrae, Calif.: Celestial Arts, 1976, p. 26.

PERLS, F. S. *In and Out the Garbage Pail.* New York: Bantam Book edition, 1972.

MCCLELLAND, D. "Managing Motivation to Expand Human Freedom." *American Psychologist,* Vol. 33, March 1978, p. 201.

TERKEL, STUDS. *Working.* New York: Avon Books, 1972, p. 500.

true confessions

its a drag to live with desires
that are out of balance with the world

always
> *to keep a lid on it*
> *god don't like it*
> *mommy and daddy don't like it*
> *boy scouts don't like it*
> *Sylvia don't like it*
> *Ms. magazine don't like it*

nobody likes it
> *now I hate it*
> *now I have much anger*
> *now I will shower and shave*

now I will smile

SIDNEY MILLER

Male Mid-Life Decline

STANLEY D. ROSENBERG
AND
MICHAEL P. FARRELL

The phenomenon of dramatic mid-life change in men has a long tradition in Western culture. Aside from the obvious example of Gauguin, we have Michelangelo, who produced his "David," "Moses," and the roof of the Sistine Chapel between the ages of 29 and 40, then virtually nothing for the next fifteen years. Bach, following a pattern like that of Gauguin, did not begin his creative career until he was 38. Rossini was an artistic giant for his first forty years and a recluse for his last thirty-four.

Today, similar changes, referred to as "mid-life slump," "mid-life crisis" or "male menopause," are presented as being as common as adolescent identity crisis. For several years, the authors have been gathering detailed and representative data on the changes in emotion, attitude and personality that men undergo in mid-life.

This transition, which generally takes place between the ages of 39 and 43, creates problems for many men. We estimate about half of all males at this stage of life experience depression, despair and confusion about themselves and their lives. These feelings are reflected in behavioral changes and in the emergence of pervasive, but unsubstantiated, concerns with death, disability and illness. We characterize these concerns and feelings, combined with evidence of emotional withdrawal from friends, family and work, as a syndrome of psychosocial decline. Men in the decline syndrome vary in their emphasis of symptoms or changes but tend to combine several of them. It is notable that these men deny negative changes which are obvious to those around them. They insist that they are "doing fine" and are "in their prime" while showing evidence of distress and disorganization.

We find that the changes associated with mid-life are influenced by social class and environment. In a large survey conducted in 1973, young men (23 to 28) were compared to men approaching mid-life (35 to 48). The young men readily expressed feelings of alienation, dissatisfaction or anxiety while their middle-aged counterparts did not. The mid-life respondents tended to minimize any negative features they perceived in themselves or their lives. The exception to this rigid denial was found in the working class. These men were far more forthright in expressing their disappointment and distress but blamed their families, their neighbors or their work organizations. They often expressed their unhappiness through psychophysiological complaints (sweaty palms, trembling hands and headaches) and vague but insistent fears of fatal illness. Their outlook on the world became increasingly dour, and they became more prejudiced and punitive toward anyone different from themselves.

In contrast, the middle-class males refused to recognize that they were middle aged. Most claimed to be "young" and "in their prime." They indicated that their lives had measured up to youthful expectations, that they had few problems or complaints about their marriages, and that they rarely discussed personal problems. They were also the group with the highest incidence of alcoholism and were a high-risk group for peptic ulcer, hypertension and heart disease.

These findings were puzzling. Were the middle-class men truly satisfied and in harmony, or were they caught up in the need to appear strong, successful and in control? To find out, we studied twenty mid-life respondents. The following composites of those cases illustrates our findings and contrasts the ways working-class and middle-class men respond to mid-life.

These two men claimed to be non-symptomatic, self-fulfilled and situated in stable, congenial families. They are millworker Ed Fielding, 42, and electronics engineer John Brodsky, 44. Both married early and are still married to their first wives.

THE FIELDING FAMILY

We visited the Fielding family at home one evening. The time of the visit had been agreed upon, but the family was unprepared to receive us. Ed Fielding was still at work, the house was in disarray, and Joan Fielding was ironing. She was congenial and responsive, speaking freely about her life and marriage despite the presence of the younger children (two older children had already left home). She revealed dissatisfaction with most of her married life, particularly the early years when she was tied down with young children. Recently, she had gotten out from under by finding a job and taking a lover.

Ed's arrival brought a change in the emotional environment. The children quieted down and Joan became tense and circumspect, while Ed seemed less than delighted about our visit. During that evening and in subsequent interviews, some of the relations between Joan's reemergence and her husband's involution became evident.

Early in the marriage, she had accepted his demands that she remain enmeshed in home and family. The first child had come early and Joan found herself anchored to the home. Ed felt it unseemly to help with housework and demanded care and attention at the end of the working day. He was to be the breadwinner, she the nurturant mother. He still defends this pattern.

This existence precipitated her into years of depression. She yearned for a social life, but Ed hated socializing. He was also hostile, suspicious of their acquaintances, and reluctant to leave the children with anyone. For many years, he ruled the family with an iron fist. A major tool in his control over Joan was the fact that she could not drive. Quite suddenly, in his late thirties, Ed began to fear that he would be stricken by a heart attack. To assure himself swift transportation to the hospital, he demanded that Joan learn to drive. Her new mobility blossomed into a job and a boyfriend.

The irony of this situation cannot be appreciated unless one recognizes the fantasies which fueled Ed's efforts to control and isolate his wife. His distrust of others and dislike of socializing were reactions to a fear of his wife's possible infidelity. The victim of an unhappy childhood and inconstant mothering, he looked to his wife to "always be there." This desire was destructive not only to Joan but to their children because he could never accommodate to "sharing" her with them. He lived with this conflict by trying to identify with the children and to give them the "close family life" that was withheld from him. In reality, however, he could bear little real intimacy with his children and could not talk to or understand them.

This highly isolated, patriarchal family structure began to erode as the children matured. Joan would not confront Ed alone but found allies in the two eldest children, who also chafed under their father's heavy hand. The mother and eldest son became particularly close. As the conflict between father and son escalated, the boy left school and moved away. Of all the elements of Joan's bitterness toward her husband, this memory evokes the strongest feelings.

The remaining children are open (when seen individually) about their feelings toward their father. They feel he neither understands nor cares for them. Joan is feeling a sense of her own strength and freedom. She is unwilling to hurt Ed by leaving him or by acknowledging her infidelity but is unable to keep her rage in complete control. She is alternately deferential and derisive. When Ed said, "I don't like to go out at night and leave the children with a baby sitter," Joan responded, "We certainly don't need to hire a baby sitter when we have a sixteen-year-old daughter."

They are now leading almost parallel existences. Their sex life is all but over. Mother and children pursue interests outside the home while Ed sits home, drinks beer, curses the neighbors, and broods. Always withdrawn, he is becoming more isolated and morose as the years pass. He is disappointed in his work, where he has made little progress and found no friends. He has remained in a semi-skilled spot for years, while others of his age have moved ahead. He feels estranged and hostile toward the younger workers around him whose values and behavior he finds incomprehensible and repugnant. He hates his employer for not showing him the respect and appreciation he deserves. Ed takes tranquilizers to get through his work day.

He sees Joan and the children as his last refuge in a hostile world and must deny the anger and family dissolution which is clearly underway.

THE BRODSKY FAMILY

John Brodsky, like Ed Fielding, portrays himself as being in perfect health but does a much better job of maintaining the facade. Initially, after entering his gracious, custom-built home and being entertained with easy small talk, good liquor, and a sophisticated family dinner, we found it easy to assume that John is what he declares himself to be, a successful man epitomizing the rewards of hard work and achievement. The entire family is careful about not betraying any chinks in this armor.

Only after several hours of talk does Loraine Brodsky reveal that her husband has been an alcoholic and recently suffered a nearly fatal kidney shut-down. John explains that he "never really had a drinking problem," but rather "an unusual sensitivity to alcohol." Despite medical warnings that continued drinking will probably kill him, he has an occasional cocktail. He claims to be in perfect health because he has "recovered" from his kidney problems. This illustrates his ability to deny any evidence which contradicts the image he attempts to foist on himself and the world.

In his decline, John has become emotionally estranged from his family. We hear once again of a marriage which began in the traditional mode. John worked and Loraine stayed at home. She had begun a teaching career before the marriage, but after the arrival of their first child, she agreed to stop working full time. However, there was a period when she agitated to work part time, a move John resisted. Eventually, she stopped protesting. These conflicts were most overt in the first six or seven years of the marriage.

This issue represented an axis around which many elements of their family life crystalized. John, an ambitious man with a lower socioeconomic background than his wife, became the family achiever. He demanded her help in his work, and their joint effort was the basis of their marriage. This joint effort supported and, therefore, increased his achievements, and he won a reputation as a young "comer." For upward mobility and to maximize advancement, he switched from company to company, rarely staying in one location for more than a year or two.

This period was very good for John in comparison to the present and to his youth. He came from a hardworking, emotionally distant family and never received much affection. Consequently, he attempted to "prove his worth" to his family through school achievement. He was competitive and found it difficult to be close to others. His wife was the first person who meant very much to him, and he invested his emotional life in his relationship with her and his work. By providing emotion, warmth, and the capacity for interpersonal relationships, Loraine gave her husband the opportunity to work primarily in two spheres—the marriage and his job.

This arrangement came under increasing stress as John entered mid-life and his career advancement stopped. He could not move from engineering to management because he did not have leadership skills. The final blow came when the company he worked for closed down. For months he underwent trial by interview. His current job is far less prestigious and well-paying than his previous ones.

In the Brodsky family, mother and children form a muted alliance. They are not in combat with John, but they are determined to have warmth and enjoyment in spite of his emotional limitation. Both children feel that he has always been distant and that they were raised by their mother. They also identify with her enthusiasm for life. The three share interests, activities and friendships. This emerging pattern has left John isolated.

He began drinking heavily in his mid-thirties, during a period when the family power structure and coalition patterns were changing and before the period of his occupational stagnation. He used alcohol as an escape from the depression and isolation he experienced as his status was deteriorating. With no positive human relationships, occupational achievements were not enough to sustain him.

When his career stopped, his remaining defenses crumbled and he could no longer keep his wife at home. She went to work for a community college and after several years became the director of its adult education program. This work keeps her out all evening, and John has gravitated to a pattern of early retiring and early rising. They rarely take a meal together or speak to each other. This is a radical departure from the almost constant companionship that marked the early years of their marriage. Surprisingly, their sexual relationship survives.

While the husband declines, the wife ascends graciously, protecting him from any implication that he is less of a man than he was. He seems much older than his 44 years and, after a few hours of contact, becomes depressed. Loraine acts like an elder daughter, showing respect to him while essentially being his caretaker. He watches television, plays solitaire, makes jig-saw puzzles and claims it is a rewarding routine.

John clings to his myth of success and vitality. His middle-class status and intelligence contribute to this illusion. He finds some solace in his relative success and affluence and harbors ideas of an occupational comeback. His family plays along with this illusion and privately acknowledge its false quality. During the interviews, however, they treated him with kid gloves and rallied to protect him from embarrassing questions. John, in a reversal of form, confided privately that he wished he had the time to tell the psychologist all that was on his mind. Each segment of the family seemed obligated to protect the other from reality.

CONCLUSIONS

A substantial minority of men in our culture (perhaps one third or more) undergo a decline at mid-life. These men exhibit certain common characteristics. The specific style of each man's decline fits with his earlier life patterns. The despair represents an exacerbation of the struggles and central concerns of their lives. These struggles take on a special prominence at the time of mid-life transition. The experience is depressive for this subgroup and filled with images of death, illness, disability, and decay. These images are used as condensed symbols for an experienced diminuation of self.

This mid-life crisis is precipitated by changes in the man's lifestyle, age and societal expectations. Young men have certain beliefs about self-fulfillment and most strive for achievement, believing it will bring them feelings of wholeness and love. Early adulthood is a period of spontaneous effort based on these assumptions. By mid-life, a man can assess where that effort has left him in terms of his work and his relationships to community and friends.

Equally significant, he experiences changes in his relationship to his family. This relationship may be as much symbolic and mythic as it is real, but it is a crucial aspect of his sense of self. To the man who has bullied and coerced his wife and children into acting like an ideal "happy family," the mid-life crisis represents the stage when these enactments begin to fall apart. The wife and children begin to talk back, a transition precipitated by their own developmental changes. They are also fueled by the man's inability to maintain the domestic tyranny which earlier characterized his marriage. The failure to develop close affective bonds leaves a heritage of bitterness, anger and disappointment. There is very little basis to support the family's efforts to build a new life.

As his ego defenses crumble, a man experiencing the decline syndrome feels lost and stagnant. He tries to bind up his psychic wounds and to engage in some analogue based on patterns of early adulthood. Fundamentally, he often tries to envision a new period of successful striving. In this new venture he will once again be absorbed in tasks and efforts to conquer his environment. In reality, he lacks a strong conviction in such a possibility and has difficulty envisioning a life structure more congruent within his present experiences and current life-stage.

Our cases illustrate some typical responses to the dilemmas of mid-life. These men characteristically resort to denial, interpersonal withdrawal and manic activity as modes of ego defense.

During the crisis, these defenses become less useful to the victim and less appropriate to the other family members. It is difficult for men whose egos are dependent on family support, and who also have no capacity for intimacy, to adapt to these developments. Their lives have represented a continuous striving for power, strength and control. Abandoning these goals is a form of death, the death of a posited self. It remains to be seen whether the victims of this crisis can move beyond the patterns of decline and fulfill their fantasies of reemergence and transcendence.

What Time Is It in My Life?

Inexorable clock;
*   with your numbered face*
*   and black iron hands*
*   your ticking, clicking is sickening me.*

What mathematically perfect mind
*   made you so imperfect?*

In the youngness of my life,
I raced demonlike at breakneck speed,
through every moment,
but the clock hardly moved.

Now,
when I think,
stop and stand,
and look longingly
at the color of your eyes, skies,
puddles at the curb.

Now,
the calendars have gone wild,
my pauses are engulfed by whirlwind,
the clocks are possessed,
and life is flying by.

Can young boys and aging men,
ever know
what time it is in their lives?

SIDNEY MILLER

part two

SOCIALIZATION INTO MALE SEX ROLES

Motivation

Demonstration

SOCIALIZATION INTO MALE SEX ROLES

Explanation

Imitation

According to Yankelovich (1974), 80 percent of male workers in the United States see their jobs as meaningless and onerous. Although men may be victimizers of women and other men, we have seen in the preceding section that men can also be the victims of constraining and demanding role expectations. This section examines many of the ways that men are socialized into male sex roles from infancy through adulthood. It also points to one of the results of this socialization, which is sexism. It is a small, hollow privilege that most men get from sexism and the continuation of many of the traditional sex roles for either men or women.

Socialization into male roles begins very early for boys, as it does for girls in our society (Hartley, 1959). According to the author of the first essay, many preadolescent boys (as well as some girls) are conditioned into traditional male roles through social institutions such as Little League. Fine, a participant-observer of boys' interactions on Little League teams, examines some of the ways in which Little League reinforces and channels the traditional male sex role. Boys are taught to be tough and competitive; they are taught that girlfriends are to be "used," that girlfriends must be physically attractive, and that boys must be seen as "macho." Little League, therefore, teaches traditional roles through the boys receiving scornful comments about their "lack of masculinity" as well as through their identification with adult role models in the person of Little League coaches.

According to Kirshner, many comic books which children read present superheroes such as Superman, Captain Marvel, the Hulk, and Spiderman. Through the glorified stories of these superheroes, boys especially are taught to become the "Big Wheel, the Sturdy Oak, and Give 'Em Hell male with a minimum of the sissy stuff" (David and Brannon, 1976). Kirshner's study of past as well as more current comic-book heroes is an intriguing analysis of changing sex roles for males. An alternative proposed by Kirshner to the superhero of yesteryear is the "Common Man hero" who has no supernatural powers but "manages under pressure to call upon all of his natural resources." The author thinks that such an alternative may present contemporary children with more realistic, less sexist, and more attainable ideals.

Hantover argues that men become anxious when they are unable or fear that they cannot meet masculine expectations. Why are so many men anxious about their masculinity? Hantover suggests a social-psychological theory of masculine anxiety and rejects biological determinism. Masculine anxiety is grounded in male experiences of early childhood, adolescence and adulthood and is for many boys and men partly a result of role ambiguities and denials of opportunities to play optimal roles. Two ways are suggested by this writer for reducing this anxiety in boys and men: (1) the seeking of new ways to reaffirm traditional male roles and (2) the redefining of masculinity and giving "males more positive and self-affirming, not alienating, goals."

Another cost of traditional sex-role socialization is chauvinism. Carter in "Male Chauvinism: A Developmental Process" traces some of the factors which lead to the development of male chauvinistic behavior: (1) the continual higher valuing of the male than the female by society at large and (2) parental reactions to male infants, such as in rougher handling of boy than girl children. In conclusion, Carter also examines some of the consequences of chauvinism for men, women and society.

Another cost of most male learning, according to Balswick, is the socialization of many men either to be unaware of their feelings or to be unable to express many feelings. Men become inexpressive, that is, they do not express positive feelings toward others, as a result of the roles they have been taught. Male inexpressiveness is categorized on the basis of (1) whether there are feelings present, (2) whether there is an attempt to pretend to express feelings, and (3) whether the object of expressiveness is a female or a male. The resulting six types of inexpressive males which emerge from these three dimensions include cowboys, good ol' guys, playboys, locker-room boys and parlor-room boys. (The use of the word *boy* is intentional, since it more truly conveys the lack of maturity which is displayed by males who fall victim to one of these role constellations.)

Men are even taught to value some spaces above others and therefore are often left with an impoverished sense of personal space. In the final paper of this section, Tognoli examines some of the reasons why men feel ill at ease and even alienated in their own living spaces, their homes. As a child, Tognoli himself never perceived his parents' home as a place in which he could relax, especially with friends. Parental practices and social expectations also helped to produce discomfort and detachment from many of his living spaces throughout his life. One negative implication of the detachment which many men experience in their living spaces, according to Tognoli, is that they may move into "outer space" (interest in science fiction), become too comfortable living with sexist values, and may even physically move out and away from women and children.

Little League Baseball and Growing Up Male

GARY ALAN FINE

When the final history of the American Republic is eventually written, Little League baseball will probably receive no more than a footnote. However, this corner of American leisure has raised controversy worthy of the great issues of our day. Former pitcher Robin Roberts, recently inducted into baseball's Hall of Fame, has criticized Little League baseball as a "monster." And, if the plot of the recent popular film, *The Bad News Bears,* can be believed, the passions aroused are worthy of the Shakespearean stage.

During the period between ages eight and twelve, children (preadolescents) learn much of that which is necessary to function in a *social* world, and preadolescence has been termed the chumship period or the gang age. By this age most essential physical skills have been mastered, and the child has developed a considerable language repertoire and educational background. However, social competency, at least in the details of proper social interaction, is still being developed, and during preadolescence the emphasis in socialization is decidedly social. Little League baseball is one setting in which socialization occurs for the contemporary American preadolescent, and this situation contributes directly to conditioning the player into accepting the traditonal male sex role. It is this function of the American spring ritual, Little League baseball, that we shall examine in this paper.

For the years 1975 and 1976, I conducted in-depth field research with two leagues in the New England area.* This research consisted of intensive participant-observation (as a scorekeeper and as an adult friend to the players) bolstered by in-depth interviews with players and by short questionnaires distributed several times during the season.

Most Americans have probably had some contact either directly or indirectly with Little League baseball teams or players, the Little League being one of the major recreational organizations in contemporary life. The first Little League baseball league was founded in 1939 in Williamsport, Pennsylvania, with three teams having the goal of providing a sense of team belonging for the players by supplying a regular field, uniforms, and the trappings of a professional league. In addition, it was hoped that by having adult supervision, boys would learn more about the mechanics of the game of baseball.

The organization succeeded more than could ever have been imagined at the time. From the three teams organized in 1939, the league has grown to include 7,000 Little Leagues with approximately 42,000 teams, not including the softball programs or senior league programs run by the organization. Little League became as American as apple pie, and was granted a national charter by Congress in 1964. Despite a barrage of criticism by some parents and other interested parties, it cannot be denied that the overwhelming majority of the participants enjoy the Little League program. In one league in southern Rhode Island all players were asked during the last week of the season how much they had enjoyed playing Little League baseball. Of the 94 percent (98 players) who completed the questionnaire, 60 percent enjoyed playing Little League baseball "extremely much," another 28 percent said "very much," only 10 percent enjoyed playing "much," and 2 percent enjoyed Little League "only a little." Interestingly enough, none of the players responded that they did not enjoy playing at all, and only three boys quit Little League competition after the opening of the season. The satisfaction gained by players (mirrored in most parental comments) is quite impressive. Preadolescent boys by all available criteria enjoy participating in Little League baseball.

Of course, individual boys have negative experiences in Little League. Some individuals after several years come to regret their experiences, and in considering their youthful athletic exploits do not perceive them so grandly in retrospect (see Candell, 1974). However, the immediate psychological damage to the individual from participating in Little League is minimal.

*Part of this research was sponsored by the National Science Foundation through Grant SOC75–13094.

That Little League baseball helps to socialize boys into the male sex role seems beyond dispute, and with the recent acceptance (1975) of girls into the program, it may also begin to socialize girls into the male sex role.

Based on my research experience, I will first discuss the development of the male sex role based upon the informal interaction of boys nine to twelve years of age; then I shall examine the ways in which the Little League organization channels and develops these attitudes and provides them with a social legitimacy.

The Preadolescent's Developing Sense of Cross-Sex Relations

Freud described the period of preadolescence as one of sexual latency, perhaps the only period when the individual's sexual desires are relatively inactive. This view is supported by observations of children's play—boys and girls traditionally play separately (Lever, 1976; Furfey, 1930) and may publicly scorn or tease each other.

While there are occasions on which boys and girls do not have much contact, recent literature has indicated that no strongly felt sentiment exists on the part of preadolescents to separate on grounds of sex (Lewis, 1958). Sociometric research (Broderick and Fowler, 1961) has indicated that fifth-, sixth-, and seventh-grade students name a considerable number (17.1 percent) of children of the opposite sex as best friends. An interest among preadolescent boys in the opposite sex does exist—based on the physiological awakenings of puberty and in part on the boy's desire to fulfill the requirements of the male sex role in our increasingly eroticized culture. Both the teasing and proto-intimacies that boys feel (or feel they feel) stem from an emulation of their older companions and their media idols.

Preadolescent boys in both leagues mix surface hostility toward girls (teasing) with surface affectionate protectiveness (a manly concern about protecting one's girlfriend). These behavior patterns are similar to the aggressiveness that men show in attempting to "keep women in their place" and their sometimes patronizing (if well-meaning) affection.

In both leagues, girls go to the games to watch their boyfriends, generally without being publicly acknowledged by the boys. For one Rhode Island team this was particularly prevalent, as a small group of giggling girls would be present at many of the team's games and practices. The boys on this team (Sharpstone,* named after a local car dealership) never acknowledged their presence by as much as a wave or a hello. Their arrival did not pass unnoticed, however, as boys on the team would tease the recipients of their interest. As one boy said to one of the objects of

*All names in this report are fictitious.

their affection, "Hey, here comes your audience." Within the context of this all-male activity these outsiders could play no role other than as a source of embarrassment or as a point of negative comparison.

The response to girls in this situation must not be taken to suggest a complete lack of interest in girls. In both leagues, some twelve-year-olds and a few of the eleven-year-olds showed the beginnings of dating relationships (cf. Broderick and Fowler, 1961). These relationships were very important to them but exposed them to teasing from their peers (as is true for adult males as well). First, a boy could be embarrassed if caught displaying affection in the presence of another boy. One of the younger members of one of the Rhode Island teams was chased, though not attacked, after he had caught an older team member "taking care of business" (kissing his girlfriend). Second, the boy becomes vulnerable to comments that while he goes out with girls, he is unable to "score." Interestingly, the baseball metaphors of "getting to first base" (kissing) and "getting to second base" (non-genital petting) were common in a Boston suburban league, though not in Rhode Island. Perhaps due to the inability of the preadolescent male to express intimacy in other than euphemistic terms, or perhaps as a result of my presence (as an accepted adult, but an adult nonetheless), direct descriptions were not used. Thus, both being intimate with and not being intimate with a girl lead to teasing. The latter is the more serious charge and often is accompanied with scornful comments about lack of masculinity. The former, while teasing on its surface, implies respect and admiration in terms of the preadolescent male's value system, and the boy spied upon was considered by all players and coaches as one of the team's leaders.

The young male who has a relationship with a girl also may face teasing scorn about the girl's attractiveness (or physical attributes). One twelve-year-old was even teased by his friends for dating a flat-chested girl! A common putdown is to compare a friend's girlfriend to a dog. So on one occasion when a dog was spotted, one preadolescent asked another, "Why don't you say hello to your girlfriend?" When a strange dog showed up at Sharpstone practice and began barking, Whit, a handsome eleven-year-old and a member of the team's elite clique, was told that "that was his girlfriend"; and the dog was named Laurel, after Whit's current girlfriend. The ultimate insult is reserved for the boy considered unable to get dates other than with his sister or mother.

Boys can also be teased because of the real or imagined unfaithfulness of their girlfriends. Reporting to a boy that his girlfriend has been seen with another is designed to diminish the boy's status as an attractive, competent male. An excessive interest in girls or unfaithfulness to one's current girlfriend may also produce joking. Several boys, including Whit, were described as two-timers for spending time with girls other than their "official" girlfriends. The number of girls that a boy has or has had is a legitimate subject for teasing, frequently in conjunction with their lack of attractiveness. Justin, another member of the Sharpstone elite clique, remarked, "Whit has a lot of experience with dogs. He's been out with more than ten of them." Being over-attached to a girl is also grounds for teasing: Whit teased his friend Harry for daydreaming about his girl instead of playing baseball, and it was publicly noted that Whit cried after Laurel left for the summer, a point which Whit stoutly denied to the amusement of those around.

One of the central developmental tasks of the preadolescent male is learning to interact properly with the opposite sex. Even at this age, before dating becomes serious and passionate, boys are mastering the "rules of the game." The boy discovers that affection must be private; but that in order to avoid being considered ineffective, he must be willing to "kiss and tell," and because the behavior is private, there is no embarrassment if he tells more than he kisses. He also finds that girls are to be used—they need not always be treated as peers; at times they must be ignored for their own good or for the boy's reputation—one would not want others to think that he preferred talking to girls than to boys. Further, a boy learns that the physical attractiveness of his girlfriend and his "success" with her is how his masculine prowess will be judged. These themes were brought out in a letter I received from one of the Sharpstone players I knew well (Justin, the most popular member of the team). Justin, who at the time of the letter had just turned thirteen, wrote in answer to my question of whether he still saw his summer girlfriend, Carol:

Carol is old news. I just dumped my new girl friend (Karen). She could make out good though she wasn't that pretty. When I went out with Carol we never used to make out that much, but I make out with Karen everyday. I'm trying to go out with the prettiest girl in seventh grade. (I'm making progress). She is excellent. . . . Whit isn't going with Laurel any more. He was going with with Jean (Very Pretty. One of the best). But she dropped him. I think it was 'cause he never made out with her. [Punctuation regularized]

To show remorse at the end of a relationship is considered poor form. It is legitimate at this age to cry when one strikes out in baseball, but not if one "strikes out" in romance.

Preadolescent teasing does not always, or even usually, imply personal hostility. The remarks are generally traded in a good-natured fashion, with the target generally returning the barb in kind. Yet, despite the outward signs of merriment, these remarks serve as a mechanism for internalizing the appropriate male sex role.

One other aspect of the preadolescent sex role deserves mention: the emphasis on "macho" and toughness, and the desire not to be a sissy, baby or fag. For preadolescent boys being a member of any of these three groups is to be avoided at all costs. One must not be thought to be a girl (a sissy, prissy, bambi), a baby (a child), or a homosexual (fag, faggot, homo, Fig Newton, durv). All have identical implications—these are individuals who are not successfully portraying their male sex roles—they are too weak, quiet, thoughtful, friendly (in a gentle way), awkward, silly, happy, or generally non-conforming to the standards of their peers. This constellation of attitudes represents a covert denigration of all three groups. Because it is perceived that homosexual behavior is voluntary and is based on conscious deviance, that form of condemnation is the most severe. It is also the only one which adults generally do not use directly to preadolescent boys. Adults tell preadolescents to stop behaving like a baby or like a girl, but do not overtly raise the issue of homosexuality. Because this terminology is not sanctioned by adult usage, it is more precious and more denigrating when used by preadolescents.

The Channelization of the Male Sex Role Through Little League Baseball

It would be ludicrous to suggest that the creation and extent of the male sex role is caused only by the behavior patterns learned in Little League baseball. Preadolescent boys are placed in numerous circumstances in which similar masculine role identities are taught. Many fathers emphasize to their sons both in word and deed the importance of being a man (Cannell, 1974), television and movies are readily available sources of sex-role behavior, and peers in informal situations are of tremendous importance in teaching the boy others' expectations of him (Hartley, 1959).

Little League baseball, however, serves as a microcosm of these pressures. Because one of the defined goals of playing Little League is to win as a team, and to play as well as possible as an individual, the emphasis on competition is strong and this competition is seen as concomitant to the male role. In addition, because of the structure of the organization with a number of coaches and adult leaders assigned to each team, the preadolescent sees the adult male in a situation in which (1) the emphasis of the adult's behavior is on competition and winning; (2) informal interaction between adult males, outside of the presence of women, can be observed; and (3) the adult male has as a formal requirement of this role to teach the preadolescent about competing successfully. These factors collectively channel the behavior of the preadolescent. In addition, peer interaction is in this situation highly oriented toward winning, and weakness is not merely considered undesirable but also is directly frustrating to the goals of the other boys. In such frustrating situations some form of aggression is common (if not inevitable). Thus, Little League baseball and related athletic groups (such as Pop Warner football or Midget hockey) provide a structure in which many pressures—both organizational and behavioral—orient the boy to the male sex role, with its competitive emphasis (Pleck, 1976).

The Sharpstone team discussed here is a particularly vivid case study of this process, although the basic dynamics, if not the explicitness of the verbalizations, apply to virtually every Little League baseball team I have observed.

Sharpstone has a reputation of playing competitive, heads-up, hard-nosed baseball, and they have been one of the best teams in their league for several years. The players enjoy playing on the team, and many players on other teams are disappointed that they were not chosen by the Sharpstone coaches. The coaches, unlike those for other teams in the league, are not fathers, but two college students (Peter and Dave) majoring in physical education at the state university. Both are excellent athletes and are well-regarded, even envied, by other adults associated with the program.

Part of their method for teaching baseball and for dealing with their all-male team is to emphasize that players must not behave like girls. These comments, often not expanded upon, relate the concept of femininity to inadequacy in physical ability. Thus, Peter told his starting right fielder (a middle-status member of the team), "You throw like a girl." Later, when the starting catcher, Whitney, fell down reaching for a ball, Pete told him, "Get out there, Whit, you look like a girl." Of course, at that point another player (Harry—one of Whit's close friends) retorted, "He is." The effects of this behavior are apparent: A week after the incident Harry tells Whit in throwing practice, "You look like a girl," and other players use the term *girl* in this setting to mean incompetent. Both coaches when dissatisfied refer to the team as a bunch of girls, and a sincere compliment is to say of a boy that he is "a tough kid" (see Pleck, 1976:255). The coaches felt responsible to toughen their players, and the players wanted to be tough. Justin, the acknowledged team leader, was known as a "Kamikaze" on the base paths. The coaches tried to build this spirit up, to the point of teaching the team how to slide into a base to disconcert the opposing fielder.

The desire to be tough and masculine is strong, not only on this team but on virtually all teams. This view is often explicitly encouraged by the coaches and is entirely consistent with the inclinations of the high-status members of the team, who are physically well-developed for their age. The form of this behavior will depend upon the personality and needs of the individual adults and children, but the interrelationship between male adults and male children generally produces similar behaviors and attitudes.

Playing to win is associated with this masculine attitude, as is the importance of hustling, playing hard, and competition. While many coaches explicitly tell their teams that they can only ask them to do their best, the criteria for judging is whether the team wins or loses. An unsuccessful team is in the coach's implicit definition a team that is not trying. This places great pressure on the team that is not as able as other teams in the league (sometimes a result of poor coaching or poor choice of players by the coach). Because defeat is equated with a lack of desire, the losing team has its collective self-image threatened in terms of physical ability and team character.

On Sharpstone an additional factor influenced sex-role adaptation: the interest of the Sharpstone coaches in the sexual and proto-sexual behavior of their players. Most father-coaches never raise this dating behavior as an explicit topic of conversation; however, since the two coaches of Sharpstone were college students with no responsibility for monitoring the sexual behavior of their players and have close friendships with their players, joking on this topic was permissible. While never explicitly condoning the behavior of their players (for example, dating, kissing games, making out, and giving rings to girlfriends), their interest implicitly sanctioned such behavior and implied that this behavior was appropriately masculine. As in the case of the parent who does not punish the male child "because boys will be boys," socialization can occur by the boy observing adult inaction despite awareness, or through adult amusement. The teasing banter that concerned these subjects served to legitimate them. These preadolescents were not being taught directly by the coaches; however, their behavior was implicitly being sanctioned.

A similar situation is found regarding adult behavior toward preadolescent pranks. Again, the coaches on Sharpstone encouraged this type of behavior by their interest. At one point during the spring a number of boys went streaking through their neighborhood (that is, they ran around totally naked). The coaches were informed of this activity, and rather than being disapproving were vastly amused and asked those involved numerous questions about this episode—perhaps experiencing a vicarious thrill from their players' behavior. This type of behavior and other similar examples (throwing eggs at houses, darting through traffic) are typical of preadolescent males in America (Knapp and Knapp, 1976) and England (Opie and Opie, 1959), and it is not entirely dependent on the reactions of adults. Indeed, it has been argued that pranks may have value in developing social competence (Dresser, 1973).

The Little League context, both formally and informally, serves to channel male behavior by the structure of the league, with its emphasis on winning, by the examples set by the coaches, and by the reactions of the coaches to the team members' behaviors. Because currently only a small percentage of preadolescent girls play Little League baseball, the environment of the games and the practices is that of an all-male club—the rowdiness found on adult males' sports teams is mirrored to a surprising extent in Little League baseball.

Girls Will Be Boys:
The Decision to Allow Girls
to Compete in Little League

One of the most widely publicized victories for the Women's Rights Movement in the 1970's was the capitulation of Little League Baseball, Inc., in allowing preadolescent girls to play in the same leagues as boys. This was achieved over vehement objections from the supporters of Little League baseball, who believed that allowing the "weaker sex" to play would seriously compromise the integrity of the game and would destroy Little League. However, in the face of a barrage of lawsuits and considerable unfavorable publicity from feminists and journalists, and after an unfavorable 1974 court decision in New Jersey, girls were allowed to compete for positions on Little League baseball teams.

The arguments against admitting preadolescent girls dealt with the physical, psychological, and social. Some claimed that girls are not as physically well developed as boys—their bones are more fragile, and their reaction times are slower. However, child-development experts agree that until puberty there is no substantial physical differences in strength between the sexes. The proposed argument that girls hit in the chest would develop breast cancer, while psychologically interesting, was found to have no medical support. If anything, girls may be slightly stronger before puberty because of an earlier growth spurt (Tanner, 1972). The physical evidence did not support the desirability of isolating boys and girls during preadolescence.

Psychological damage was also seen as a possible outcome of the mixing of the sexes. One letter writer to *Sports Illustrated* noted: "I have small children of both sexes and I believe that most sports should be kept separate . . . because the young boys who are inferior to some girls will be harmed psychologically for the rest of their lives" (Wren, 1974). The sentiment is touching, but the writer makes a number of unfounded assumptions. First, the Little League experience is seen as more traumatic than it could reasonably be. A boy *may* suffer some public embarrassment by being bested by a girl, but that embarrassment is minor, and quite likely psychologically healthy. He will be surpassed by others; it is well to learn this lesson early. Also, the same girl may be able to better several or more boys; in this case, it is the girl who may be potentially harmed by the boys' collective resentment. The other assumption in the letter is that for men to be less competent than women is socially undesirable. With society changing rapidly in the direction of greater sexual equality, boys must realize that they cannot necessarily surpass girls in traditionally masculine activities.

If sports serve as a microcosm of American society, Little League baseball may be an excellent location for equality between the sexes.

The third element of the debate involved the social aspects of the game. As noted, many of the central values of Little League baseball are related to the male sex role—and to males' idyllic visions of their own childhood. Deford (1974) has argued that men feel that women are trying to steal their childhood—the golden days when boys could be free of societal restraints and propriety. The presence of girls, it is felt, would destroy this spirit. Some have argued that Little League managers are attempting through their involvement to recapture their lost childhood, the sanctity of the male-male bond. The presence of girls on the team would mean that the coaches would be forced to be self-conscious about the "propriety" of their behavior. Part of the dilemma of the male role is that among the middle class it consists of several mutually contradictory roles. The content of appropriate male behavior in the presence of other (equal-status) males differs enormously from the content of male behavior in the presence of females. Thus, coaches and some players felt that the presence of girls would "cramp their style." It is therefore not surprising that the coaches of Sharpstone did not want any girls on their team, and at one point said so publicly.

This social argument is harder to answer, since the presence of girls *is* likely to alter behavior. Yet we cannot estimate how much and in what direction. Male behavior may be altered by the presence of girls, but girls are more likely to alter their behaviors to conform to the actions of male coaches and male players. It is difficult to imagine many teams with a majority of girls or a large number of female managers; thus the dominant behavior patterns will be based on male behavior, and male sex-typed behaviors may become common among girls in Little League. This is speculative, and even if it is an accurate depiction of the future, it is questionable whether this would be beneficial over time.

As of 1978, girls have not rushed to play Little League baseball. Of four leagues of which I am aware, a total of six girls played "Major League" Little League in the first two years girls were admitted. The percentage of female Little Leaguers seems to be about 2 percent, although in the "Minor Leagues" (reserved for less talented players), the percentage of girls is higher—11 percent in one league.

There are several reasons for these relatively low figures. First, some leagues have responded to the feminists' challenge by setting up softball programs, which satisfy parents worried about having their daughters playing hardball but who want their children to have some form of athletic exercise. Many parents have not supported their daughters who desire to play Little League baseball (Peterson, 1974). Thus, girls find that they not only must overcome objections of managers and league officials, but also objections within their own family.

Some girls have internalized traditional beliefs of the proper behavior of young ladies. Girls are told that they will develop unfeminine muscles, and that boys will not want to hold hands with girls with rough hands (Ravage, 1975). Despite a growing feeling that people should be encouraged to behave as they wish regardless of traditional sex-role stereotypes, many females are anxious about the possibility of being defeminized through competitive team sport.

In typical American homes the father will take his son to the park or backyard and will teach him the fundamentals of baseball as early as the child can walk. Girls are given no similar encouragement by their parents, and not surprisingly most girls cannot play baseball as well as most boys. Indeed, from my observation, the average girl who tries out for Little League baseball is not as qualified as the average boy her own age because of this lack of experience. Until early sex-role training in the family changes dramatically, it is unlikely that girls will have a substantial numerical impact on Little League baseball.

Finally, some managers resolutely refuse to have girls on their team. They can do this because girls still have to be chosen in a competitive tryout, followed by a Little League "draft" or "auction" in which each manager chooses those players who he feels will most contribute to the team's success, and some managers expressly refuse to choose any girls. Since affirmative action has not yet affected Little League baseball, little can be done to remedy this situation. Fortunately, most leagues have some managers who welcome preadolescent girls on their teams, and so qualified girls are chosen. One hopes teams which choose the most qualified players regardless of gender will be more successful, and seeing this and seeing no unusual disharmony, other managers will change their drafting practices.

How do the Little League players feel about this commotion? As with any group of individuals, they disagree; but generally the male players do not mind girls playing on the same team if they are considered talented. This sentiment is more widely shared among the eleven- and twelve-year-olds than among the nines and tens, who would be most likely cut if girls played in great numbers. Two girls who played on the same team in the suburban Boston league I observed in 1975 created no friction resulting from their presence. As one boy on another team reported: "Well, the other players can't complain too much because they (the girls) are the best players on the team." However, not only skill contributes to acceptance— all girls in the leagues I have studied have been integrated into their teams, and boys unanimously claim that the girls have been accepted and have no problems fitting in. Girls agree with this assessment.

The problems predicted by opponents of sexual integration simply have not materialized; the great debate was a non-issue. When I asked players on all eight teams in the Rhode Island league six months after the season had ended what made their teams different from other teams, not a single player on the two teams for which girls played mentioned that their team was special because girls played on the team. Girls were accepted with little more difficulty than a boy of equal ability. Boys and girls have had the opportunity to work with each other in school, and so in the sports context the same patterns of cooperation are easily transferred. The preadolescent boy's interest in sexual matters and sexual behavior does not interfere with his task-oriented behavior on the baseball diamond. However, to the best of my knowledge none of the girls playing Little League baseball had boyfriends in the league, and, though I have no evidence for this, we might speculate that they were not considered suitably feminine to be dating partners, as is sometimes true with adult females in male-dominated occupations.

On the basis of the meager evidence available it is not clear in what specific ways girls alter their behavior to fit in with the team. However, since the teams on which girls play do not seem dissimilar to the other teams in the league, it is a reasonable hypothesis that girls are behaving in accord with the preadolescent male sex role in terms of competition and striving for success at all costs, and my observations of the few girls supports this view.

Summary

Little League baseball is a crucible in which the emotions and behaviors of preadolescence are displayed. In this article the preadolescent male's interest in sexual matters was described as a result of his sex-role training and as a result of bemused adult tolerance. Little League baseball serves as a channeling mechanism for appropriate male sex role behaviors through the identification with adult role models provided by the coaches and through adult reinforcement of preadolescent behavior.

Despite the emphasis on toughness and skill, girls are able to fit into Little League baseball with little difficulty. Boys see baseball as a goal-oriented activity, and any help toward that goal will be viewed with favor. The only difficulty in terms of complete acceptance of girls into the Little League structure comes from parents who insist on maintaining traditional sex-role stereotypes despite the greater flexibility of their children.

However, since the Little League system as it is currently structured is based upon competition and the need to win, Little League baseball may have the effect of teaching girls the basic tenets of the male sex role in terms of competition. The effects of this remains for future generations to determine.

References

BRODERICK, CARLFRED B., AND STANLEY E. FOWLER
    1961 "New patterns of relationships between the sexes among preadolescents." Marriage and Family Living 23 (Feb.): 27–30.

CANDELL, PETER
1974 "When I was about fourteen . . ." Pp. 14–17 in J. H. Pleck and J. Sawyer (eds.), Men and Masculinity. Englewood Cliffs, N.J.: Prentice-Hall.

DEDFORD, FRANK
1974 "Now Georgy-Porgy runs away." Sports Illustrated 40 (April 22): 26–37.

DRESSER, NORINE
1973 "Telephone pranks." New York Folklore Quarterly 29 (June): 121–30.

FURFEY, PAUL H.
1930 The Growing Boy. New York: Macmillan.

HARTLEY, RUTH E.
1959 "Sex-role pressure in the socialization of the male child." Psychological Reports 5:457–68.

KNAPP, MARY, AND HERBERT KNAPP
1976 One Potato, Two Potato: The Secret Education of American Children. New York: W. W. Norton & Co., Inc.

LEVER, JANET
1976 "Sex differences in the games children play." Social Problems 23 (April): 478–68.

LEWIS, GERTRUDE M.
1958 Educating Children in Grades Four, Five and Six. Washington D.C.: U.S. Office of Education, U.S. Department of Health, Education, and Welfare.

OPIE, IONA, AND PETER OPIE
1959 The Lore and Language of Schoolchildren. Oxford: Oxford University Press.

PETERSON, ROBERT W.
1974 " 'You really hit that one, man!' " New York Times Magazine (May 19): 36–7, 90.

PLECK, JOSEPH
1976 "My male sex role–and ours." Pp. 253–64 in D. S. David and R. Brannon, The Forty-Nine Percent Majority: The Male Sex Role. Reading, Mass.: Addison-Wesley.

RAVAGE, JOHN M.
1975 "Should your daughter go out for football?" Family Circle (Oct.): 36, 124.

TANNER, J. M.
1972 "Sequence, tempo, and individual variation in growth and development of boys and girls aged twelve to sixteen." Pp. 1–24 in J. Kagan and R. Coles (eds.), Twelve to Sixteen: Early Adolescence. New York: W. W. Norton & Co., Inc.

WREN, LARRY L.
1974 "Little League lasses." Sports Illustrated 40 (April 15): 40.

I Sit Frozen on the Couch

I sit frozen on the couch,
arm around her shoulders.
It is time to take the Next Step
but I am too scared to move.
The seconds tick off my embarrassment,
hanging from my eyes like tears of lead
dragging me down, down.
There is no way forward
and no going back
so we sit . . .
frightened boy,
passive impassive girl . . .
stone statue that I am supposed to want
to touch,
that I do want to touch.
Nothing comes from you
    no help
    no clue
    no heat
    no warmth
yet for fifteen years I will hate myself
for not being able to make love
to a succulent corpse.

DAVID STEINBERG
Copyright © 1979 by David Steinberg

Masculinity
in American Comics

ALAN M. KIRSHNER

A short while ago my son asked me to buy him his first comic books. I had not read a comic book since the 1950's. I immediately noticed a number of changes in the roles of the superheroes. Since I was already teaching a course on masculine roles, I decided to examine how comic books might be mirroring changing masculine values.

Comic books can provide a fantasy world through which children will reinforce roles or values while sheltering themselves from their feelings of insignificance. Children hero worship in order to shield themselves from such fears as floating down the drain in the bath tub, a very prevalent childhood nightmare. The protecting heroes of childhood are real ones like their parents or imaginary ones like Superman. Centuries back youngsters could identify with or fantasize themselves as gods and goddesses and the heroes of the myths and legends of their societies. More recently, folk heroes such as Paul Bunyan or John Henry fulfilled this task. Today's mythological heroes are found in the comic books and to a lesser extent the comic strip, which as a whole seems to be written to entertain adults rather than children. Millions and millions of comic books are sold every year to these small people searching for fantasy heroes who would help them cope in a world of uncertainty. Most children have perused comic books at some time in their lives. Whether the effect of comic books has been positive or negative is open to debate.

An article on action figurines ("Dolls Are for Girls") in the *New York Times Magazine* a few years ago struck my fancy, as the author argued for the positive growth of children playing with Spiderman, Batman, The Hulk—all derived from the modern folk heroes found in the comic book. The writer argued for the escapism and dream world these dolls (action figurines) provided for the growing child. If the child can identify with the super powers of Superman, then the child can ward off all evil; the child can fantasize himself as superior to the giant, threatening world around him. Most of the superheroes, be they The Hulk, The Thing, The Falcon, or Spiderman, appear indestructible, exactly the way a child wants to be while waiting for maturity: waiting for those muscles of steel that can be imagined by identifying with the perfect forms of the superheroes, or for the more adventuresome, by sending in a dime to Charles Atlas.

Superman, Captain Marvel, The Hulk, and other Marvel or D.C. comic superheroes are "superior in kind" to the ordinary mortals. The need for the "superior in kind" hero still remains in our young; yet I believe our youth today tend to identify or escape more readily with the "superior in degree" hero. The belief in the perfect or "superior in kind" hero went out with the sixties, with the tell-it-like-it-is generation. The "superior in kind" hero is "greater" than the child and is significantly different. It is as if he were of another species—witness Superman's descent from another planet or Bruce Banner's transformation into The Hulk as the result of a gamma bomb explosion. The perfect hero can control his world in ways in which the child cannot, although the child can still fantasize. The "superior in kind" hero can defy "natural laws." To identify with such heroes, the child must reach out to his most extreme fantasies.

In contrast to this Super Man hero is the more practical, at least for the child, Supreme Man hero, the hero "superior in degree." This hero is (or appears to be) human—Batman, for example—more powerful than the child, yet real. A Batman, capable of making mistakes (but seldom does), physically vulnerable (but seldom hurt), and ultimately mortal (though the child can sometimes feel that the hero is immortal). The Supreme Man hero can no more defy natural laws than the child can; yet he may seem to.

I have been discussing these superheroes in the masculine because traditionally they have been masculine or empowered with masculine attributes. In recent years a myriad of women superheroes have appeared. In my generation only Wonder Woman existed, and we simply passed her off as a lesbian, which many of my hard-hat friends still do to any woman who joins their occupations. Girls have usually found their champions in the likes of Lois Lane. For boys early in life learn the role of protector, while girls learn the role of being protected.

In the comic books the superhero, be he a Super Man or a Supreme Man, is a Real Man. He protects the woman. The young boy, in fantasizing about his folk hero, becomes the folk hero in order to defeat the forces of evil—the world of the unknown. In so doing, he saves the weak, pious, pure, well-endowed female from the same dangers. Ah, those many dreams I had as I grew up of saving the poor maiden in distress, wearing my mask and cape (my fantasy identity) and obtaining her gratitude—a peck on the cheek. I flew off not wanting more, knowing in my masculine way that if I wanted or needed more than that peck on the cheek, my superpowers would evaporate. I, like Samson whose hair Delilah cut, would then be in the hands of a woman, and therefore at the mercy of the evil forces in the world, never again able to defeat the villains. I feared the ultimate result of a woman's control—always remaining small, petite, feminine, a sissy! I, like boys today, in reading comic books, had my role spelled out: I was to be strong, silent, aloof, decisive, rational, and of course success would follow.

And, what of those girls I dreamed of rescuing? They found their security in the comics, too—evil could be warded off, the unknown conquered, and maturity finally achieved if they could win over a male superhero to protect them. Young girls learned and learn the way to obtain this protector, this man of steel, this Doc Savage: Be pious, pure, domestic, submissive, sweet, demure and develop a 40-inch bust—Charles Atlas versus Mark Eden!

Young girls tried to fill their bras as Lois Lane and the heroines of the romance comics obviously did, although endowments were seldom emphasized, as this would have called into question the demure image. Only insecure girls, who obviously could never find a protector to guide them through their young years, became exhibitionists. For the Charles Atlas protege, exhibitionism was expected. A boy needed to show how aggressive, assertive, and strong he really was by following the pattern set by his hero in the comics. He rolled up his sleeves and displayed his bulging biceps. A girl would swoon, dream of romance, and wait to have her door opened for her. The boy would ignore the girl while saying, "Daddy, feel my biceps!" Comic books taught a boy to be a man, not a sissy, and a girl to be a true woman.

What is a Real Man, then? Earlier I alluded to some of the accepted roles of masculinity in our culture: A man must be aggressive, dominant, assertive, strong, silent, and success oriented. Deborah S. David and Robert Brannon, who have edited a book of readings called *The Forty-Nine Percent Majority: The Male Sex Role*, inform us that a small number of themes prevail which ultimately define American masculinity—the masculinity so often portrayed in the comics:

1. *No Sissy Stuff:* The stigma of all stereotypes are feminine characteristics and qualities, including openness and vulnerability.

2. *The Big Wheel:* Success, status, and need to be looked up to.

3. *The Sturdy Oak:* A manly air of toughness, confidence and self-reliance.

4. *Give 'Em Hell!:* The aura of aggression, violence, and daring.

"The Big Wheel," "The Sturdy Oak," "No Sissy Stuff," "Give 'Em Hell!"—these masculine roles are what a boy learns and men in later life continue to confront. The role is reinforced in the media and by friends and relatives. Men can talk about sports, sex, business, and politics in a cold, calculating manner providing the image of the Big Wheel, the Sturdy Oak, Give 'Em Hell, but always avoiding the Sissy Stuff.

There is no difference in the comic books: Spiderman starts out as Peter Parker, "bookworm, professional wall flower" needing to be fattened up. Peter Parker, who wears glasses and is more interested in attending an exhibit at the new science hall, can't win the admiration of the girls so necessary to young boys entering puberty. How does this sissy obtain his success? He doesn't need to take the Charles Atlas course advertised at the back of the comic. Luck, in the form of a radioactive insect, transforms him into a miraculously strong, agile Real Man who only now that he is physically strong can take advantage of his knowledge of science and achieve respect as Spiderman.

How about the comic books' sissy of sissies, Clark Kent? Well, involvement with women is never permitted for a Real Man. Women chase him, he ignores them, and once in a while he releases his sexual spleen faster than a speeding bullet. Clark Kent is a whimp. He would do anything for Lois Lane. For almost forty years Clark has been saying the same basic words as he said in a 1943 comic: "Lois—I hate to be insistent, but won't you please tell me once and for all if you care for me?" and Lois's response has remained the same: "I like you, Clark, but how could I really care for a man like you when I've associated with someone as confident, outspoken, and assertive as SUPERMAN!" "Confident, outspoken, and assertive"—Clark simply can't learn his role as a man—that masculinity he needs to conquer a woman.

Believe it or not, times have changed—at least a little. Clark seems finally to have made the scene with Lois Lane and they have recently married. How did that sissy Clark Kent finally score? OK, all you Woody Allen rejects, do you want to know the secret of success? Clark lost his temper and dumped a table full of food on a fellow TV commentator (times have changed, so Clark Kent's old reporter job with the Daily

Planet has been replaced with the more glamorous and playboy-like position of a TV anchorman). Later, he even decks his fellow TV commentator with one punch. He has become the Big Wheel, the Sturdy Oak, Give 'Em Hell man with a minimum of the Sissy Stuff. His transformation takes place in full view of Lois Lane. Clark Kent can play the role of protector to this great cook and homemaker who has a body to match. She gets the message and so do America's boys. At the end of this story in the March 1976 edition of *Superman Comics,* they are behind closed doors and we read: "All right, Clark . . . no more SHOP TALK tonight!" To which Clark slyly responds: "Want to see something, Lois? I've got this great romantic view of the apartment across the street. . ."

Clark Kent, successful TV commentator, darling of millions of viewers, has learned to be assertive, aggressive and dominant: Good-by mild-mannered Clark Kent? It is Clark Kent who marries Lois Lane, not Superman. No Real Man gets married. That is sissy stuff. Clark Kent returns to his wimp status. Marriage is a True Woman's dream. For the Real Man, the bachelor's life is ultimate bliss. Most unmarried comic-book heroes are adventurers, swashbucklers, loaded with virility. For the Real Man, to marry would be to castrate him, to eliminate his virility, to prove him a sissy. The married man might try to preserve what remains of his swashbuckler adventuresome spirit by having a few affairs on the side with his secretary or when he is out of town at a convention with a bar maid. Yet in most cases the married man can only assert his masculinity by having male friends over on the weekend to watch sports on TV, for now as the provider and protector of a woman he feels he hasn't time to participate. His memorized sports statistics, his can of beer and his poker game serve to prove to the boys that he is not "pussy whipped." Yet, the Dagwood Bumstead image prevails.

Being a Dagwood Bumstead scares (dare I say it?) the pants off of most unmarried men. Dagwood Bumstead, disinherited from his masculinity through marriage; browbeaten by a domineering and assertive wife; abused by his boss; and generally a failure in everything he tries, although his intentions may often be generous. Dagwood Bumstead may once have been a debonair playboy, but marriage has made him impotent. The Real Man—the Big Wheel, the Sturdy Oak, Give 'Em Hell male—unmarried, is never inadequate, for he has a nine-inch phallus (read any pornography). Married men, or single men like the former mild-mannered Clark Kent—sentimental, emotional, wearing glasses—always project the imagery of a three-inch penis, obviously inadequate in life; ask any teenager in the gym locker room. Yet, when a Clark Kent can assert his masculinity—punch a colleague in the nose—it is interesting, better said, tragic, how his organ gains six inches. He is ready for Linda Lovelace, or she for him. But poor Dagwood, all he can do being married is use his three inches to do his assigned job, breeding. Once he does that, the sex life of the former swashbuckler son of a rich man ceases to exist. He can only sublimate through the sandwich he made famous. No secretaries, no bar maids, no reciting sports statistics, nothing to flavor the few remaining drops of his former virile self—Dagwood Bumstead All-American husband, cuckold.

Dagwood Bumstead, Clark Kent, and Peter Parker are the type of men young boys learn they must never become. Much better to try and be a Superman, Batman or recently a Spiderman. As adults, men will in their subconscious still idolize the masculinity of the superheroes, but the realities of life will probably have matured them into Clark Kents. If this truth fails to create conflict toward their masculine roles, then certainly the changes in society since the 1950's, also reflected in the comics, will.

I grew up in the fifties, the era Alvin Toffler, author of *Future Shock,* identified as the apex of the industrial age, the era of uniformity. Boys confronted two worlds, Fonzie's or Richie's, the hood and blue-collar worker, or the collegian and man in the gray flannel suit. Each group appeared to dress alike and to groom alike. Sure there existed a few pariahs, outsiders like the beatniks who demanded diversity on their terms, but most of us only had the choice between two roles. College-oriented boys sported flat-tops, wore saddle shoes or white bucks, chinos, and button-down collar shirts with buttons on the back. Boys headed for blue-collar occupations wore blue jeans, tee shirts with the cigarettes held tight against the shoulder by rolled up sleeves, motorcycle jackets, garrison belts and engineer's boots. This was the culmination of a civilization born of the Industrial Revolution: each boy stamped out of the same mold in order to adapt to a factory society based upon mass production. Individuals formed into the nation, thereby becoming a focal part of the country's industrial output. Men existed as tools of the nation as well as of the industrial society. The media ignored the pariahs of society, the outcasts, the marginal individuals, as knowledge of them might tend to draw the nation apart or throw a wrench into the machines of mass production.

The sixties brought change, unprecedented change. Toffler speaks of the new age as the coming of super-industrialism, the era of diversity. For example, in the fifties, during the height of industrialism, men piled layers of cloth together and the machine cut out, let us say, one hundred suits in one minute, all the same style of grey flannel. Presently, a laser can cut out one hundred suits in half a minute, each suit completely different. In this super-industrial age the choice between alternatives is immense. Today's man (and woman for that matter) can choose among hundreds of diverse lifestyles and patterns of dress, and I advance that this is only the beginning. Looking at the boys of the eighties, we can see long hair, short hair, beards, mustaches, various styles of side burns, tee shirts, wide-collar shirts, button-down collars, loose pants, tight pants, no pants, and on ad infinitum.

During the fifties, boys attempted to be like Jack Armstrong, All-American boy. They believed in the Horatio Alger myth. Any man could achieve success, provided of course he showed no Sissy Stuff (feminine characteristics and qualities, including openness and vulnerability), learned the roles of the Sturdy Oak—that aura of aggression, violence, and daring—and in reality were white, blonde, Protestant, and blue eyed. The era of uniformity bred skin lighteners, hair straighteners, name changes, as minorities tried to conform. Identity crises, especially in the males, became intermixed with Friday night drunk spells, big cars, or a hundred and one other escape valves.

The sixties brought a revolution. People on society's fringes demanded participation in the wealth of America while maintaining their cultural identity. Women insisted on their equality to choose between being pious, pure, domestic, and submissive or being aggressive, assertive, dominant, and successful, or between any combination of these traits. Finally, many men began to question the roles they had been forced into. Why couldn't they "tell-it-like-it-is"? The "success objects" had higher percentages of ulcers, high blood pressure, heart conditions and suicides than the "sex objects." Men became more distraught and distressed after divorce than women. They had power but not happiness. Men couldn't tell-it-like-it-is because the roles they had learned only allowed them to talk sex, politics, guns, and cars. They couldn't express their personal feelings, emotions, sentiments—either positive or negative—for fear of being vulnerable and therefore failing in their role as providers, protectors: success symbols. Men had to give the impression of being perfect, of having nine-inch cocks, of being Superman in the guise of Clark Kent. First the gays and then some heterosexual men began to demand out of this box—Gay Liberation, Men's Liberation.

As the super-industrial age has produced confusion in choices, it has also created anxieties about roles. In recent years, the comic books, like other forms of popular culture, began to mirror some of this confusion, some of these anxieties, and a bit of the change. Comics began to provide more alternatives for men. Perhaps only a minimum of what is needed in this age of diversity, but at least the false perfectiveness of the fifties and earlier has been replaced by a touch, mind you only a touch, of reality.

The perfection of the Superman and Captain Marvel of the fifties is giving way to the conflicts and anxieties of Spiderman and The Hulk. The WASP image of Batman has been joined by the diversity of the likes of the black man who is The Falcon. The comic book hero of super-industrial age of diversity can show Sissy Stuff along with the Big Wheel, Sturdy Oak, and Give 'Em Hell images. What could be more relevant, more inspiring, than a hero like Spiderman? A hero who constantly questions his motives, expresses his vulnerability, and even washes his own costume. A hero who sells autographed photographs of himself in order to pay his college tuition. Boys can learn from reading the new comic books that they no longer need money to be successful, nor do they have to be humble.

There is nothing innately wrong with success if you determine what your success should be. With most men the drive for success and the type of success has been dictated by others. The results are usually self-destruction. Today, boys are growing up in and men are living in a new society that is offering a myriad of alternative lifestyles, and males are questioning the traditional masculine values, as are their counterparts in the comic books. Not all men who begin to question their roles and direction toss the traditional values aside for a new life. Actually, many find the society-directed roles fulfilling for them. Yet, they have made their decision after questioning and admitting their fallibility. Even this new approach to masculinity—admitting anxieties, questioning, searching, feeling, and deciding upon a new direction or returning to one's previous goals but finally understanding why—is also being portrayed in the contemporary comics.

In December 1974, Captain America became distressed. How could he continue to fight for the red, white, and blue, considering Nixon and Watergate? Americans had faced crisis and scandal before, but none had driven Captain America to query his American superhero status. Captain America now questioned his ability to fight for good in the American way when he concluded that the American way in reality was corruption, abuse of power, and Catch-22 phraseology. He decided he had no alternative but to hang up his uniform and shield. Yet once a superhero always a superhero. He rapidly realized that he still needed to fight evil. So Captain America concluded that he must take a new identity and battle evil as a world superhero. He became the Nomad. He made himself a black and yellow costume and decided he needed a cape. He could never understand why Captain America failed to be given a cape—a real superhero always had a cape. Well, society's reality soon struck him in the face. For as the Nomad he went after the supervillains in his first assignment in his new identity and he tripped on his cape, fell flat on his face and knocked himself out cold. When he awoke and realized the supervillains had absconded he said, "Now I understand why Captain America never had a cape." And reflecting that new masculinity that permits vulnerability even of superheroes, he concludes, "Well, even a superhero is entitled to a mistake!" The young boys of today no longer need to match the Perry Mason success rate of all wins and no losses.

Later, the Nomad became confused as he learned of another Captain America battling evil. He soon encountered the pretender—a Puerto Rican youth, symbol of the new America. By the April 1975 issue of Marvel Comics' *Captain America and the Falcon,* "Cap's Back!" Why? Well, after some heavy thought, The Cap said: "But being the Nomad was no MISTAKE! Being forced into a greater awareness of CORRUPTION,

DECEIT, and the madness of POWER was no mistake—even if the initial SHOCK was almost more than I could BEAR. I did react more with my HEART than my HEAD—but it forced me into a greater awareness of MYSELF, as a MAN—And as a SUPERHERO, apart from the LIVING LEGEND I had become, I learned what makes me TICK—something I could NEVER have done while I was living my life trapped deep in a RUT! I never intended to go BACK to being C.A., but it was only through stepping OUTSIDE myself that I could gain a PERSPECTIVE on going back in! No, I may not ALWAYS have made the BEST decisions, but NOTHING I did can be called a MISTAKE! I've BROKEN AWAY from the BLINDNESS of the past, which can only mean a better FUTURE for both MYSELF—and the COUNTRY!"

Captain America, similar to many men today, is able to contemplate, feel, and even be vulnerable. He finds himself and likes himself on a more mature level. He has been disabused of his naive optimism, entering a state of pessimism, and finally arriving at a condition of mature optimism. Yet, there is still a long way for Captain America to go, just as there is for most men in our society. Today a man or superhero can express thoughts of love; yet he still can't permit himself to be "pussy-whipped," nor is he allowed to relax and contemplate for too long. He still must follow his drive for work and success. Masculinity, then, as portrayed in today's comics, is providing some alternatives to the traditional No Sissy Stuff, Big Wheel, Sturdy Oak, and Give 'Em Hell values. The American male is changing, and the comic-book media is reflecting this transformation. The range of acceptable performances, the roles men are permitted to play, certainly has been expanded, and in my mind that's for the better. Yet neither in the comic books nor in society as a whole do I feel men are provided a wide enough range of alternative roles to select from.

In Webster's *Seventh Collegiate Dictionary* we find a superman defined as a "superior man that according to Nietzsche has learned to forego fleeting pleasures and attain happiness and dominance through the exercise of creative power." Perhaps it is time to forego the image of the Super Man or Supreme Man hero and construct the Common Man hero as Roger Rollin in his introduction to his 1973 book *Hero/Anti-Hero* defines him: an individual possessing "no more power than we do and no more virtue or skill." I believe the tell-it-like-it-is generation has invested us all with a greater sense of self-worth, and those who are mourning the loss of heroes fail to understand the creation of a healthy, productive, participatory society where we are each our own heroes. The Common Man hero in a sense is the "hero of the moment" rather than a "hero by inheritance" or a "hero by radioactive accident." According to Roger Rollin, "the Common Man hero has never been endowed by nature with any special powers, but rather has managed under pressure to call upon all of their natural resources." It is time for all people and especially men to call upon all of their natural resources. When men can finally become relevant males by allowing their masculinity to reflect sentimentality, vulnerability, emotion, tenderness, openness, closeness to other men, and weakness, then our male comic-book heroes will no longer need Charles Atlas bodies, nor for that matter will the female heroines require Mark Eden busts, and our young will mature warding off evil from within, deciding their own direction for success.

The Way to Be a Man

I get tired of being all together, whether that's the way I feel or not,
Tired of being Superman, to stand alone with feelings that I've got,
But I was told when I was small, never cry, to stand up tall,
Back up straight against the wall, no time at all to fall,

    The way to stand, the way to be a man.

Talk of women who are pretty, in the cities, in the towns,
They walk and ride beside you and you long for love you hide beneath
    a frown,
Talk about the football games, helpless dames, and planes and trains,
Heroes' names and will it rain and silently no one complains,

    The way to stand, the way to be a man.

I give to others every day, to help them find the way they say they're
    looking for,
To show them how they must be strong, to carry on a life they've never
    had before,
Bring the feelings from inside, shed the fears you want to hide,
It's time to ride the great divide, time to open and confide,

    The way to stand, the way to be a man.

I get tired of being all together, whether that's the way I feel or not,
Tired of being Superman, to stand alone with feelings that I've got,
I need a friend to call my own, to care for me when I'm alone,
To call me on the telephone and visit me when I'm at home,

    Together stand, the way to be a man.

    Together stand,
        hand in hand,
            the way to be a man.

WORDS AND MUSIC BY BILL FOULKE
Copyright © 1980 by Bill Foulke
Used by permission

The Social Construction of Masculine Anxiety

JEFFREY P. HANTOVER

Men no longer come "forward as representatives of the universal." Their gender role is scripted by society and not by some extrasocietal force (whether it be God or their chromosomes). We have come to recognize the cultural grounding of the male role. We need to explore with more discrimination how men respond to problems of sex-role performance. Why do men become anxious about their masculinity?

This paper attempts to develop a social-psychological theory of masculine anxiety. It rejects biological determinism, the determinism often implicit in theories of differential early childhood socialization, and a purely reactive male-female model of anxiety. I do not deny the developmental consequences of early childhood socialization experiences, but they are the first layer of anxiety disposing events which males undergo as they progress through the life cycle. Adult masculine anxiety flows from the experiences of early childhood and adolescence but is independently generated by events in adulthood. However, we must move away from a restricted perspective which sees men anxious about their masculinity solely in reaction to the assertiveness of women and their demands for previously male-only prerogatives. This is only one aspect of adult masculine anxiety. Men become anxious when they are unable to meet cultural expectations and social opportunities. The restriction of opportunities may occur independently of the action of women.

Anxiety is produced in childhood, adolescence, and adulthood. In childhood it flows primarily from the unique aspects of male sex-role socialization. Early childhood anxiety is basically an anxiety over goals. So is adolescent masculine anxiety, but in this stage the focus shifts from the parents to the peer group. Males in the peer group suffer from pluralistic ignorance—each is unaware of the other's doubts about the meaning of manliness. For adults, in addition to continuing doubts about the proper goals of manliness, there is an anxiety of means. Men committed to the culture's goals of manliness do not have the excuses of youth; and when they are unable to meet these goals, they can become anxious.

I am not arguing in support of present role prescriptions when I speak of anxiety flowing from the discrepancy between goals and means. I am arguing that an individual who has a "high masculine sex-role preference" may react anxiously when unable to meet the culture's sex-role standard.

A General View of Masculine Anxiety

Anxiety, let alone masculine anxiety, is an elusive concept in its causation and expression. I will use masculine anxiety as a theoretical construct to explain a defensive reaction in attitude and action to threats to the perceived integrity of sex-role norms and to the individual's felt ability to meet these normative demands. The anxiety expresses itself in the increased saliency of gender in social life and in a compensatory emphasis on the assertive and aggressive side of the male role. The man "protesteth too much" is the commonsense recognition of what behavioral scientists term defensive masculinity or compensatory masculinity. Salience refers to an increased concern over what is proper male and female behavior and the tendency to see sex-role differentiation at stake in a wide range of issues from birth control to whose head should be higher on the pillow.[1]

The definition of masculine anxiety used here focuses on two aspects of role strain. The first is ambiguity. The individual is unclear about what kind of person he is to be, what he is expected to do. The script is sketchy and he must improvise. Ambiguity is distinguished from role conflict, in which the person is faced with conflicting role demands: I am supposed to be masterful and dominant but I am also told to be convivial, a good mixer, and one of the boys. This conflict can lead to anxiety, but this paper

---

[1]Komarovsky (1976, p. 29) writes of one male undergraduate: "His sensitivity to sex roles was seen in his remark that, if his head happened to be lower than his fiancee's on the pillow, he readjusted his position."

concentrates on other forms of anxiety which appear more prevalent with males.

The second type of anxiety arises when the individual has a well-written script, knows his part, wants to perform, but is denied the opportunity to act. The fault lies not in the individual's commitment to the role, his capabilities, or motivations, but in the social structuring of opportunities or what Komarovsky calls the "socially structured scarcity of resources for role fulfillment." The focus on the opportunity structure gets away from an overly individualistic view of anxiety: The individual lacks personal resources or reacts to women whose demands for equality have made him feel threatened. It is more helpful to consider the behavior of women within an opportunities framework. Their behavior may restrict the opportunities for males to behave as culturally expected, or changes in social structure independent of female action may limit this structure of opportunities.

A final preliminary point about masculine anxiety: Though it is an individualistic concept, an individual may become anxious not solely because of experiences which occur to him personally but also because of the experience of members of a group with which he identifies. He may not lose his job to a woman, or he may not find his job one of passivity and dependence; but if other men who serve as a reference group undergo these things, he may feel the "naturalness" of masculinity is being undermined.

The Physiological Fallacy

Often in the discussion of masculinity and femininity a dichotomy is made between doing and being. The argument goes that a woman naturally achieves gender fulfillment by physical developments. A woman is told she is female by the natural development of her body; true to the stereotypic view of women in our culture, a woman need simply be passive and femaleness is conferred on her. Men, on the other hand, have no such natural signposts; and they must constantly, through their actions, prove their masculinity. The need for active confirmation of one's masculinity is a cultural fact of life in American society. The danger is to consider such a need as a physiological predisposition.

The doing-being distinction and the concomitant anxiety when things are not done is not a function of physiology but a function of culture's response to physiology. A woman receives sex-role reassurance from her body because her body has been taken as the central defining element of her sex role; the reassurance of childbearing rests on her reproductive functions being the key determinant of womanhood.

For a man, his body is not an end but a means for the performance of culturally prescribed behaviors. Biological change does not signal that a man has achieved masculine confirmation, but that he is now ready to meet the challenges of masculinity, is ready to prove that he really is a man.

Physical change and appearance are related to masculine anxiety, but not in a deterministic way. Physical development is an important element in how fathers and peers interact with a young male. A father's perception of his son and his motivation to interact with him are influenced in part by the boy's physical ability (Biller, 1971, p. 53). Among his peers, a boy with a mesomorphic physique and good coordination is likely to have more success in male activities; thus, there would seem to be a physiologically based process of mutual reinforcement between secure sex-role identity and peer acceptance. This connection is, however, far from biological determinism. It does not explain differences in adult male anxiety over time and across social space and does not explain why certain performances are considered crucial at various periods of social history. To get at these differences we must look to the sociological production of anxiety throughout the male life cycle.

Early Childhood Socialization
and Masculine Anxiety

Considerable research has been done on the differences between male and female early childhood socialization. Three aspects of this differential socialization are related to the generation of masculine anxiety: the nature of demands, the setting in which these demands are made, and the process of identification.

Males are required at an earlier age than girls to exhibit sex-role-appropriate behavior; the range of accepted behavior is narrower; the socialization messages are expressed in more negative injunctions; and the socialization demands are enforced more punitively. Lansky (1967) reports that both parents expressed more negative attitudes toward boys for their cross-sex choices of toys, while being more neutral and positive in their reaction to the cross-sex choices of girls. Parents of boys exhibit more polarized attitudes about sex-role behavior, while the parents of girls show more casualness and neutrality about their daughters' choices (Rubin, Provenzano and Zella, 1976).

By kindergarten, boys are restricted to masculine activities, but girls can amble for the next five years in the prescribed direction to femininity. We have a legitimate transitional social role for these female "amblers"— tomboys. A father may even take pride in the athletic prowess of his ball-throwing ten-year-old daughter. But there is no acceptable social role for boys who slowly make their way to the cultural goals of masculinity. No father observes his delicate, aesthetic son and exclaims with pride what a "sissie" he has for a son.

The early sex-role demands on boys are primarily negative in nature, what David Lynn has called divergent feedback. The boy is told more what not to do than what he should do. There is more discouragement of inappropriate sex-role behavior than rewards for appropriate behavior (Lansky, 1967). Ralph Turner perceptively comments on how self-respect is tied to notions of masculine self-respect. Parents and teachers challenge a young boy's masculinity as a way of controlling signs of childhood weakness, and the accusation of femininity is a "pervasive threat" behind a broad range of activities (Turner, 1970, p. 295).

The setting for male sex-role socialization is primarily feminine. It is the mother and the female primary school teacher who are the major instructors in, and enforcers of, masculine norms. The young boy is taught to reject all that is feminine, but he is under the control of women; he is told to be independent but to obey his mother and his female teachers. This occurs at an early age when he has already learned of the higher status of masculine activities (Biller, 1971, p. 40).

The setting and the process of identification are interrelated. In order to be masculine, the boy must differentiate himself from this feminine matrix and identify with an abstract cultural ideal rather than a concrete role model.[2] A young girl has the concrete role presence of her mother. The boy has a cultural ideal which is transmitted by his mother. The boy sees himself as different: He is not like his mother, but neither fully like his distant father (Roessler, 1971). Talk of the absent father can be overdone, and one can indulge in the myth of "the classical family of Western nostalgia," but studies by Lynn (1964, 1966) and others make a good argument for the qualitative and quantitative absent father. He shares less intimate activities with his son like toileting, preparation for bed, nursing when ill. Lynn likens the father as a model to a map showing only outline but not detail. Thus, the boy must abstract the appropriate identification goals, which are often phrased in negative terms; he must translate these warnings into principles defining proper role behavior (Lynn, 1966).

The socialization of boys is "effective," but at a cost. Boys do express stronger preference for the masculine role than girls do for the feminine role (ages three and one half to ten and one half) (Brown, 1958). Boys make earlier and more clearcut choices of sex-appropriate activities and toys (Rabban, 1950; Minuchin, 1976; Biller and Borstelman, 1967). Yet there are empirical findings and theoretical arguments to suggest that this socialization brings with it the costs of anxiety.

David Lynn (1964), in his discussion of divergent feedback, elaborates the possible anxiety-producing consequences of negative socialization. In addition to possibly generating hostility toward the punisher, such socialization may require more negative instances than positive ones

---

[2]This may be especially difficult when, as Fagot and Patterson (1967) report, female preschool teachers reinforce feminine behaviors in boys and girls.

to convey the same information and may lead to the repression, not the elimination, of disapproved behavior. The identification process is discontinuous for boys: They must shift behavioral gears from a nurturant and dependent relationship to one of detachment and independence. There is also a strong tradition in personality and culture studies which argues for the generation of anxiety from the conflict of primary feminine identification with a later secondary identification with males.[3] One consequence is the repression of this feminine identification and a resultant feminine hostility. The more complicated task of teasing out the principles and goals of masculinity may be anxiety producing; and Roessler (1971), drawing on Lewinian field theory, suggests that in such an uncertain field, the male is likely to be more open to cultural cues in the definition of his role. As we will see, these cues tend to be black and white and may raise more anxiety than they quell.

The young male is thus faced with intense pressure to be a male but without the proper directions as to what this means. Before he can worry about accomplishment, he must distinguish goals. But it is just these goals that seem elusive. As the child's social world expands, he turns to his peers to relieve this anxiety, but the experiences of the adolescent peer group may exacerbate the problem.

Adolescence and Masculine Anxiety

The early adolescent male turns to his male peers for masculine models and specific information about masculine behavior. Yet, masculine anxiety and membership anxiety which lead one to peer dependence at the same time interfere with the expression of one's self doubts and recognition of the possibilities of male behavior. A system of shared misunderstanding about the adolescent experience and the nature of masculinity is produced. I am speaking primarily of early adolescence; Komarosky's (1976) work on college students indicates that an opportunity structure perspective is more applicable to older adolescents, who strive to meet the cultural requirements of vocational achievement, responsibility, and heterosexual competency.

Boys form collectivities while girls associate more in dyads (Holter, 1970, p. 232). It is to these age peers that boys turn to fill the gaps in information and models left by familial socialization. But the peer group provides neither the sustenance nor the setting for a firm anxiety-free sex-role identity. In *Crestwood Heights,* peer group life among the upper middle class is examined. The authors write that boys find their occasional male teachers and principal

[3]For a good discussion of this perspective, see the works of John Whiting (1960, 1961).

in partial or even marked contrast to the masculine values for the male role in his culture. The boy, even more than the girl, is therefore thrust into a dependency upon the peer group for his masculine models, and this group, in turn, has a tendency, in upper middle class culture, to select as its model the athletic hero or the currently popular movie or TV star. (Seeley, Sim, and Loosley, 1956, p. 97)

The mass media image the peer group promotes accentuates the bipolarity of sex-role stereotypes and overemphasizes the physical and athletic side of the male role. It is unlikely that such emphasis and unrealistic goals will relieve adolescent anxiety.

This anxiety not only leads boys to specific forms of overcompensation such as body building and weight lifting. It also functions to limit discussion of one's feelings. David Matza (1964) writes of the shared misconceptions held by lower-class gang members about the other members' commitment to delinquency; each believes the others are more committed than they really are. "Sounding," the verbal derogation lower-class youth engage in, maintains this pluralistic ignorance. Most boys of all classes are desirous of being accepted as members of a group and being thought truly masculine.[4] This desire for membership generates a similar form of pluralistic ignorance which is maintained by "putting down," the barbed joking common to all classes of adolescents. If a boy was to express his doubts about the narrowness of the male image, he could anticipate being "put down," "cut," or made the target of sexual jokes. A lack of self-confidence is defined as unmasculine. These barbs are not necessarily a reflection of peer commitment but are means of alleviating stress and sex-role anxiety. Each boy dwells in ignorance of the others' doubts and sees his own doubts as deviant. A self-perpetuating system of pluralistic ignorance, anxiety, and sex-role rigidity is produced. This rigidity is even more accentuated by the fact that these adolescents stand on the "threshold of manhood, and consequently they are more obsessed by the postures and poses that symbolize and confirm it" (Matza, 1964, p. 156).

Masculine Validation and Adult Anxiety

Men do not suffer masculine anxiety because of some childhood or adolescent experience. These experiences may set the stage, but they are

[4]I would take exception to Jerome Kagen's contention that "many sex-typed skills involve solitary practice for which the boy does not require the reactions of others in order to assess when he has reached an adequate level of mastery. . . . The boy receives from these solitary endeavors information that strengthens his convictions that he is acquiring masculine attributes" (1964, p. 152). I would argue that shooting baskets or fixing a bike must still be validated by public performance and peer acceptance.

not determinant. To think otherwise would be to disregard adult psychological processes and to devalue the impact of social and cultural changes. A central element in understanding adult masculine anxiety is the relation of cultural expectations to socially structured opportunities for their fulfillment. The social structure must provide men the opportunity to act in the way the culture dictates that they should. If goal commitment remains constant, then changes in the opportunity structure will affect one's sense of sex-role identity. The question to be asked is, does the individual have the opportunity to develop sex-role attributes consonant with the ideal scripted by the culture? Opportunities may be restricted by women consciously demanding resources previously held by men, and also by changes in spheres of masculine validation unrelated to these demands.

Suzanne Keller (1975) states that the core masculine role consists of vocational achievement, the assumption of responsibility, and heterosexual competency. Traditionally, men have looked to work, the family, and sex as arenas for masculine validation. Men have exhibited anxiety when unable to fulfill sex-role expectations by activities in these areas. A cartoon in the *New Yorker* several years ago showed a middle-aged man leaving for work with briefcase in hand, his wife stands at the door saying to her bemused husband, "Farewell, brave lover! Come back either with your shield or upon it." Neither he nor many men today can expect such heroic challenges at work. The shift to bureaucratic white-collar jobs has not brought with it a parallel redefinition of masculinity. Men are still to be autonomous, active, independent, and masterful. But as C. Wright Mills (1951) observed, "a bureaucracy is no testing ground for heroes" (p. 263). Competition turns into "grubbing and backbiting," activity and self-reliance into passivity and following orders, and mastery of men and nature into compulsive niceness ("brown nosing"). Changes in the nature of work deny men the arenas for the performance of valued masculine attributes, and this change occurs independently of the entrance of women into the work force. The definition of masculine attributes has lagged behind changes in the nature of work demanded by a bureaucratically organized and service-oriented economy.

A man must assume responsibility to be a man; this is especially the case for "his" women and children. The unwritten contract of marriage, the one found in statute and court decisions, makes the husband the head of the household and the person responsible for its maintenance. The young college students in Komarovsky's 1969 sample felt quite anxious about their continuing economic dependence upon their parents and the possibility of having to depend on their wives for support for graduate study. One student stated that to depend upon his wife would "cut my masculinity." Others expressed similar concern about maintaining a dominant role, and they found themselves caught between not wanting a housefrau for a wife but fearing a wife more successful than themselves. The assumption of responsibility in one's household exemplifies the larger need for reciprocity in the validation of role identity. Others, both men and women, must allow men to play the traditional role or anxiety may ensue—the centrality of reciprocity may explain why such seemingly minor issues like the holding open of a door is so important. For a woman to open a door for a man is to deny him the reciprocity of behavior on which his sex-role identity is built.

Sex is also a central arena of masculine validation. The virgins in Komarovsky's college sample were anxious about their lack of dominance and their inadequate masculinity. Sexually active students felt the pressure of masculinity, of having to be a "fantastic lover." The need for self-validation is fused with the wish to provide their partners with sexual pleasure. An even more anxiety-provoking aspect of increased female sexuality was the possibility that the women would be more experienced than the men.

According to traditional sex-role stereotypes, "good" women were not expected to play an active sexual role, to have any special sexual skills and competencies, or even to enjoy too intensely (Salfilios-Rothschild, 1977, p. 108).

Men traditionally were the experts in bed, but the increase in female premarital sexual experience threatens this cherished male ascendancy.

Sexual mastery is not simply a concern of young males, but as Rainwater's (1960) study of fertility among the lower class suggests, is an aspect of masculine self-identity. Men, denied the respect and validation of their maleness in the world outside the home, seek sex-role confirmation in the conjugal bed. Fathering a string of children comes to represent a kind of defiant demonstration that they are in fact real men (p. 85). "The sexual arena is one in which their culture supports their [lower-class men] right to be in control, to have the main voice in deciding the way things are to go" (p. 94). Other classes of men may feel unfulfilled by their jobs and respond by demanding at home the power and respect culturally ascribed to males.

All social roles, including sex roles, require a stage on which they can be actualized. If not, actors wishing to perform suffer strains and anxieties. This analytical perspective does not, however, address the issue of whether the role should be played at all, whether the script should be rewritten.

The Future
of Masculine Anxiety

This framework for analyzing for masculine anxiety is presented strictly as a non-normative analytic tool. It suggests, however, that if one wishes to reduce masculine anxiety, there are two broad alternatives. First, the traditional definition of masculinity can be retained and new ways sought to reaffirm it. Or, we can redefine what we mean by masculinity, recognizing the behavioral and emotional possibilities open to men. The emotional costs of the old definition, from heart attacks to affective impoverishment, would alone argue for redefinition without even considering the practical impossibility of finding valid forms of confirmation for the old masculinity in our changed social and economic environment.

Redefinition will not come easily. The initial reaction to change is most often a reaffirmation of old identities and modes of behavior. Nor will redefinition eliminate role anxiety. But it should free it from the narrow confines of gender. Young males can be given positive and self-affirming, not alienating, goals; adolescents can become freer to disclose self-doubts and express feelings now denied them. Men, as social beings, will still be concerned with status and self-presentation, but one hopes they will not feel their masculinity at stake so often. I am not one to approach social change with utopian visions, and my sketch of the future may not be magnetic in its appeal. View redefinition as a start. If we recognize the real source of anxiety and discontent, we can begin to remove the bars from the "iron cage" of masculinity.

References

BILLER, HENRY B.
　1971 *"Father, Child, and Sex Role.* Lexington, Mass.: Heath Lexington Books.
BILLER, HENRY B., AND LLOYD J. BORSTELMANN
　1967 "Masculine Development: An Integrative Review." *Merrill-Palmer Quarterly* 13 (October): 253–94.
BROWN, DANIEL G.
　1958 "Sex-Role Development in a Changing Culture." *Psychological Bulletin* 55 (July): 232–42.
FAGOT, BEVERLY I., AND GERALD R. PATTERSON
　1969 "An *In Vivo* Analysis of Reinforcing Contingencies for Sex-Role Behaviors in the Preschool Child." *Developmental Psychology* 1 September): 563–8.
FLING, SHEILA, AND MARTIN MANOSEVITZ
　1972 "Sex Typing in Nursery School Children's Play Interests." *"Developmental Psychology* 7 (September): 146–52.
HARTLEY, RUTH R.
　1959 "Sex Role Pressures and the Socialization of the Male Child." *Psychological Reports* 5 (October): 457–68.
HOLTER, HARRIET
　1970 *Sex Roles and Social Structure.* Oslo, Norway: Universiteforlaget.

KAGEN, JEROME
1964 "Acquisition and Significance of Sex Typing and Sex Role Identity." Pp. 137–67 in *Review of Child Development Research,* edited by Martin L. Hoffman and Lois Wladis Hoffman. New York: Russell Sage Foundation.

KELLER, SUZANNE
1975 *Male and Female: A Sociological View.* Morristown, N.J.: General Learning Press.

KOMAROVSKY, MIRRA
1976 *Dilemmas of Masculinity: A Study of College Youth.* New York: W. W. Norton & Co., Inc.

LANSKY, LEONARD M.
1967 "The Family Structure Also Affects the Model: Sex-Role Attitudes in Parents of Preschool Children." *Merrill-Palmer Quarterly* 13 (April): 139–50.

LEWIS, ROBERT, ROBERT CASTO, WILLIAM AQUILINO, AND NEIL MCGUFFIN
1978 "Developmental Transitions in Male Sexuality." *The Counseling Psychologist* 7 (4): 15–19.

LYNN, DAVID B.
1964 "Divergent Feedback and Sex-Role Identification in Boys and Men." *Merrill-Palmer Quarterly* 10 (January): 17–23.

———
1966 "The Process of Learning Parental and Sex-Role Identification." *Journal of Marriage and the Family* 28 (November): 466–70.

MATZA, DAVID
1964 *Delinquency and Drift.* New York: John Wiley.

MINUCHIN, PATRICIA
1976 "Sex-Role Concepts and Sex Typing in Childhood as a Function of School and Home Environments." Pp. 206–22 in *Beyond Sex-Role Stereotypes: Readings toward a Psychology of Androgyny,* edited by Alexandra G. Kaplan and Joan Bean. Boston: Little, Brown.

PLECK, JOSEPH H.
1976 "The Male Sex Role: Definitions, Problems, and Sources of Change." *Journal of Social Issues* 32 (Summer): 155–64.

RABBAN, MEYER
1950 "Sex-Role Identity in Young Children in Two Diverse Social Groups." *Genetic Psychology Monographs* 42 (August): 82–158.

RAINWATER, LEE
1960 *And the Poor Get Children.* Chicago: Quadrangle.

ROESSLER, RICHARD T.
1971 "Sexuality and Identity: Masculine Differentiation and Feminine Constancy." *Adolescence* 6 (Summer): 187–96.

ROSALDO, MICHELLE Z.
1974 "Woman, Culture, and Society: A Theoretical Overview."

Pp. 17–44 in *Woman, Culture, and Society,* edited by Michelle Z. Rosaldo and Louise Lamphere. Stanford, Calif. Stanford University Press.

SAFILIOS-ROTHSCHILD, CONSTANTINA
1977 *Love, Sex, and Sex Roles.* Englewood Cliffs, N.J.: Prentice-Hall.

SEELEY, JOHN R., R. ALEXANDER SIM, AND ELIZABETH W. LOOSLEY
1956 *Crestwood Heights.* New York: Basic Books.

SIGAL, BERNARD W.
1962 "Male Nurses: A Case Study in Status Contradiction and Prestige Loss." *Social Forces* 41 (October): 31–38.

TURNER, RALPH H.
1970 *Family Interaction.* New York: John Wiley.

WHITING, JOHN W. M.
1960 "Resource Mediation and Learning by Identification." Pp. 112–26 in *Personality Development in Children,* edited by Ira Iscoe and Harold W. Stevenson. Austin, Texas: University of Texas Press.

———
1961 "Socialization Process and Personality." Pp. 355–80 in *Psychological Anthropology,* edited by Francis L. K. Hsu. Homewood, Ill.: Dorsey Press.

ZIEGLER, HARMON
1971 "Male and Female: Differing Perceptions of the Teaching Experience." Pp. 74–92 in *The Professional Woman,* edited by Athena Theodore. Cambridge, Mass.: Schenkman Publishing Co.

Beneath This Calm Exterior

When my eyes are bleeding,
when terror scrapes its claws across my gut,
it is not enough to hear you say
everything's gonna be all right.

When my stomach spasms
and thrashing does nothing to keep the water
from closing over my head,
it is not enough to be hauled up onto land
and left alone to dry.

If I knew how to scream
maybe then you would hear me.
But my voice freezes,
terror takes my breath away.
I scream with my eyes:
no one sees.
In time bravery grows to virtue,
submission descends to defeat.
Layer on layer on layer
I paint this cell the colors that bring praise
     and distance.

Before you say this house is pretty outside,
remember that I clean the walls
by eating spiders.

DAVID STEINBERG
Copyright © 1979 by David Steinberg

Male Chauvinism:
A Developmental Process

STUART CARTER

The idea of what traits and behaviors are characteristically male has been described in many ways and generally constitutes a pervasive group of characteristics that most people have come to expect.

Parsons and Bales (1955) described two characteristic personality types, the female "emotional-expressive" type and the male "instrumental" type. Their instrumental personality closely resembles Kagan and Moss's (1962) description of the traditional masculine model as actively sexual, athletic, independent, dominant, courageous and competitive. Rosenkrantz et al (1968) conducted research which revealed that men and women agree almost perfectly as to the distinct traits pertaining to men and women. Their research showed that traits stereotypically ascribed to men can be interpreted as reflecting "competency." Traits included in this group are independence, dominance, activity, competitiveness, ambitiousness, logical thinking, and objectivity. A relative absence of these traits characterizes the stereotypic perception of women who are seen to reflect "warmth-expressiveness" with such qualities as tact, gentleness, ability to express tender feelings and kindness.

Tiger (1970) identified similar characteristics when he compared the traits observed in male primates and male humans. In addition, Tiger found that "male-bonding," an exclusive status-bound male-to-male relationship, and "dominance-submission hierarchy," a kind of command-chain or pecking order, are particularly male characteristics. Bonding excludes "non-member" males and females from the "group." Competitive ability, aggressiveness, leadership qualities, and ability to enlist the aid of others for a cause are important skills for advancement to the top of the dominance-submission hierarchy where, presumably, each male controls the behavior of the one below him. In sum, there appears to be a generally accepted and expected notion that men are dominant, competitive, active, courageous and adventurous, and independent.

Having identified what is understood to be typical male characteristics, three questions become important:

1. What constitutes male chauvinism in terms of the relationship to expected male qualities?

2. What factors are important in the development of male chauvinistic behavior?

3. What are some of the consequences of chauvinism?

Chauvinism historically meant militant and boastful devotion to one's country. It was coined from the life of Nicholas Chauvin, one of Napoleon's soldiers who, though wounded many times, was satisfied with rewards of military honors and a small pension. Retaining a simple-minded devotion to Napoleon, Chauvin came to typify a cult of military glory that was popular after 1815 among veterans of Napoleon's armies (Woods, 1976). Chauvinism ultimately came to mean fanatical patriotism and almost any kind of ultra- or super-nationalism.

Similarly, the contemporary idea of male chauvinism has to do with being ultra- or super-masculine and having a blind allegiance and simple-minded devotion to one's maleness. Chauvinists often perform male behaviors to the extreme, emphasizing dominance and aggression as an expression of their masculinity. The following studies show that chauvinists are not necessarily the ideal representation of the conventional conception of their sex role.

Woods (1976) felt that male chauvinism is mixed with open or disguised belligerence toward women, usually associated with an attempt to ward off anxiety engendered by women. He felt that male chauvinists maintain their beliefs with great tenacity and resist any contrary data.

Nadler and Morrow (1959) found that high school and college men who had high masculine stereotyped behavior preferences had authoritarian attitudes and a tendency to devalue women. Worell and Worell (1971) investigated the psychological makeup of men opposed to the women's liberation movement. They found four major characteristics of the opposing males. (1) They are principally motivated by the desire for social recognition. They want to be held in high esteem by their acquaintances and have a reputation which warrants admiration and respect. (2) They are relatively high in harm avoidance, tending to maximize their personal safety by self-protection and cautiousness. (3) They tend to be controlled by the opinions of others and have a lowered confidence in their ability to guide their own destiny. (4) They demonstrate very high authoritarian tendencies. In dealing with others, they tend to be rigid, conforming, inflexible and submissive to authority.

Adorno et al (1950) found high positive correlations between traits such as status concern, personality rigidity, tendency toward conventional values and repression of feelings of weakness and passivity.

Miller (1972) found that male self-esteem was related to attitudes toward women's rights. Where attitudes toward women's liberation were more conservative, male levels of self-esteem were found to be lower. Woods (1976) suggested that male chauvinists were in a precarious position with respect to their own masculine self-esteem.

A male chauvinist, then, is a person who performs what he considers the important behaviors to an extreme degree and who has a devotion to his own masculinity. He tends to be conventional, rigid, overtly or covertly belligerent toward women, concerned with status and cautious. He may have concerns about weakness and his self-esteem.

How does this syndrome develop? I see the answer to this question in terms of two related issues. One is the apparent difference of valuation between male and female roles, with the male role having more value. The second is the related societal pressure on men to conform to the expected role.

Despite the alleged American distaste for ascribing status, there remains a difference of valuation between male and female traits. The literature indicates that men and male characteristics are more highly valued in our society than are women and female characteristics.

Gallup (1955) found that between five and twelve times as many women as men recall having wished they were of the opposite sex; similarly, D. Brown (1958) found that boys and girls between the ages of six and ten years express greater preference for masculine things than for feminine things. Sears, Maccoby and Levin (1957) report that mothers of daughters are happier about a new pregnancy than are the mothers of sons. Investigations have also found that the interval between the birth of the first child and the conception of the second is longer when the first child is a boy than when it is a girl, and that the likelihood of having a third child is greater if the first two are both girls than if they are boys (Pohlman, 1969). Research by Broverman et al (1970) found that clinicians considered traits characterizing healthy adults as more typical of men than of women, with female clinicians showing as much bias as their male counterparts.

These points are but a few that suggest that our society feels it is a little better to be a male than a female.

That there is an apparent higher premium placed on the male role is important when considering the societal pressure on males for masculine behavior, particularly during the developing years. Consistent with the expectation, men must perform the male role at least adequately to receive the value implicit in being male. If a man exhibits behaviors that are uncharacteristic, particularly those deemed feminine, he will probably receive some type of punishment because he appears to spurn a role that is highly desirable and expected by society. Thus a man knows well enough that he is not "supposed" to be without the status that comes from being a man and performing the male role adequately. He knows this because he has been taught a certain set of prescribed behaviors since infancy.

Goodenough (1957) asked parents what they expected their male and female children to be like. From their girls they expected feminine interests, gentleness, submission, sensitivity and emotion, social awareness, coquetry and affection. From their boys they expected masculine interests and movements (for example, a swagger while walking), aggression, obstinacy, power and suppression of emotion. Parents conform to the prevailing conventional opinion of what boys and men are like, and they expect the appropriate behavior from their children. That parents are the first in a series of conditioning agents to teach their sons what is expected of them can be seen from reviewing a few studies.

There is a consistent trend for parents to elicit "gross motor behavior" from their sons. Lewis (1972) reports that mothers are more likely to respond to a son's large muscle movements than to those of a daughter. Moss (1967) and Yarrow et al (1971) report that parents are more likely to handle boys roughly and pull their arms and legs vigorously. Tasch (1952) interviewed fathers who reported engaging in more "rough and tumble" play with their sons than with their daughters.

In terms of parental warmth toward children, both parents and children report more warm feelings between mothers and daughters than between mothers and sons (Sears et al, 1957; Bronfenbrenner, 1960; Siegelman, 1965).

With few exceptions, boys receive punishment more often than girls, even for the same infraction. Their punishment is harsher and more physical (Tasch, 1952; Sears et al, 1957; Bronfenbrenner, 1960; Siegelman, 1965; Newson and Newson, 1968; Minton et al, 1971).

In terms of encouragement of sex-typed activity, both parents more strongly encourage sex-appropriate behavior and discourage sex-inappropriate behavior in sons than in daughters (Fling and Manosevitz, 1972).

Lansky (1967) presented parents of preschool children with hypothetical situations in which a boy or girl chose either a masculine or feminine activity. When a girl chose a boyish activity, neither parent seemed especially concerned. When a boy chose a girlish activity, however, both parents reacted quite negatively, and this was especially true of fathers. Fathers were also quite likely to show positive reactions when a boy chose boyish activities. R. Brown (1965) discusses the tendency of many parents to think that they have not been sufficiently insistent on behavior appropriate to biological sex when their child behaves uncharacteristically. He claims that parents are likely to "deal with the problem" by firming up the definition of the role. Therefore, they undertake more detailed, explicit and rigid instruction as to what boys do and what girls do.

The knowledge that boys and girls are encouraged toward sex-appropriate behaviors that closely model expected stereotyped behaviors is not so terribly disconcerting in and of itself. It is the intense conditioning and related effects on boys particularly that is startling.

Several studies have reported that boys consistently prefer masculine things earlier than girls do feminine things (D. Brown, 1957, 1958). While girls do not make consistent sex-appropriate preferences for feminine things until about age 10, boys make consistent sex-appropriate choices as early as 3 years of age (D. Brown, 1957, 1958; DeLucia, 1963). Rabban (1950) reported that boys consistently choose masculine things and reject feminine things as early as 30 months of age. Hartup and Moore (1963) found that boys were more likely to strongly avoid sex-inappropriate toys than were girls. This information supports the contention that boys are aware of their gender identity earlier than are girls and that a significant part of the identification process has to do with disdaining those things that are associated with girls and femininity. This appears to be so because boys are subjected to more socialization pressure, much earlier than are girls, to adopt behavior and attitudes that are consistent with the prevailing beliefs.

Hartley (1959) discusses the fact that boys are aware of what is expected of them, because they are boys, at a very young age. Boys restrict their activities to what is suitably masculine as early as kindergarten, while girls amble gradually in the direction of feminine patterns for several more years. Hartley feels that the harshly enforced stringent demands not to perform undesirable behaviors impresses the small boy with the danger of deviating from behavioral prescriptions he does not quite understand. This situation provides practically the perfect combination for inducing anxiety, particularly around male issues. Youngsters are learning in a negative way that male behaviors are good and that anything else is bad.

Cohen (1966) feels that this pattern continues, peaking during adolescence, when boys show greater evidence of social and sexual anxiety than previously. Indeed, a great many boys do give evidence of high anxiety related to the area of sex-connected role behaviors, an anxiety which frequently expresses itself in over-straining to be masculine, in virtual panic at being caught doing anything traditionally defined as feminine, and in hostility toward anything even hinting at femininity, including females themselves. If it is true that this method of socializing men causes extreme anxiety, particularly during childhood, why do men become, in many cases, so fanatically masculinized later on?

Cognitive dissonance theory may help us to understand this process. Simply stated, Festinger's theory (1957) suggests than an individual strives toward inner consistency. Opinions and attitudes exist in clusters that are internally consistent. When an experience or idea enters the person's field, it will stand out by contrast. The person will become active in the search to reduce the dissonance. This activity can take a number of forms ranging from avoiding the situations or information that creates the inconsistency, as in denial, to changing behavior or opinions. Further, the harder one works at something or the greater the hardships endured in accomplishing something, the greater the dissonance generated by any suspicion that the goal has not been worth it, the greater the necessity of believing the effort has been worthwhile. Although boys and men may not completely understand all the subtleties of the effects of socialization on them, they understand all too well what is expected of them and they feel the pressure to conform to the expectation. Applying the concept of cognitive dissonance to gender identity development in light of the given description, we see that many men endure considerable hardships while learning the male role. Therefore it is necessary for these men to believe in this role and often even more necessary for them to resist any inconsistency or assault on their behavior or beliefs.

A chauvinist is a person who often sees himself as a "super" man, performing the role society has taught him to the extreme, resisting any inconsistency or assault on his behavior or beliefs, and denying opinions other than those he "knows" are right. A chauvinist may look imposing, but he cloaks his needs beneath the masculinity image. This cloaking along with the rigid adherence to a belief system not based on a well-developed sense of self causes severe difficulties.

The difficulties referred to primarily involve the potential for disappointment in developing fulfilling interpersonal relationships. Mussen (1961, 1962) reported that boys with high masculine preferences experience insecurity and inadequacy as adults in terms of interpersonal skills. Kupferer and Knox (1971) identified the fact that the highly masculinized behaviors rewarded during infancy and adolescence serve little purpose interpersonally for the bearer during adulthood. Given the harshness with which deviation from "masculine behavior" is treated in the growing boy and given the social sanctions against giving up highly valued "male" traits and behaviors in favor of less valued "female" traits and behaviors, it is little wonder that as adults many men have difficulty accepting their "warmth-expressive" qualities or even seeing value in these traits.

Thus, men are locked as much into a confining, rigid pattern of behavior as women used to be. Men are as much victims of socially imposed standards as are women, possibly more so. As attitudes change toward women exhibiting behaviors which are stereotypically male, one hopes men will experience fewer sanctions against exhibiting stereotypically female behaviors.

It may be possible to accelerate the process of social change if we know why some men are capable of expressing traits and behaviors which are not rewarded in males, that is, concern for others, cooperation, showing emotions, expressing hurt feelings. My suspicion is that these are men who were allowed to "be themselves" as boys, who were rewarded for being affective, warm and competent human beings, rather than those who were punished for not being "masculine." What is needed is research into the factors which allow boys to grow into "androgynous" men who incorporate positive "male" traits and positive "female" traits into their self-concept and behavior.

"Male Chauvinism: A Developmental Process" was presented at the annual convention of the Massachusetts Psychological Association, Boston, Mass., April 10, 1976. This paper was part of a symposium entitled The Psychology of Victimization.

The author wishes to thank Dr. Inge K. Broverman for her many helpful suggestions in the preparation of this paper. The author also wishes to thank Dr. Lisa Anne Krock, without whom this topic never would have been confronted.

References

ADORNO, T.W., FRENKEL-BRUNSWIK, E., LEVINSON, D., AND SANFORD, R.N.
1969 *The Authoritarian Personality.* New York: W. W. Norton & Co., Inc.
BRONFENBRENNER, U.
1960 Some familial antecedents of responsibility and leadership in adolescents. In L. Petrullo and B.M. Bass (Eds.), *Studies in Leadership.* New York: Holt.
BROVERMAN, I. K., BROVERMAN, D. M., ROSENKRANTZ, P. S., AND VOGEL, S. R.
1972 Sex role stereotypes: A current appraisal. *Journal of Social Issues, 28,* 59–78.
BROWN, D. G.
1957 Masculinity-femininity development in children. *Journal of Consulting Psychology, 21,* 197–202.

1958 Sex-role development in a changing culture. *Psychology Bulletin,* *55,* 232–241.

BROWN, R.

1965 *Social Psychology.* New York: Free Press.

COHEN, M. B.

1966 Personal identity and sexual identity. *Psychiatry, 29* (1) 1–14.

DeLUCIA, L. A.

1963 The toy preference test: a measure of sex-role identification. *Child Development, 34,* 107–117.

FERNBERGER, S. W.

1948 Persistence of stereotypes concerning sex differences. *Journal of Abnormal and Social Psychology, 43,* 97–101.

FESTINGER, L.

1957 *A Theory of Cognitive Dissonance.* Evanston, Ill.: Row Peterson and Co.

FLING, S., AND MANOSERVITZ, M.

1972 Sex typing in nursery school children's play interests. *Developmental Psychology, 7,* 146–152.

GALLUP, G.

1955 *Gallup Poll.* Princeton: Audience Research, Inc.

GOODENOUGH, E. W.

1957 Interest in persons as an aspect of sex differences in the early years. *Genetic Psychology Monographs, 55,* 287–323.

HARTLEY, R.

1959 Sex-role pressures in the socialization of the male child. *Psychological Reports, 5,* 457–468.

HARTUP, W. W., AND MOORE, S. G.

1963 Avoidance of inappropriate sex typing by young children. *Journal of Consulting Psychology, 27,* 467–473.

KAGAN, J., AND MOSS, H. A.

1962 *Birth to Maturity: A Study in Psychological Development.* New York: John Wiley.

KNOW, W., AND KUPFERER, H.

1971 A discontinuity in the socialization of males in the United States. *Merrill-Palmer Quarterly, 17,* 251–261.

LANSKY, L. M.

1967 The family structure also affects the model: sex role attitudes in parents of preschool children. *Merrill-Palmer Quarterly, 13,* 139–150.

LEWIS, M.

1972 State as an infant-environment interaction: an analysis of mother-infant behavior as a function of sex. *Merrill-Palmer Quarterly, 18,* 95–121.

MILLER, T. W.

1972 Male attitudes toward women's rights as a function of their level of self-esteem. Paper presented at annual convention of the American Psychological Association, Honolulu.

MINTON, C., KAGAN, J., AND LEVINE, J. A.

1971 Maternal control and obedience in the two-year-old. *Child Development, 42,* 1873–1894.

MOSS, H. A.

1967 Sex, age and state as determinants of mother-infant interaction. *Merrill Palmer Quarterly, 13,* 19–36.

MUSSEN, P. H.

1961 Some antecedents and consequents of masculine sex typing in adolescent boys. *Psychological Monographs, 72.*

————

1962 Long-term consequences of masculinity of interests in adolescence. *Journal of Consulting Psychology, 72* (26), 435–440.

NADLER, E., AND MORROW, W.

1959 Authoritarian attitudes toward women and their correlates. *The Journal of Social Psychology, 49,* 113–123.

NEWSON, J., AND NEWSON, E.

1968 *Four Years Old in an Urban Community.* Hammondworth, England: Pelican Books.

PARSONS, T., AND BALES, R. F.

1955 *Family Socialization and Interaction Process.* New York: Free Press.

RABBAN, M.

1950 Sex-role identification in young children in two diverse social groups. *Genetic Psychology Monographs, 42,* 81–158.

ROSENKRANTZ, P. S., VOGEL, S. R., BEE, H., BROVERMAN, I. K. AND BROVERMAN, D. M.

1968 Sex-role stereotypes and self concepts in college students. *Journal of Consulting and Clinical Psychology, 32,* 287–295.

SEARS, R. R., MACCOBY, E. E., AND LEVIN, H.

1957 *Patterns of Child Rearing.* Evanston, Ill.: Row, Peterson.

SIEGELMAN, M.

1965 Evaluation of Bronfenbrenner's questionnaire for children concerning parental behavior. *Child Development, 36,* 163–174.

TASCH, R. J.

1952 The role of the father in the family. *Journal of Experimental Education, 20,* 319–361.

TIGER, L.

1969, 1970 *Men in Groups.* New York: Vintage Books.

WOODS, S. M.

1976 Some dynamics of male chauvinism. *Archives of General Psychiatry, 33,* 63–65.

WORRELL, J., AND WORRELL, L.

1971 Supporters and opposers of women's liberation: some personality correlates. Paper presented at the annual convention of the American Psychological Association, Washington, D.C.

YARROW, M. R., WAXLER, C. Z., AND SCOTT, P. M.

1971 Child effects on adult behavior. *Developmental Psychology, 5,* 300–311.

The Sherpa's Wife

She is good at following,
following the trails of men
far into the clods,
bringing the milk
of the yak she milks
to those whose milk
is the clear white milk
of mountains,
the blinding snow at the upper ridge
of their search to reach
above themselves, and be lost
in a greater finding.

She is good at following,
following the trails of men,
men who do not thank her much
or even bother for her touch,
as, lost to their beginnings,
they search upwards for the finish.

But there will be no finish,
and she knows that.
The men are always going
upward—upward and away,
like clouds that do not stay
in the same shape
in the same place.

They are going,
so she must be going
after them—with milk,
with milk
and nodding
and few words,

and only a smile to herself
singing in her eyes
like secret silken birds.

GABRIEL GIRISHA HEILIG

Types of Inexpressive Male Roles

JACK O. BALSWICK

Much of that which constitutes masculine behavior is presented as something males should not do rather than as something they should do. One of the characteristics of males in American society which is defined in negative terms is inexpressiveness. An inexpressive male is one who does not verbally express his feelings, either because he has no feelings (or at least is unaware of his feelings and therefore is viewed as having no feelings) or because he has been socialized not to express his feelings.

This paper is based upon two assumptions: (1) that it is better to express positive feelings toward another when he or she is present than it is not to express these feelings, and (2) that the reason men often do not express positive feelings toward others is because of the role they believe they are expected to play in society. Based upon these assumptions, six types of inexpressive male roles will be discussed: "cowboys," "good ol' boys," "playboys," "conboys," "locker-room boys," and "parlor-room boys."

The concept of *role*, as it is used within the sociological framework of symbolic interaction, traditionally allows inexpressiveness to be viewed not only as a personality trait but also as behavior which results from interaction between the individual personality and others. Although it is not possible to fully develop the role theory approach here, I would suggest that the concept *role* serves to explain inexpressiveness as that which results from the ego's conception of himself, his perception of the alter's (potential target person's) role, and his perception of the alter's expectation of him.

A male's self-conception begins to form at the time he is born. There is perhaps no role which is stronger in shaping one's self-concept and behavior than one's gender role. In learning to be a man, the boy in our society comes to value expressions of masculinity and to devalue expressions of femininity. Masculinity is expressed largely through physical courage, competitiveness, and aggressiveness, whereas gentleness, expressiveness, and responsiveness are often scorned as signs of femininity. The family, peer group, and mass media converge to help shape the male's view of masculinity—his self-concept.

The ego's perception of the alter's role and his perception of the alter's expectation of him are important factors in understanding inexpressiveness because they widen the boundaries used to explain expressiveness from the ego (the individual level), to interaction with the alter (the social level). Turner (1962), for example, suggests that "role-taking" shifts emphasis away from the simple process of acting out a prescribed role to devising a performance on the basis of an imputed other role. Interpretation of the social situation is a key variable in understanding inexpressiveness.

Although it will be impossible to fully present the social-psychological process whereby different forms of inexpressiveness can be understood, an attempt will be made to discuss the various forms of inexpressiveness in terms of role behavior.

TYPES OF INEXPRESSIVE MALE ROLES

Male inexpressiveness can be categorized on the basis of at least three criteria: first, whether or not feelings are present in the male; second, whether or not there is an attempt to pretend to express feelings; and third, whether the potential object of expressiveness is a female or a male. As seen in Table One, there are three groups of inexpressive male roles, each of which contains two inexpressive roles.

Feeling, Verbal Roles:
Expressive Male Roles

A totally expressive male is one who has feelings and expresses those feelings to both females and males. However, it is not uncommon for males to express their feelings to one sex and not the other. While some

Table One.
TYPES OF INEXPRESSIVE MALES' ROLES

		FEELING	NON-FEELING
VERBAL	Toward Females	EXPRESSIVE MALE (Parlor Room Boy)	PLAYBOY
	Toward Males	EXPRESSIVE MALE (Locker-Room Boy)	CONBOY
NON-VERBAL	Toward Females	COWBOY	LOCKER-ROOM BOY (as seen by females)
	Toward Males	GOOD OL' BOY	PARLOR-ROOM BOY (as seen by males)

males are expressive toward females and inexpressive toward males, others are inexpressive toward females and expressive toward males. A more full discussion of these two types of incomplete expressive male roles will come later under the non-feeling, non-verbal type of inexpressiveness.

Feeling, Non-Verbal Roles: Cowboys and Good Ol' Boys

Some males are inexpressive because they have feelings but either cannot or will not verbally share those feelings with others. Feeling, non-verbal males play the role of cowboy toward females and the role of a good ol' boy toward males.

The Cowboy Role: The feeling, non-verbal male learns to relate to females by assuming the strong, silent, rugged he-man role. Perhaps the best portrayal of the cowboy role can be seen in any one of the typecast roles played by the movie actor, John Wayne. Around women, Wayne, in his films, appears to be uncomfortable and often unable to speak, especially if he really cares for the woman. He seems more comfortable around his horse than around "his woman." Any display of affection is likely to be disguised, rarely issued in a pronouncement of "I really love you." Such open verbal displays of affection would be out of character for the type of rugged frontiersman who supposedly won the West.

It would be a mistake to think of the cowboy as non-feeling. Even the rugged cowboy portrayed by Wayne has emotional feelings—toward women, toward small children, and even toward other men, *but* they are never expressed directly. The cowboy type is feeling but is non-verbal in his expression of these feelings.

Upon entering marriage, the cowboy type may actually be relieved of expressive expectations. By presenting the marriage as evidence of his affection ("Would I have married you if I didn't love you?"), a husband can reduce the pressure to express such emotions.

His wife too can infer the existence of such emotions in the marriage ("He must love me or he never would have married me"), thus reducing the requirement for him to continually demonstrate affection and tenderness toward her. If together long enough, most couples develop shorthand symbols, such as an arm around the shoulder, a certain look, or a pat on the derriere, through which they express certain emotions and desires. These symbols come to represent the emotions which the husband has but is unable or unwilling to verbally express.

However, marriage can also represent added role strain for the cowboy, who is ill-prepared for a companionship-oriented marriage. Wives today are much more likely to expect their husbands to be expressive in the marital relationship than were wives in the past. Several researchers have commented on the male role strain which can result from con-

tradictory demands and expectations males experience in their socialization and adult life (Hacker, 1975; Hartley, 1970; Knox and Kupferer,
1971; Bem, 1975; Pleck, 1976). American society "inconsistently teaches
the male that to be masculine is to be inexpressive, while at the same time,
expectations in the marital role are defined in terms of sharing affection
and companionship, which involves the ability to communicate and
express feelings" (Balswick and Peek, 1971: 366).

The Good Ol' Boy Role: The term *good ol' boy* is primarily a Southern
expression which has recently been popularized by the mass media's
interest in President Carter's brother, Billy Carter. Billy and the male
friends with whom he sits drinking beer and swapping stories constitute
good ol' boys to each other. Good ol' boy relationships do not arise
overnight; rather, they often begin during childhood and are nurtured
through the trials and triumphs of growing up together. The good ol' boy is
completely loyal to the other good ol' boys, who together form a strong in-
group or primary group. A good ol' boy will stick with you "through thick
and thin."

Although good ol' boys spend much time talking together, they
rarely communicate their personal feelings to each other. If asked why he
didn't talk about his feelings, the good ol' boy is likely to reply that it
wasn't necessary. He may also say, "Man, if you have to say it, the feelings
must not be there." He believes that the expression of feelings is a
"womanly" trait. The man who is expressive of his feelings is likely to be
laughed at and joked about by the good ol' boys as one who is "too
feminine" or lacks "manliness." Good ol' boys do have deep feelings for
each other which are enduring and show in the supportive *action* they will
take on behalf of each other.

Good ol' boy roles are both fostered *by* and perpetuators *of* a male
subculture. This subculture is a storehouse of folk philosophy, humor,
wisdom, stereotypes, which is transmitted to males as they begin to learn
the good ol' boy role. By the time adulthood is reached, each good ol' boy
has a common storehouse of memories, stories and wisdom which makes
lengthy conversation unnecessary. A brief statement or comment can
serve to conjure up a common memory in the good ol' boys which will
result in a collective laugh or response and then lead the group to another
memory which they all share. It is difficult, if not impossible, for a woman
to become a part of this subculture, as it would be for another male who
does not share this heritage.

Non-Feeling, Verbal Roles:
Playboys and Conboys

Non-feeling, verbal roles call for a display of feelings when in reality
the male has no feelings within. The male who plays these roles must become skilled at pretending to have feelings. In relating to females, the non-

feeling, verbal male assumes the playboy role, while in relating to males he plays the conboy role.

The Playboy Role: Although the playboy role can be considered to be a modern version of the cowboy role, it departs from the cowboy role in that it calls for the male to be verbal but also non-feeling. A movie example of the playboy would be James Bond. As Bond interacts with women, it is with a cool air of detachment. They fall passionately in love with Bond, but he remains above it all. It is interesting to note that in the one film where Bond does "fall in love" with the heroine, she dies—no doubt the tragic consequence of Bond's shedding his emotional detachment.

As reflected in the philosophy of his namesake, *Playboy* magazine, a playboy "is a skilled manipulator of women, knowing when to turn the lights down, what music to play on the stereo, which drinks to serve, and what topics of conversation to engage in" (Balswick and Peek, 1971: 265). The playboy reduces sexuality to a packageable consumption item which he can handle because it demands no responsibility. The successful encounter with a woman is when the bed is shared, but the playboy emerges free of any emotional attachment or commitment. When playtime is over, the plaything can be discarded in a manner that is fitting in our consumer, disposable-oriented society.

The Conboy Role: Webster's defines the term *con* as a swindler or as an attempt to direct the course of another. The conboy role describes the types of manipulative behavior we associate with the "con-man," "con artist," or "wheeler-dealer" in our society. The conboy becomes a skilled manipulator of other males through his ability to convice them he really likes and cares for them.

Certain occupational roles, such as the traveling salesman, may place one in the conboy role. To the extent that the techniques of selling involve flattering and building up the ego of a would-be client, the salesman is playing the role of the conboy. In the competitive structure of much of the work-a-day world, males learn to be on guard against such manipulative behavior in other males.

The conboy's attempt at verbal manipulation may even be ethically justified within certain male subcultures. The conboy learns to rationalize his manipulation of other men by believing that the "sucker" or naive "mark" deserves to be taken advantage of. The skilled conboy may even achieve status in such a subculture because of his reputation as a skilled manipulator of others. Conboys may well agree with W. C. Fields's famous line, "Never give a sucker a second chance."

The ethics and philosophy behind the conboy role are those of a modified type of rugged frontier individualist who makes it to the top on his own. Instead of succeeding purely by hard work, self-discipline and honesty, the conboy models his behavior after the equally hard-working folk hero who had to scheme, connive, and sometimes "claw" his way to the top. The fact that many men report they feel suspicious of other men and have a difficult time trusting them may be indicative of the extent to which the conboy role is used by males in our society.

Non-Feeling, Non-Verbal Roles:
Locker-Room Boys and Parlor-Room Boys

To be both non-feeling and non-verbal undoubtedly results in few meaningful interpersonal relationships. There is not much that can be said to describe the behavioral roles of such males, other than to say that they are inexpressive because they in fact have no feelings to express. As such, their behavior is more consistent with their emotional state, which is that of the playboy or conboy. Many males, however, may learn to express their feelings toward members of one sex but not the other. Males who are non-feeling and non-verbal toward females but expressive of their feelings toward males will be viewed by females as locker-room boys. Males who are non-feeling and non-verbal toward males but expressive of their feelings toward females will be viewed by other males as parlor-room boys.

The Locker-Room Boy Role: This role calls for the expression of feelings to men but not to women. There is a certain extent to which all inexpressive male roles allow the male to feel more comfortable around men than women, that is in the security of a male subculture. The locker-room boy is dependent upon such "masculine" subcultures as men's athletic clubs, sports teams, bars, and gaming rooms. In such environments, where masculine identity is secure, the locker-room boy is better able to express his more gentle feelings and even physical affections.

Examples of locker-room boy behavior transcend the boundaries of social stratification. After a few beers at the neighborhood tavern, men who have spent the day working in a factory will begin to share their feelings and concerns with each other. Such emotional sharing does not take place between them and their wives (Balswick, 1970; Hurzitz, 1964; Komarovsky, 1962; Rainwater, 1965).

Football players will enthusiastically hug each other following the scoring of a touchdown. In the locker room, they will openly weep following defeat or express affection or love for each other following a victory or defeat. Following one of the 1976 World Series baseball games, the New York Yankees' fiery manager, Billy Martin, announced to the media that he *loved* his ball players. Since the athlete's masculinity has been established through his physical prowess, he is free to *be* expressive of his feelings without having his masculinity questioned. The locker-room boy is more comfortable and also more able to share his feelings with certain other men in sufficiently "masculine" environments.

The Parlor-Room Boy Role: This role calls for a greater expression of feelings toward females than toward males. There is much within the male subculture that encourages a male to take on the parlor-room boy role—competitiveness, power grabbing, aggressiveness, and a general striving toward "one-up-manship." To be comfortable in such a male subculture, one must be sufficiently competitive and aggressive so as not to feel threatened or overwhelmed. The male who has an insufficient quantity of these "masculine" traits may find himself more comfortable around females than males.

There is some evidence to suggest that a male's greater ability to relate to females may originate in the home. Several studies have found that fathers are more expressive toward their daughters than toward their sons (Bronfenbrenner, 1961; Emmerich, 1959; Johnson, 1963). Johnson (1963) noted that while mothers have an expressive attitude toward male and female children indiscriminantly, fathers are expressive with their daughters and instrumental with their sons. Because of the role model provided by their father and the greater expressiveness shown to them by their mother, male children may become freer in expressing their feelings to females than to males.

Much of the literature on male relationships suggests that males often fear and distrust other males. Sattel (1976) suggested that males are inexpressive as a conscious effort to maintain power in a relationship. This implies that a male will become vulnerable when he expresses his feelings to another male. The fear exists that another male cannot be trusted to use such revelations in a non-exploitive way. Given these fears, and the reality that many males are capable of assuming the conboy role, it is understandable that a male may decide it is safer to restrict expressiveness to females.

Conclusions

This paper is based upon a major value assumption and a major theoretical assumption, neither of which can be completely discussed apart from the other. The implied value assumption is that behavioral maturity involves expressing feelings to another person when such feelings are present. The careful reader will have realized by now that the inclusion of the word *boy* in the title of each of the six types of inexpressive male roles is intentional. However, it is easy to misinterpret this value assumption as meaning that inexpressiveness is simply the result of the lack of personality development within certain males.

This leads us to the theoretical assumption, namely, that male inexpressiveness can best be understood within the interactive social process, rather than merely within the individual. Although individuals behave inexpressively, they do so within socially perceived and prescribed situations. The interrelatedness of the theoretical and value assumptions can perhaps best be summed up in the following statement: *Resorting to the type of behavior called for within any of the inexpressiveness roles is to operate on an immature behavioral level.* This statement accepts the implication that inexpressive behavior is immature, while at the same time understanding that this behavior may be called forth by roles which exist within the social structure of our society.

Dear Brothers

Dear brothers,
it is not enough to want to change,
it is not enough to try,
it is not enough to wish,
it is not enough to cry.
Words do not cover
the colors of the quiet places.
Excuses do not erase
the lost possibilities.
Brothers, you may die tomorrow:
what are you waiting for?

DAVID STEINBERG

Men in Space

JEROME TOGNOLI

My father's occupation as a building contractor had a strong influence on all three of his sons. My youngest brother entered the same profession and my middle brother recently finished his own adobe house in the Arizona desert with my father's help. I took a more academic route—studying social psychology in graduate school, then focusing on an interest in environmental psychology and sex-role development, and finally combining these interests to explore the relationship men have with houses. More specifically, I was interested in why men often felt ill at ease in their own houses. I often felt uncomfortable, especially when entertaining male friends there on my own, yet I would feel quite comfortable if a woman was there to share that responsibility with me. I don't think it was simply a function of believing in the adage that the house is the woman's domain. As I talked with more people and thought about the issue, complexities emerged which pushed me to dig deeper.

Writing about houses, Gaston Bachelard acknowledges a female/male inside/outside dichotomy, saying, "In the intimate harmony of walls and furniture it may be said that we become conscious of a house that is built by women, since men only know how to build a house from the outside." Bonnie Loyd writes that "it is the man who designs the architectural shell within which the woman operates." She clarifies this by also saying that "the homescape traditionally falls to the woman" but that "a man who stays at home is labeled less than a man." I suspect that this model is foisted on children at an early age. Women friends have mentioned to me that when they were kids they often felt shut in compared to boys they knew. Passivity and learning to make do with quiet at-home activities were the rule for them, while boys, who supposedly had so much energy to burn up, were encouraged to be outside the home. I was like that. I was often not at home if I didn't have to be, and I still recall being spanked at the age of six by my mother for forgetting to come home one evening until 9:00. I was playing at a friend's house, and it never occurred to me I had to be home. My memory of those early years in northern New Jersey is of playing in the woods and by the Saddle Brook near my house, and of getting to know the outdoors in the different seasons.

Being inside during the day meant standing inside looking out—standing in the living room waiting during late winter afternoons, waiting for the street lights to come on, waiting for my father to come home from his wartime job at the airplane factory in Hackensack, waiting in front of the window and slowly gnawing on the white painted sill and the wood strips between the panes.

But my room at night was a haven because it took me into outer space. I had two glow-in-the-dark pictures on my bedroom walls, as well as stars pasted on the ceiling. When one of my parents would come to turn out the light at night, I couldn't wait, lying in bed watching. First the stars in the ceiling came out and then the moon and stars in the pictures. As they faded I would be drowsing off to sleep.

During my high school years, after reading in my room after school and then bolting down dinner, I would go back to my room and hide away there doing homework. The room was a retreat. It held no positive social significance. In the summer, I was usually out with friends every night after dinner. Often we went bowling, hung around the teen center, called on friends, or just drove around for hours in one of our parents' cars. Sometimes we would drive down to Miami Beach (my family had moved to Florida), where I would gorge myself on french fries and a root beer float. Sometimes we would wander around hotel swimming pools and nose around the lobbies. I never saw my house as a place to relax in, especially with friends. My parents were hurt that I spent so much time away, and yet I saw being at home as boring. I felt restless, and I thought of my parents' house as totally uninteresting.

I recall often feeling dissatisfied with the ordinary furnishings in their house and wished that my parents had the "opulent" taste that the parents of some of my friends had—swimming pools, and decor which included pink carpets and all-white sofas, and gilt rococo lamps and mirrors. Today I would judge all this as vulgar, but at the time it represented an elegant adult world. For compensation I would occasionally rearrange my bedroom and the living room—shoving sofas and armchairs into different positions and hanging new pictures. I always asked my mother's permission but never asked my father, not even once.

My father did build me a desk for my bedroom, but, like the plastic "seersucker" curtains with baseball and football players printed on them which my mother hung in my room, I hated the desk too. It was a table really, and it wobbled. I remember whining and putting up a fuss, but neither my father nor my mother went out to buy me the solid desk I had been expecting. In fact, my father built two more, one for each of my younger brothers who had to share a room.

At the age of eleven or twelve I remember distinctly attaching a negative sense of covert sexuality to my being in the house—in my room in particular. I had just learned about masturbation from a boy in the neighborhood. I was fascinated and terrified simultaneously. I was afraid of being discovered by my parents, who had never talked about sex of any sort with me. I remember a few times, knocks on my bedroom door accompanied by words like "what are you doing in there with the door locked?" and "you ought to be outdoors playing." I confessed this to the priest, and rather than feeling a sense of ease through absolution, I felt guilt—and lots of it. Even on those occasions when I was in the bathroom for long periods, sometimes only having an extra-long shower, there would be shouts from the door to hurry up and come outside. All this probably didn't go on for more than a few years. By then, I had learned to stay away, to play outside, to see friends, not in my own home, but elsewhere. I was dating and spending time at girlfriends' houses.

Years later, when I finally had a place of my own, I found that I felt uneasy cultivating friendships, especially with men, there in my own space. I felt a sexual tension and a fear of being discovered. But discovered doing what, and with whom and by whom? By a parent? The church? I had imposed my own internal sanctions on any situation where a male friend would visit. I created a sexual apprehension where none was necessary. I never experienced this tension with women, since my involvement with girlfriends was originally not attached to being at home. I always felt easier with them, and of course at their places. I was experiencing what Gregory Lehne calls homophobia and was learning to attach my fear of men to particular settings.

For four years in graduate school I maintained minimal involvement with each of the four places I lived in. I ate some meals there and slept there, but otherwise I felt a great sense of detachment. I studied in my office and ate out a lot. Social life occurred at other people's places— mainly women's. I defined their places as life centers.

My first apartment in graduate school was furnished, and the only embellishment I did was to tack three innocuous prints onto my bedroom wall and toss my red plaid bedspread (from my college days when my roommate and I trotted off to the University of Florida with matching bedspreads) onto the bed. I didn't even have a desk in the apartment, though Alan, my roommate, did. Our commitment to the place could not have been more minimal. He married in June, and we saw increasingly little of each other.

The next year, in another apartment (this time unfurnished), I stored some of my books there on a makeshift brick-and-board bookcase. I bought myself a used bed and dresser. The bed was maple, single, ascetic, and it had four posters, reminding me of "The Three Bears." The room was warm, brightened by the red plaid bedspread, which years later became cafe curtains, and after that cushion covers. But I only used the room to sleep in because I had to share it with Larry. My friend Art had his own room because his woman—Eileen—would come down to stay on weekends, and neither Larry nor I had steady women friends. Art and Larry provided an old couch which didn't have any legs, and I made a dining room table out of a sturdy packing crate and a seven-foot-long plywood board. I stained it a dark mahogany color. I hung a pastel drawing I had done on one wall, and Art added an oil painting that Eileen gave him. We ate meals together but rarely used the apartment aside from that. I am sure that we all knew that the one year together would be all there was. In June, I left for England, Art and Eileen married, and Larry quit the graduate program. Art and I remained friends and years later formed a men's consciousness-raising group out of which some of my ideas about "men in space" began to develop.

The two years that I was in England were the first I had ever lived on my own, and I felt awkward in my social life. Gradually as I began to make friends, I found that I felt self-conscious about inviting them over to my flat for a drink or dinner. I was assuming full responsibility for cooking for the first time in my life, and although I enjoyed it, this new skill was not part of a role I had been trained for or had seen my father perform. When a woman friend would come over to share the entertaining with me, I immediately felt relief as well as welcomed invisibility. Attention would be diverted away from me, and the woman would become the focus.

I moved house several more times after leaving England and coming back to America. The pattern was always the same. Alone, I was uneasy in my apartment and therefore spent most evenings out. Only when Helen and I took an apartment together was I relieved of this sense of discomfort. I became dependent on her social organizing, but eventually my dependence became unbearable for her. I began to see a pattern emerging: I would tend to avoid those situations in which I would singly invite friends to the house and be solely responsible for their entertainment. Significantly, once when I did ask a man friend to have lunch with me, we talked about my sense of discomfort and I discovered that he felt similarly. I had never visited him in his house in the two years I had known him. I began to understand that for many men, getting together socially is limited. If married, they hardly ever entertain a woman friend; and if they are single, women are not entertained but seduced in the bachelor pad. I suspect that the occasions in which men get together with other men in their own homes is formalized into structured situations such as card playing and television watching of sports. This becomes the defense mechanism of homophobia. The house does not serve as the place to relax in with friends or by oneself. There *are* men who claim to have no desire to get out, but often they do not see many people in their homes. It becomes a retreat.

There are many living situations which men experience that need to be examined. The following groups will each be considered with respect to their domestic space: elderly men, men committed to living alone, divorced or single men looking for a mate, and gay and straight men living with other men.

Sandra Howell writes about housing for the elderly and the problems of readjustment, especially for men. The move to a new location for a couple is often difficult. With the man retired and at home much more, there are often arguments—a result of feeling uncomfortable with the space, alien territory, and not the male work place. Howell describes the adjustment of widows and widowers to new housing. Women usually keep as much of their old furniture as they can, often crowding it into apartment rooms much too small to contain all of it. The result can often be claustrophobic for someone entering that space for the first time. Men, on the other hand, often end up having their furniture taken by their children, who convince them they don't need it. In fact, Howell reports having tried some consciousness raising with her own father, who claimed he didn't care about his home furnishings. He *did* care, but he appeared to be out of touch with these feelings. Again, men traditionally are not meant to have much concern for the inside of a house, and as long as the spouse is alive, it never really becomes an overt issue.

If a man is living alone and searching for a mate, it is fairly likely he will begin to develop a sense of rapport with the house because no one else is there to make decisions about the household—decisions concerning its decor, how often it is cleaned, how the space is filled and how it is organized and used. Even if the house is decorated to provide a setting for sexual seduction (I think here of the playboy image of the man as cook and interior designer), there is bound to be much behavior which eventually becomes functionally autonomous.

There are some rather revealing statistics on divorced men and the length of time they live on their own. Herbert Goldberg reports that it's not very long, and in fact the lifespan of a divorced man who does not remarry or live with a woman again is considerably shortened. Women in this situation fare much better living alone, perhaps because they have learned to cope more effectively with interior space. This probably relates to their early socialization as girls learning to be passive inside the house. Traditionally, divorced women often assume the responsibility of raising children, which may provide a structure and meaning in their lives that men don't have. As legal situations involving divorce and child custody tend more toward granting custody to men, it will be interesting to examine statistics on life span (and incidences of remarriage) for these men.

I expect that those men who live alone and are not actively searching for a mate develop a strong identity with the house. By virtue of their being on their own, they will have developed a more intense involvement with the house than men living in a relationship with a woman, for example. Social pressures not to live alone are fairly strong, and therefore I feel such individuals are rare. It might be few people define themselves as one type (searching or not searching) all of the time, and that it is much more accurate to view them as people who move in and out of such states. They probably also move back and forth in terms of levels of intensity in their relationship with interior space, as do most of us.

A final issue concerns men living with other men. These are gross generalizations based on the observations of a few instances: My feelings are that straight men living together define themselves to be in a sort of limbo state in which involvement in the house is a compromise with masculinity and the espousing of feminine (and negative) values. As a result, cooperative straight all-male living situations reflect minimal self-expression, homophobia, and a lifeless house. This represents the type of household I lived in as a graduate student.

The case with some gay men is different. I would like to think they feel ultimately responsible for the living situation they create because no woman is there to create it for them. Reinforcing and supporting one another, I feel they might represent a sample of liberated men who have raised their consciousness sufficiently, establishing a comfortable rapport with their environment and feeling unthreatened by both the physical and social implications of living within it.

*   *   *

One implication of the detachment I feel most men experience with the physical and social environment at home is that they move as far away from it as possible, both physically and psychologically—to outer space.

There is a fascination in science fiction literature with depicting a traditionally sexist male-dominated world in which intimate social relationships are absent. Ursula LeGuin's work is an exception, but then she is writing from a female consciousness. A typical pattern in this science fiction format is for the main character—a man—to set out on an adventure to an alien world leaving his wife at home to take care of the children. This is evident in Frank Herbert's classic *Dune* and in films like Nicholas Roeg's *The Man Who Fell to Earth* and Steven Speilberg's *Close Encounters of the Third Kind.* David Bowie's lyrics from the song "Space Oddity" summarize the same theme: Captain Tom, thousands of miles away from earth in his spaceship, relays to ground control love to his wife, whom he has obviously left behind. Ideas espoused by Timothy Leary on space migration support the move of men out and away from home. He advocates that humans have evolved for travel to outer space to fulfill a sort of genetic destiny—to live out life spans of three hundred years. Ignoring the complexities of relationships on earth and the limitations expressed through the male-dominated notion of space travel, Leary fails to recognize the possibility for redressing the social issues mentioned here.

Almost in direct contrast to the flirtation with space exploration is the dream we men have had to be architects and builders—nest builders and settlers. There is the fantasy of building by hand that cabin in the woods—the dream house—but never really living in it. I wonder how many women imagine themselves building their own house or dream cottage. Or, are they more reality based? I suspect that women don't go as far afield as men because as children, girls have real houses and doll houses to play-act in. There is also a proliferation of home-decorating magazines whose main readership is women. The ideas and suggestions in them are concrete and often require little expenditure of money. Building codes, on the other hand, make house construction difficult and inaccessible. The result for men, therefore, might only be fantasy and then frustration. As a boy of eight, I had a hut which I built in the woods out of some old boards and two saw horses. I used it as a hideout and a place to go to read comic books. Once, a neighbor gave me some plates, cutlery and cooking pots for the hut. "Let's make potato salad," I told a friend. After cutting up potatoes and serving them up on a plate, I was shocked when I bit into them. They were raw, and I felt really sad. The bubble had burst. I didn't know about cooking. I had an earlier experience as cook at the age of three. I was pretending to make liver in the broiler by tearing up pieces of corrugated cardboard. I had forgotten to tell my mother the cardboard was in the oven, and the next thing I remembered after she lit the oven was her tossing the large flaming pieces of cardboard out the kitchen window. My fantasy of home was one of frustration and failure.

There is a wide world separating the world of science fiction, dreams of rustic cabins and the concept of house as physical structure on the one hand, and the experiencing of the day-to-day realities of living in one's own space, house, skin, on the other. I expect that as work pressures push men farther and farther away from their own homes and into outer space, they will ultimately have to confront that loneliness. Perhaps they will be fortunate enough to have men friends to talk with, as I did, to begin to attach a language to such experiences and to realize that they are not unique and also not alone.

References

BACHELARD, GASTON
  1969 *The Poetics of Space.* Boston: Beacon Press.
GOLDBERG, HERBERT
  1976 *The Hazards of Being Male.* Plainview, N.Y.: Nash Publishing.
HERBERT, FRANK
  1965 *Dune.* New York: Ace Books.
HOWELL, SANDRA
  1976 Recent advances in studies of the physical environments of the elderly. Talk given at the City University of New York Graduate Center, Environmental Psychology Program, New York City, April 29.
LEARY, TIMOTHY
  1976 Space migration. Talk given at C. W. Post College, Greenvale, N.Y., October.
LEGUIN, URSULA
  1969 *The Left Hand of Darkness.* New York: Ace Books.
LEHNE, GREGORY K.
  1976 Homophobia among men. In Deborah S. David and Robert Brannon (Eds.), *The Forty-Nine Percent Majority: The Male Sex Role.* Reading, Mass.: Addison-Wesley.
LOYD, BONNIE
  1975 Woman's place, man's place. *Landscape,* October, *20* (1): 10–13.

part three

FEMINISM AND MEN FACING CHANGE

Even daddies get sick

What's good for
the gander . . .

Housespouse

FEMINISM AND MEN FACING CHANGE

One egg or two?

The observation has been frequently heard by those of us who have been members of male consciousness-raising groups that most men have been "sent there by their wives or women friends." This comment is a reference to the fact that those women touched in some way by the values of Women's Liberation often must either change their husbands or men or exchange them, since it is difficult to live with unchanged men after their own lives have been so definitely altered.

Mitchell describes in her essay, "Difficult Times for the Family: Change Hurts," many of the difficulties which arise in family and other relationships when individuals have their consciousness raised. Mitchell describes in several case studies of men she has come to know, men who have unsolved dilemmas. For example, there is Chris, a young man in his twenties, who modified his behavior toward his women friends only to find that they later began to prefer men who were "success objects." Another example was Tony, 50 years old, who has over time accepted equalitarian sex roles and is more active in household tasks but finds no praise nor support for these changes from his wife, since "isn't this what women have had to do for so long?" Solutions to these relationship problems are not easy and therefore are not freely offered by Mitchell. She does suggest that equal partnerships are best worked out where each person does that which he or she does best or most easily, rather than because of stereotypic role expectations. However, change often does hurt; and relationships where the rules have changed or one or both persons have changed their values must again be built in very idiosyncratic ways.

Many men are caught between a rock and a hard place, according to Marciano, since men have been taught in their earlier socialization to expect women to be dependent, and now they may be pressured by their women to reexamine these beliefs. Marciano presents the summaries of two studies which suggest that men do not have an easy time understanding some women today who expect equality in their relationships. What will be the long-range effects of Women's Liberation upon males' actions and attitudes? This author does not claim to be able to predict the future. She, however, sees many confused and bewildered men, such as the male who relates to one woman in male-dominant ways and seems to be appreciated for this but then is accused by another woman of being a male chauvinist. Marciano suggests that "men lack group memberships where they receive positive cues . . . for living in equality with women." In summary, she suggests that men must find peer support from other men, if they are to find encouragement for their own changes in attitudes and behavior, or they must be incorporated into women's consciousness-raising groups, wherever there are no groups for men.

Benson in "Talking Our Way Out of It: The Rise and Fall of a Men's Group" describes one men's consciousness-raising group of which he was a member. This group of feminist-oriented men met every week for more than three years to explore the implications of their feminist values and to receive emotional support from the others for solving their personal and relationship problems. Although this group dissolved in time, it seemed to provide support to those men and their attempts to change their lives and their relationships.

What is it like to be a man in a society that no longer covets extreme physical strength? This is a question which Boyer attempts to answer in "Changing Male Sex Roles and Identities." "In the sexual and feminist revolutions, the male has been cast as the 'enemy' . . . Obviously, any significant change in women's roles has a definite and immediate effect on men and their behavior expectations. . . . [However] as long as men feel that equality with women will emasculate them, this is precisely the effect that Women's Liberation will have on them," writes Boyer. One solution, according to this writer, is a new masculinity which is predicated not upon male dominance or driving ambition, but upon a man's sense of responsibility toward others, that is, upon how well he manages his life and treats others according to equalitarian values.

Difficult Times
For the Family:
Social Change Hurts

JOYCE SLAYTON MITCHELL

No one likes social change. Men don't like it. Women don't like it. Children don't like it. Even though feminists desperately want a different social structure where equality of the sexes is the basic assumption, most would admit that the process of this change hurts. Sex-role stereotypes in a sexist world are easier to deal with. Knowing what the rules are and what the parameters of our behavior are—regardless of the effects of those rules and parameters—is not so difficult. Everyone in his or her place has an order about it that brings less conflict and more energy to other things. Changing our places, changing the rules, changing the options for relationships and upsetting the sex-role stereotype is what these difficult times are all about.

It comes as a shock to many of us when we realize that human rights for girls and women will be a social change. It's not easy for men or for women to counter a basic preference for boys in our social institutions of family, school and church. It brings on difficult times to go against what we were all brought up to feel (sometimes we get the idea that only boys get the message to boys, and that only women get the message to wives, for instance; but of course we all get all the messages, and both men and women learn what a wife is like, and what a real man is like and what a real boy is like).

Social change brings on difficult times for everybody. What really happened to get this change started? It was only a few women who decided that because the role stereotype was not what they were like or was not valued by society (dependent, passive and emotional), they wanted out. And a few men decided they had a right to be out. Then a few men decided that they wanted out of the acceptable and valued stereotype for men (independent, logical and active). When women wanted out of their stereotype and said it was OK for others to be out of theirs, the stress and strife began. The rules and parameters were broken down and the struggle was on: struggle for survival, for oneself (a person's identity outside the stereotype), and with that certainly a struggle with our partners. When the partner was a marriage partner, things were even worse because of all the traditional economic, legal and child responsibilities, and holiday customs, and relatives, and extended-family pressures and expectations which remained the same and over which we had little control.

Women, looked, analyzed and wrote about how they had been socialized into their passive, dependent roles. It has been a very short time since men recognized the consequences of being a success object, and then they too began to notice just as little girls are programmed, little boys are taught to fear in themselves and to have contempt for each other if they show their feelings, are less than brave in any adventure, or show affection to anyone. The socialization of young boys is often accomplished by the accusation, "You're acting just like a girl!"

The masculine mystique insists on dominating relationships rather than those that are based on cooperation and sharing. Guys must measure themselves against and compete for sports, grades and girls. Dating puts men in constant competition with each other to be taking out and making out with the most desirable girl. Marc Fasteau, author of *The Male Machine,* says that making it with a woman is so competitive that this readiness to perform at all times is one reason why men retreat and segregate themselves from women, as they do in sports, or in drinking parties, and nights out in order to "relax with the guys." While many young men are socialized to look at young women as "sex objects," young women are often as narrow, as they see males only as "success objects." In place of seeing a man as a total person, many women see only the potential career, or the prestige in sports and clubs, or what college he is going to, or his car, or how much money he has to spend.

The problem with being a "success object" is that as soon as a young man accepts the success system with the right to control others, he in turn can be controlled *by* others. The price of controlling other people, rather than participating in an equal partnership with others, is that the young men's classmates, their brothers, and ultimately the men they work with, will always be in fierce competition with them to be on top, to be making it, to have just a little bit more power than they have. The very power system that says they must be in control of relationships with women is the same system that pits young men against each other.

Going through the process of becoming aware of our socialization is different for men than for women. At first, to some men, liberation seemed to be women's liberation in reverse—until we realized that men and women start from such different places. After all, it's OK for women to be more like men, but we all know that it is *not* alright for a man to be more like a woman. A sexist world means that the male stereotype is valued so much that anyone can be like it. At a workshop on the implications of feminism on male liberation (The Second National Men's Conference in Philadelphia) some personal issues for liberating men were vividly brought out. Chris, a young man in his early twenties, described his dilemma. He said he had dropped out of college and the competitive career race and was trying to be less competitive, less aggressive, more human, and more loving. He said that at first the young women in his life all encouraged him and he felt good about changing his life style around trying to find what was right for him. Then, all of a sudden the guys his age were out of college, in graduate school, in training programs for bank and corporation executives, or in good jobs. The women he liked were also in the competitive job world. Chris was completely left out. Feeling as if he had been had. Cheated. Lied to. A Fool. The feminists, who he felt had led him astray, were now interested in the silent, cool John Wayne type with great career potential—just as always. No longer the valued male stereotype—the success object—he agonized about his choices, and about the price he was paying for them.

Peter, a recently divorced man in his mid-thirties from Kansas, represented a lot of men when he explained that his women friends said they wanted to be treated equally, but from his perspective they never acted equal in terms of social behavior. "For instance," said Peter, "I'd take out a woman who talked a liberated line, and when I'd take her home, I'd make a point of saying 'call me sometime.' If I waited for a woman to call me, I'd be sitting home every night. I've tried a lot of ways but can never get them to call me. This is just an example, and I find that [women] taking the initiative in any way in social relationships just doesn't happen. I know women take the initiative in their work and career situations, and I keep expecting it to happen on dates."

Another viewpoint was expressed by Lenny, who talked about several women he knew who he said were taking on role reversals—male mainstreaming. To many women, liberation meant that they had to be very aggressive and competitive. Lenny felt that if women did not want him to be that way, they shouldn't be the so-called male stereotype either.

In other words, competitiveness and aggression were not good for anyone—male or female. The problem with this concept, for feminists, is that labeling the so-called male traits doesn't mean that the traits *really* ever do belong only to men. After all, women can be competitive and aggressive and still be female. For feminists, to object to all men having to be competitive all the time is quite different from approving that people can be who their experiences lead them to be. Women have a right to any and all personality characteristics available to humans. And men do too. The male stereotyped characteristics don't belong exclusively to men! *Being a liberated male doesn't mean all men have to give up competition and assertiveness.* It means that their life doesn't have to focus on those characteristics just because they are men. Certainly we can agree on certain mature characteristics for all people. One of them would be assertiveness, the standing up for one's own rights without putting others down, as opposed to aggression, which means standing up for one's rights by putting someone else down.

It was interesting that no one in the workshop directly talked about the pain of social change, though many expressed it in their voices and through their questions. The struggles that couples have as they try to work out social change in terms of an equal partnership take all the energy they can muster. You should know that the immediate rewards for working toward social change are very few. Some families do work for change, yet they get very little social support and have a hard time finding a support group. The community (the family, church and school) have always been for the status quo; they do not support sex-role stereotype changes. The partnership that takes on the challenge is very much alone—with many "you must be crazy" accusations coming in from all around most of the time, *especially* directed to the men.

As crazy as it seems to others, there are a few who are trying to change their families and relationships, who are trying to break from the husband-father stereotypes, who do want to live with equal partners, who want to raise their children in an equal-partnership environment. What happens to them as they try to bring about sex-role changes? What goes on between a man and a woman who were both raised in a sexist culture? And what are the implications for their children?

Dan, a Ph.D., dropped out of full-time work in higher education because he was convinced that he wanted to turn the traditional marriage around and have an equal partnership with his wife, Pat. She worked while he got his degree; then he worked while she got her degree and the necessary credentials for the job she wanted. While in their early thirties, they had their first child. They planned to share the financial costs of the partnership by both working part-time in order to be able to share the child-raising. The first unexpected thing that happened was that Dan didn't enjoy being with the new baby as much as had thought he would.

The second unexpected thing that happened was that when the baby was five or six months old, Pat left the home for her share of working for pay and Dan felt as if he were wasting his time "just taking care of the baby." He was really upset that he would feel this way. He especially felt this way in the mornings (previously his best-thinking and most-active time). What happened to Pat was that she was upset that Dan wasn't more comfortable with the baby and that he didn't do more with the responsibility. She was even more furious that he felt he was wasting his time! She then proceeded to hassle Dan about what all women have been talking about all this time, that "no one gives a damn about people who are home taking care of babies." It doesn't count the way selling cars, securities, or real estate, or filling teeth or teaching school counts.

Tony is another example. A professor in the social sciences who just turned 50 and has two school children and a "feminist" wife of 20 years, he is in the process of changing his marriage or ending it—neither of which he would have chosen to do. He feels that his perspective about marriage and changes in sex-roles are very logical: (1) Men his age were socialized to financially provide for their wife and family, to do the maintenance around the home, drive the car, write the checks. He does all these things very well and has always taken the responsibility toward his family as he was taught to do. Now he feels put down by his wife Rosanna for the very things he does well. (2) Tony takes on cooking, child raising, sharing his traditional role of making money, and Rosanna never gives him credit because she feels it's about time he started helping with the house and the kids, and he isn't the only one who can make money. (3) Men are socialized by their mothers and families to feel very special because they are male; their feminist wives and friends now act as if it's not only not special, but something to feel guilty about. So Tony gets neither strokes nor credit for being what he is—very accomplished in his work and a good father and husband, as he was taught to be. He is treated as if it's nothing—after all, he is a white male, so why shouldn't he be successful? All these situations have caused him to withdraw and to show little interest in social change, at least at home. No matter what task he does, Rosanna doesn't give him any credit (as his mother and teachers did); and in order for him to move toward others, he needs some recognition, encouragement and nurturing, as do all human beings. Rosanna, on the other hand, still can't get over her anger from the first ten years of their marriage when *both* Tony and she accepted a wife's place in the family as that of the one who had to do all the cooking, shopping, cleaning and laundry; who had to send out the Christmas cards, buy the gifts, wait on everyone, take care of the children, and even turn over her paycheck to her husband's account. Before marriage, Rosanna had lived independently with two other professional women for four years, and they all shared the domestic work. She learned very quickly that a sexist marriage didn't come close to the fulfillment that had been promised by the world. For Tony to help out now, after all of this time, with a few domestic chores and with the children, didn't put a dent in recovering from the anger at herself for walking right into a situation where she was taken—because she was a woman.

Fred, a very successful businessman in his early sixties, knows his wife is angry when he hears her throw the pots and pans around, pound the vacuum cleaner though their luxury home, and he asks, "What has she got to be angry about?" "She doesn't think I appreciate her or how she cooks or how she looks, but she never told me how great I was for bringing home plenty of money. I did my part for the marriage; why can't she at least keep the rugs clean that I paid for without expecting me to compliment her for it!" Maxine comes back with, "I've mothered him for all these years, told him how sharp he looked, entertained his business guests, and he hasn't given me one bit of credit or even mentioned it. Now here I am an old woman and I have absolutely no confidence in anything I do. I'm a wreck with every meal I cook for the company, wondering if it will come out OK." Both Maxine and Fred want to change in their sex roles. They are realizing that their relationship, like others, is a power struggle. When the husband had total power because he made the money, the couple's behavior was clear. Now that his so-called natural power over the couple is being questioned, they are seeing that their roles don't always work as well. Fred really wants to be more expressive in his relationship with Maxine, and Maxine wants to be more confident so that she can relax and enjoy her retirement years with Fred. Yet, they do not know how to change their patterns.

Many married people who have struggled with the hurts of working things out toward bringing human rights to women and toward a functioning equality have learned that it's not the marriage arrangement that has to go. It is the traditional role expectations, where each partner's behavior is determined only by his or her sex, that has stifled people in their marriages. A marriage where the husband has all the stress and responsibility for making money and the woman has to live within his control and his decisions is impossible for both men and women. Our culture values the making of money more than raising children and keeping house. This gives the male more prestige, but he pays for his social support with his life: Ulcers, heart attacks, and a shortened life span are often the price men have to pay for total power or responsibility.

An alternative to the traditional roles of husband and wife is an equal-partnership marriage or relationship which assumes each person may do what she or he does best, rather than what each must do because of role expectations.

Equal partnership means equal responsibility in deciding what each will do. Cooking, making money, raising children, painting the house, cutting the grass and doing the laundry are all necessary functions for the partnership. Equal partnership does not mean both partners have to paint the house or do the cleaning; it does mean they will decide who will do what on the basis of who is best at it, or who has the most time and interest in the job, or who hates it the least, instead of deciding on the basis of being male or female. Being equal partners means both people have an equal responsibility and opportunity to raise children and food, to make money and decisions. Equal partnerships are best for each member of the partnership. This is the only loving environment possible for survival of all the members.

Many of us have learned as we work toward equal partnerships within our own families that no one person in a family of transition has it made. No one gets off while another member is resenting. Good human relationships are hard to establish. It's difficult for us to live within a society encouraging stereotypical behaviors, even for men whose stereotype is valued by our society.

People do choose their problems for struggle. Those of us who have chosen to focus on social change within our family, instead of open marriage, money, recreation, housebuilding, independence, personal fulfillment and so on, must believe that the struggle is worth the price. We also believe that dealing with the present difficulties in our families as we work toward liberation from stereotypes, as we work toward equal-partnership relationships, and as we extend human rights and power to both partners . . . is a matter of human rights and justice.

I Promise to Love You Eternally . . .
till Next Tuesday

They come fully prepared,
quicksand and piranha egos
are the skulls, costumed with the skin,
of love and need.

Dinner will be served,
the main course will be you,
and no one's hunger will be appeased.

When survival turns on the axis of emptiness,
all offerings go unrecognized,
and, as the pain of my useless love
settles into my aching heart,
I look up.

With blazing eyes,
she says,
"I promise to love you eternally,
till next Tuesday."

SIDNEY MILLER

Men in Change: Beyond "mere anarchy"

TERESA DONATI MARCIANO

Turning and turning in the widening gyre
The falcon cannot hear the falconer;
Things fall apart; the centre cannot hold;
Mere anarchy is loosed upon the world. . . .
WILLIAM BUTLER YEATS, *The Second Coming*[1]

Anomie seems often to result from abrupt changes these past ten years in man-woman relationships. The Women's Liberation Movement (WLM)[2] has touched people's lives simultaneously at so many points (for example, self-concept, home life, friendship networks, courtship) that both sexes struggle to find a center which *can* hold. Frequently, however, "exasperation and irritated weariness"[3] are major products of the search for a point beyond "mere anarchy."

[1]Appreciation is expressed to Plantin Press, Ltd., for permission to reprint part of *The Second Coming* by William Butler Yeats.

[2]What is called the "Women's Liberation Movement" here is a set of *groups* (rather than a single entity) encompassing a wide range in philosophy, method, focus and membership. It is a movement in the sense that these groups do share a commitment to at least one common goal: equality with men, and then beyond that, androgyny. The range of differences among groups tends to be most visible in a group's membership (women only, men and women, heterosexual, lesbian, both, etc.) and in its method of achieving equality (e.g., legal suits, female separatism).

[3]Part of Durkheim's description of the anomic condition, in *Suicide* (1952: 357).

The effects of the liberation have been uneven for both women and men. The "Martha Movement," for example, was formed for housewives who take pride in domestic life, who resist the perceived push by the WLM to outside employment.[4]

This absence of uniform effect, in the case of men, is described in two studies. These studies link the Women's Liberation Movement to male actions and attitudes, illustrating some ways in which ideology translates into social reality. Sometimes, as will be shown, the social reality is *negative* reaction to pressure for change. (A recent instance of this is the attack on "reverse discrimination," in which Affirmative Action is held to favor women and minorities over white males.)

The first study shows that women's networks of friendship, support and definitive action (for example, working for the ERA) may produce in women a relocation and reintegration of self, where the new norms become *clearer* and support for them becomes stronger. The ways in which such women are prepared to relate to men also change—while men cannot draw upon parallel groups that might help *them* change. Male resistance, pride, dominance or the sheer unwillingness to change at all have been blamed for the slowness of normative change and the confusion men are experiencing. While any of these may be true some or most of the time, the issue here is this: How much has the *structure* of men's lives impeded their ability to join women in the movement toward equality? The first study shows that men and women are still living in separate worlds, with the women experiencing personal enrichment and support while the men are cut off from these. Such a statement may appear to be extreme at first, yet it emerges strikingly, and surprisingly, from discussions with many groups of women and with women individually, and not only from the sample findings discussed in the following pages.

Men continue to benefit, of course, from "old boy network" advantages. Yet the sense of meaning, direction, excitement and personal worth are visibly increasing among women. Women's centers become magnets when they are established on campuses. At one college, the women's center attracts men who can find no groups as congenial as that available to the women. The benefits to women are not a trade-off for the economic and social advantages of being male, but those benefits are a step toward assertions of equality that men are still largely unprepared to understand or accept.

One structural reason for this male reluctance is that men often lack group memberships where they receive positive cues, and/or personal gratification, from living in equality with women. Men's worlds still emphasize qualities of a macho type that women find increasingly

---

[4]Although based on a model from the New Testament, women of all religions, not only Christians, identify with this movement.

unacceptable as their consciousness of sexism continues to be raised.

The first study also points to the strains in the female-male encounters in personal and professional life. The women and men in that study are highly educated, holding executive and professional positions in and out of academe. The women's relations with the men are marked by frustrations for the women as they try to implement norms of equality, and for the men as they try to come to grips with changes they find threatening, "unfeminine," or simply confusing.

Males, as they try to understand and cope with evolving norms of equality in their relations with women, are the subject of the second study. There, dating and engaged couples, and young marrieds, were questioned about their expectations of each other and the negotiations between them concerning those expectations. From this study comes the idea of "the Continuum of Liberation" (see outline): On a line showing all possible attitudes toward equality and sharing with women, the men were found to stop at certain definite points. That point at which a man stops is the point at which he refuses to make further adaptations or concessions in his relations with a female partner.

That continuum indicates the amount of "give" in the relationship. The woman may fall anywhere behind, and up to, the point at which the man has stopped, without visible stress in the relationship. When the woman wishes to cross beyond the point where the man stopped, strain does become visible, and the relationship must undergo hard renegotiation, or break up. Of course, one or the other partner theoretically may simply accept the other's point: The woman may retreat to where the man stopped, or the man will advance to where the woman has advanced. This, however, was not a typical occurrence in the study that was done. The renegotiate-or-break-up options overwhelmingly were delineated by the woman's advances on the continuum. In fact, if a male was sure that the woman would not advance, he could *claim* to advance, so that it appeared that the woman had more options in the relationship than she actually had.

Both studies show that men do not have an easy time understanding or relating to many of the "new" demands women are making. The second study shows an attempt to *create* a set of norms in a heterosexual relationship, these being derived from and/or in reaction to the undermined, traditional norms.

Both studies also show that men are often "caught in the middle," between (1) their socialization to be assertive, aggressive and dominant and to look for complementary patterns of dependence in women and (2) the *re*socialization of women *away* from roles and attitudes that would complement traditional male socialization. These tend to evolve from unyielding interactions with men to work toward cooperation and partnership between the sexes.

Women are not, meanwhile, uniformly committed to WLM goals. Men may receive cues to behave in traditional ways with one woman but find that those same behaviors repel another woman. Thus "things fall apart," and anomie threatens.

The Studies (In Outline Form)

I. Executive and Professional Women, ages 26 to 55 (n = 31), and their perceptions of men who are their status and age peers.

    (1) Of the 31 women, 16 are divorced (high divorce rates typify women who have had 17 or more years of education) and 15 are married.

    (2) In all cases, male-female interactions under conditions of normative change are often made more difficult by the age factor: In dealing with older males, women find the men caught between ideals of chivalry and sexist stereotypes of women, and a desire to understand the new women.

    (3) The divorced women report that in dating-courtship processes, older men often see liberation as a sexual bonanza. They expect a woman who calls herself a feminist to be sexually free or easy.

    (4) The divorced women do not want to change their lives for a marriage; their life patterns have become a set of non-negotiable demands. These derive from

        (a) Their perceptions of divorce as being caused by sexism and lack of flexibility in their former husbands.

        (b) An unwillingness to risk entrapment into sex-typed roles in marriage.

        (c) A perceived dearth of males who do more than pay lip-service to Woman's Liberation values, as witnessed by male descriptions of what their marital expectations are (especially in regard to whose career would take precedence and the division of labor in the marriage).

        (d) A larger pool of available females than males, so that men have more apparent choices of partners than do women.

        (e) Women's career demands which, when combined with demands of children, force the women to establish priorities in which social relationships with men are secondary to career and children.

(f) Males' counter-perceptions that women want liberation *and* dependence, on their own terms.

(g) Males' concessions that more flexible, younger women pose fewer career and personal threats; also, the society glorifies youth and certain types of beauty, and men have been socialized to believe that their status is enhanced by younger, more attractive wives.

(h) A resultant feminization of women's friendship circles because women perceive it as less stressful; they opt out of many potentially "courting" relationships to avoid "wasting time" in sexual games.

(i) A result, in turn, of a further polarization of men's and women's worlds, which tends to increase tensions between women and men where women are working for policy and work-practice changes to implement norms of equality; hostility is often the result, with ensuing "confirmations" for the men of the "pushy women" stereotypes.

(j) The absence of true friendships between women and men, which is perhaps the highest cost of the preceding. Recent media reports further confirm the general patterns of these findings. Nan Robertson in *The New York Times* of July 14, 1978, reports the frustrations of single women over 30 (divorced and never-married) as they seek compatible, liberated men. Marriage as a state incompatible with career fulfillment is found among women surgeons who have succeeded that still-male stronghold. See Leslie Bennetts's article, *The New York Times* of July 18, 1978.

(5) The married women report two patterns, one of traditional marriage and one of non-traditional marriage. In the case of traditional marriage, a "schizophrenia" exists between home and work worlds, where the female is dependent and deferential to her husband at home but assertive and independent at work. The traditional marriage produces the following results:

(a) It increases the stress these women perceive in their lives as a result of the home-work split.

(b) It insulates husbands from the effects of new norms, so that the women have not succeeded in translating those new norms into personal action, while the men do not behave according to new normative expectations.

(c) Where the personal stress over the traditional marriage is low for the woman, that stress may be increased by other women introduced into the marital setting who advocate the new norms, and who sanction the traditional marital pattern in negative ways; this undermines the bonding of females in some ways, and women who perceive this threat often find themselves maintaining separations of their friends from their home lives.

(d) In traditional marriages where there are no children, the women perceived greater options for themselves than where there were children present; the security of children operated powerfully to preserve the husband's ability to resist major changes in his behavior toward greater sharing.

(e) In some cases, the *appearance* of traditional marriage was actually a marriage of great equality, where certain traditional rituals (male courtesies, female shaping of schedule, where possible, in deference to the male) functioned to provide the males with emotional security while they in turn provided support for their wives. These deceptive marriages were most thought-provoking in that they seemed to have achieved a balance, incorporating a transition between rigid, sexist traditions and greater flexibility and equality. It is these adaptations that warrant further exploration for the potential they offer to women and men to shift to more androgynous marriages.

(6) Non-traditional marriages were marked by househusbandry, active male commitment to (and work in) the WLM, a high degree of mutual sharing and consultation, an acceptance of career-induced physical separations. These marriages often were childless. In addition,

(a) They were often marked by a switch in the marriage from traditional to non-traditional patterns.

(b) They were often precipitated by the male's discontent with stereotyped sex roles which pressured them into patterns with which they were uncomfortable.

(c) These marriages showed a greater likelihood for the men to be incorporated into the friendship networks of the women.

(d) The men tended to gravitate toward social circles, among co-workers, where the men's norms accepted and rewarded those who attempted to live in greater sexual equality.

(e) In the absence of such circles, the men drew away from deep, prolonged interaction with men who held to more stereotyped sex norms.

(f) The result of this, for the men, was to make very clear the necessity of achieving continued reinforcement of the commitment to sexual equality. The study must take special note of these results, for it shows that men must be willing to forego the easy, acceptable male networks that condemn liberated males.

Above all, this study points to the critical need for *peer* support among men for change in their attitudes toward women to occur; and in the absence of male peer support, the men must be incorporated into women's circles where the new norms are being used, in order for them to receive the necessary gratifications that promote conformity to the new norms. It also points to a need for men to be willing to reach out, as women have done, to other men in the formation of consciousness-raising groups or friendship groups where deep sharing is not taboo. Men who do believe in norms of equality often find themselves isolated because first, women mistrust them in their commitments or their motives, and second, other men mistrust them for their "lack of manliness" or for their potential influence on their own lives.

The sense of anomie among men is greatest, in fact, when the distrust *is* coming from both sexes. Among women, there is disappointment or rejection when men "lapse" into sexist statements or assumptions. The commitment of both sexes to the achievement of equality as an *ongoing* process would help alleviate this. Analogies may be drawn between the need women have for consciousness raising and men's needs for that same evolutionary opportunity.

II. Younger Men on the "Continuum of Liberation": Dating,

Engaged and Married Couples (dating and engaged, n = 43, married = 12), age range: 18 to 26 years old.

(1) The clearest pattern that emerged for *females* in this study was that new norms are often confronted most strongly and adopted most readily *after* the early teen years. The "lag" and unevenness in the socialization of boys and girls to the new norms was apparent both on the campus where the dating and engaged couples were studied, and among the "young marrieds."

(2) It is a definite source of strain for the young males to encounter the new norms on the campus, as a wider variety of female attitudes become apparent. Meanwhile, the females have been exposed to women's centers, female professors who serve as role models, women's studies courses; while not all females are strong in their adoption of the new norms, those norms have definite effects, if only gradually at the beginning, upon the way in which women have begun to relate to others of their own sex, and to males.

(3) When questioned about job future and anticipated sharing of household tasks, the males, as they advanced through college, began to show crystallization of norms, a personal synthesis, to demarcate their positions vis-à-vis their perceived capacity to respond to the new norms.

   (a) The males on campus do not show an overwhelming sympathy or support for the goals of the Women's Liberation Movement, a feeling exacerbated perhaps by the feeling that the recruiters were favoring women for top-level-potential jobs.

   (b) Male groups on the campuses, where they are directed toward sports, fraternities, or preprofessional clubs, are preserves of traditional male norms.

Ballad

There was a maid of twenty-five years, who sailed across the sea
Her own true love she left far behind, and thus began her odyssey
Her love, he was sad, but he knew that she must go, so he bid her farewell
  to take her leave
With a kiss they did part, and he watched her sail away,
Her own woman, a little more to be

But while she danced and rose like the sun
Her lover, he wept in vain
For though he did know that she blossomed at this hour
He failed to share her joy because she could not share his pain
He failed to share her joy because she could not share his pain

At last she did return, but she didn't stay for long, within ten days she'd
  taken leave again
Twas for the western shores that she set off this time, but she promised soon
  to return unto him
Her love, he was sad, but he knew that she must go, so he bid her farewell to
  take her leave
With a kiss they did part, and he watched her go away,
Her own woman, a little more to be

But the weeks turned into months that the lovers were apart
And bravely he tried to understand
But the autumn nights were long and he could not come to see
How she could live apart from him and not feel incomplete
How she could live apart from him and not feel incomplete

And then one day, a letter came to him, saying "Love there is one more place
  I must go"
"We've been apart this long, we can last a few months more, I'm headed south
  for sunny Mexico"
And her love he understood, so he shed not a tear, until a month or more had
  passed him by
It was only at this time that he came to realize
That love and not dependence must survive

And it was not enough that he saw her as herself
And patiently awaited her return
For though her own woman he did need to see her as
He needed just as much his own man to become
Yes, he needed just as much his own man to become.

WILLIE SORDILL
Copyright © 1980 by Willie Sordill

Talking Our Way Out of It: The Rise and Fall of a Men's Group

THOMAS W. BENSON

I was a member of a men's group in State College, Pennsylvania, from 1973 until 1976, when the group dissolved. The experience was rich for me, and one that was for so long an important part of my life that I would like to reflect on how it came to be, how it was able to last for more than three years, and how it worked and what it accomplished.

The group had started about a year before I was invited to join. When I first entered the group, there were four members: R, J, and L, who were assistant professors of political science, and A, who had been an assistant professor of philosophy until the year before, when he had been denied tenure and dropped from the department. The group started as a fairly self-conscious attempt to recreate the experience of women's consciousness-raising groups, as a response to political conviction ("It's time to pay serious attention to sexism!"), and as a way to deal with personal problems involving work and marriage.

During the years I was in the group, L resigned to spend his time organizing a faculty union, A returned to Europe, and four more members joined the group: R, a sociologist with a special interest in personal and social development; V, a philosopher; D, a physicist who had left his wife after 19 years of marriage; and G, a colleague of mine from the speech department. We ranged in age from 34 to 43 and had in common our male gender, our training as academics, and our need for support in seeking a better understanding of ourselves. All of us are heterosexual in orientation.

What was the purpose of the group? We never did arrive at an agreement about precisely what a group like ours could do for us. In general, our model was consciousness raising: Roughly, this meant that a large part of our agenda was to talk in detail about our personal problems and then try to understand the ways in which those problems were at least partially caused or influenced by our roles as men in a male-oriented culture. We were always reluctant to use the term *men's liberation* because it seemed both ambiguous and inadequate: We did not seek sexual permissiveness, and, for the most part, we were suspicious about calls to liberation that seemed disconnected from the realities of self, family, job, and society.

We often found ourselves operating as a "support group," where our major function was to provide a structure of emotional support and reflective problem-solving for members who were having difficulties. Within this context, some of us discovered, for better or worse, problems we had not previously recognized as ours.

Although it was important to us to learn new sensitivities, we were not a sensitivity group as defined in humanistic psychology. Our experience in the group usually concerned our day-to-day lives outside the group, it tended not to be confrontational, and it operated mostly at the verbal level. Furthermore, our model of psychological health was not very clearly defined (as in "humanistic," "transactional," "sensitivity," and so on). Each of us, we seemed to agree, had the right to try to work out his own model of life, within a general consensus that our lives were some mixture of the personal and the social, the rational and the emotional, and that we were trying not to be self-destructive. I am convinced that our ambiguity about group goals and procedures was useful in helping us avoid dogmatism, but it sometimes led to painful confrontations and in the end was partly responsible for the dissolution of the group.

Although the group changed considerably with new members, new problems, and new insights, we did develop certain patterns, some explicit and some implicit. We tried to talk about our own lives, problems, and experiences rather than those of others who were not present. If a member had had a fight with his wife and was trying to understand how to respond to the situation, we tried to talk about the member rather than about the wife. And although we offered support, we tried not to choose sides: Ideally, the member who had fought with his wife was not coached on how to win the fight but encouraged to reflect on his own responsibility for creating it. Non-threatening self-criticism was an important item on our agenda.

Typically, the discussion of a marriage problem would produce two other kinds of talk: Members would share their own parallel or contrasting experiences, and the group would try to understand the structures that gave birth to such problems at the social and cultural level. Personal adjustment in marriage, we seemed to agree, depended not simply on personal good will but on real commitment to understanding the politics of the situation. There was some disagreement about this; at times members would argue that the solution to personal problems lay in looking inside one's self, getting in touch with one's inner nature, and then working out the problem from there. At times it appeared that the problem was a matter of applying interpersonal communications skills. Others argued that the problem was, at least partly, a matter of the politics of gender and culture.

Politics of gender? Most of us in the group had long considered our-selves to be "feminists": We had supported the women's liberation move-ment and had tried to learn how to avoid oppressive male attitudes and actions toward women. However, we learned that a men's group does not make sense simply as a place to feel guilty about being a white, male, Anglo-Saxon. If the group was to work, it had to work for us, and not solely as an adjunct of women's liberation. We tried to understand how man's oppressiveness toward women and other men also oppresses him. The culture we have inherited and daily reenact with other human beings provides a reasonably stable base for certain important satisfactions; it also generates a lot of pain, oppression, and contradiction. How much of our unhappiness can we expect to transcend through a self-conscious cultural revolution, and how much of it must we simply endure as the inevitable consequence of living in a society? Asking the questions in this way enabled us, I think, to see our own problems, rather than to see ourselves simply as problems for women to deal with. When a man defines his cultural role simply as a problem for women, no matter how hard he tries to expunge his male chauvinism, he is trapped in a paradox; the harder he struggles, the more he engages in the oppressive business of assuming woman's incapacity to help herself. The politics of gender required us to understand how we interacted with women and with other men; it did not require us to do something for women. This perception led to another paradox. We came to believe that, until men could learn to restructure their relationships with other men, they were likely to require the sort of support from women that women justifiably perceived as subordination.

As we learned how to talk to each other, we found our relationships with women changing. Men who can learn to opt out of constant compe-tition with other men may not need—nor want—to dominate women. However, this is not instant utopia, either: When a relationship between a man and a woman has involved domination and submission, a move toward equality requires some painful renegotiation of expectations for both partners. In our experience, a relationship in which a woman felt required to be submissive was one in which the man felt required to be dominating. This was as much a trap for him as for her, and it constituted the essence of the oppressiveness in man's role.

Once we had learned to focus on our own problems, and on our relationships with women and other men, we began to learn a lot. We learned how often each of us felt anger, and we discovered that sometimes our anger masked other emotions: sadness, depression, anxiety, fear, and even joy. We learned much about possession, and how we propped up our lives by possessing ourselves, our things, our women. We learned to admit vulnerability and found the admission fortifying. We learned to ask very clearly what would happen if the worst happened, and we learned that we could handle the worst. We learned to give and to receive permission to discover and to do what we thought was right.

Most of the talk at our weekly meetings was generated out of immediate problems. We were focused on what was wrong with the present. For example, a group member would be having trouble at work or at home and would use the group as a place to clarify what the problem was and what alternatives were available to him. Others then shared similar experiences, asked questions, and occasionally offered advice. Usually our discussions broadened to include some consideration of the causes for such problems. The group's function here was problem-solving and collective support. Often it helped just to know that others had experienced, and survived, similar problems.

Frequently, we talked about the past. We tried to reflect on how we had become what we were, on our experiences of childhood and adolescence, on our relations with our parents, on how we had learned to become men. For several weeks we structured the group around long autobiographical monologues, with each member taking an hour or so at the beginning of a meeting to tell the story of his life. There were often as many surprises in this for the teller as for the listeners.

Sometimes we tried to talk about the future. We tried to discover what shape we wanted our lives to take and what we could do to change our directions. We found that we often wasted time on idle fantasies about the future which prevented us from coping with our present situations and which were not really goals so much as mental escape hatches. I don't think we were very successful in constructing our images about the future, and it was around this issue that the group finally seemed to come apart.

We sometimes wondered whether the strong support we were giving each other in the group was merely a sort of band-aid therapy, designed to patch us up and adapt us to a life that ought to be changed rather than coped with. After years of meeting together once a week, some of us found that the group had become predictable and static—that while it provided support, it prevented radical ambitions about changing our lives. When it had reached that point, it was necessary either to change the group or dissolve it.

Two sorts of changes seemed possible. First, we wondered whether it was time to stop talking about our problems and begin to confront one another in the group, pushing to deeper layers of knowledge about ourselves and each other. Second, we realized that we could get outside the group by undertaking some common project, such as a men's resource center, or a system of cooperative work, or some sort of community. Our choices were, in effect, to deepen our therapeutic involvement with each other, to undertake a common project, or to go our separate ways. In the end, for a variety of reasons, we stopped meeting. We dissolved with some feelings of sadness, but not with a feeling of failure. A men's group could be, but need not be, a lifelong commitment. Ours turned out to be a postgraduate education in self-knowledge. I learned that I am not alone; that facing my vulnerabilities could dissipate most of the anxiety I had generated in trying to hide my conflicts and fears from myself.

An important part of the group experience for me was my attempt to confront my own marriage and its meaning for me by exploring how other men understood their own relations with women. During 1975 I produced and directed a 50-minute documentary film about three couples: Ron and Jack, both members of the group; Bill, a graduate student in my department; and Bonnie, Linda, and Ilma. For me the film was an important part, as well as a product, of the group experience. It is entitled "Couples," and is available for showings from Audio-Visual Services, the Pennsylvania State University, University Park, PA 16802. In the film, each couple explains itself to the camera, discovering in the process some surprises about the relationship. Each of the six participants describes what it means to be one's self and part of a couple. For anyone interested in starting a men's group and needing stimulus for discussion, "Couples" may be useful.

I know of one other film that may be useful for insight into the experience of being in a men's group. It is called "A Man," and it records one meeting of a men's group in which a young man describes the death of his father and asks for help. The film is also available from the Pennsylvania State University Audio-Visual Services.

These two films come from somewhat different sorts of groups and are probably more useful as starting points for discussion than as models of interaction. Each group will have to work out its own rules about what sort of talk is useful. Similarly, this discussion of communication in my men's group, of our goals, patterns of talk, and problems, may be useful as a starting point for discussion, and has been written, not to propose the correct way to run a men's group, but to provide some permission and support for men who might want to start such a group.

takin care of business

an obsessive energy
is humming me
from
places
to people
to things

got stuff to do
got stops to make

snow tires
lamp for desk
brillo
toilet paper
sylvias chair
pay the rent

and it looks like snow

many thanks to

new jersey bell
midlantic national bank
master charge
traffic court jersey city
shop-rite of fort lee

and many others too numerous to mention

don't think its easy
it takes devotion
yes even love
to get the bed made every morning
to get the garbage into the incinerator

not to forget
not to forget

to double lock the door
a place for everything
everything in its place

except me
last tuesday afternoon

what painful reassurances
I earn
from the banal chores
of my life

afraid the glue
that holds me together
would dry up
without them

would I forget how to tell time
without my late notices

would I fall
into the bottomless void
of my empty mailbox

Is it not written
across that
great computer in the sky

YOU SHALL KNOW HIM
BY HIS PAID BILLS

SIDNEY MILLER

Changing Male Sex Roles and Identities

KING DAVID BOYER, JR.

The problems arising for the American male from the sexual and feminist revolutions are now coming into a prominent position in both the personal and professional realms. An examination of the literature available and the effect certain social and technological changes have had on the male sex role will be related briefly here. Also, an attempt will be made to bring into focus the position of and the particular problems surrounding the current male role. Finally, as a prelude to my proposed work in the area of sexual therapy, the relation of male sexual dysfunctions to the confusion and problems of the changing masculine role will be discussed.

The phrase "knowledge is power" is often quoted; indeed, it is logically and practically true that knowledge *is* power, as well as success, satisfaction and a number of other positive conditions. Perhaps the most valuable subject to know is ourselves. This is the basic dilemma that faces a good many American males. In times of social change it becomes necessary to redefine roles and appropriate behavior. This process sometimes takes longer than the social change which preceded it. The situation of the male in our society is problematic for precisely this reason. What is it like to be a man in a society that no longer covets his physical strengths, agility, adroitness and other athletic qualities; a culture in which the machine, once a symbol of man's ingenuity, has evolved into the computer and vast labor-saving devices, symbolizing the loss of his individuality and personal value as a laborer? What is it like to exist in a society which faces males with a loss of identity through its pressure to conform to the "democratic group," which demands that he be a "good guy," a responsible citizen, an industrious worker and provider, as well as a satisfactory husband, father, and sexual partner? Many males feel drawn to contradictory standards of masculine behavior. On one hand the society, particularly the business-career world, expects them to have the traditionally male qualities of aggressiveness, individuality and creativeness. Yet there also exist social and psychological pressures which inhibit aggressiveness and encourage group participation and the derivation of satisfaction from other people's accomplishments. Steinmann and Fox (1974) indicate that American men expressed strong components of individual and group drives and needs. They see themselves as slightly more aggressive than inhibited, and more individualistic than groupish.

These issues are compounded by the latest social change, which is the manner in which women and "significant others" expect men to behave. The socialization of males has rendered many of them incapable of or inept at expressing their emotions to their loved ones. Balswick (1970) found that males are less able than females to express or receive companionship and support from their spouses. He also reported that the lack of expressiveness is greatest among the less-educated males. Balswick noted that male inexpressiveness is common among all socioeconomic levels, but it is particularly in the lower classes that males specifically stated that expressiveness is perceived as being inconsistent with their defined masculine roles. In keeping with this finding, Balswick and Peek (1971) have suggested that male inexpressiveness may not be entirely the result of socialization. Instead, this behavior may be caused by present perceived expectations of the male sex role. That is, the male perceives the cultural expectations as saying, "Don't express your feelings to women"; and, although he may be capable of expressiveness, he adheres to the standards of his contemporaries. Along with inexpressiveness are other personality traits that are now being expected of males that are inconsistent with traditionally masculine behavior. These include emotionality, affection, compassion, sentimentality and vulnerability. Often, males who are incapable of these behaviors are labeled macho.

It becomes apparent that the prevalent feelings that exist in males about customary and expected role behaviors add up to nothing short of a perplexed state of mind. As the male moves and develops in ways which bring him closer to what he thought were appropriate male roles, he moves further away from what women want. Conflicts and confusion concerning when to express macho or tender, compassionate attitudes are a natural experience for males in their personal and social lives as well as in their occupational interactions.

The situation that men face is a problem not only of coming to terms with their masculinity but also with their individuality. A man can no longer confidently and definitely confirm his masculinity in terms of unidimensional and sexually differentiated roles. Nor can he do so on the basis of believing in feminine inferiority in managing the practical affairs of the world. It is remarkable how two men with similar physical configurations, even when they conform to masculine stereotypes—tall, muscular and handsome—can project such divergent impressions. One conveys a feeling of confidence and ease, of a person who knows who he is. The other seems weak and easily led. It is largely in the way the man handles the choices of behavior available, indeed, whether he has the autonomy to make choices at all. That is the crux of his manly stance. In this sense there is a merging of masculinity and individuality.

Admittedly, the times are not conducive to gaining a sense of self-worth or to understanding or accepting one's sex as individualism. As long as men feel that the quality of women will emasculate them, this is precisely the effect Women's Liberation will have on them. At the same time, as long as men identify themselves so narrowly with the bread-winning role, with the competitive, driving characterization, they will be trapped in stagnant, inflexible lifestyles.

There is a new avenue toward masculinity, a different concept emerging of what it means to be a man. It has little to do with how strong the male is physically, how adept he is at ordering people around, how much wealth and status he has attained, how virile he proves to be, or how closely he identifies with the other stereotyped masculine attitudes and behaviors. This new approach to masculinity is supremely concerned with the way the man manages his life, with the way he conducts himself as a human being in terms of his partner, his children, his business associations and the co-members of his community. This male characterization refers to the courage to say no, as well as yes, to his ability to perceive and estimate the consequences of his actions and decisions. This route to masculinity-individuality is not the easy one. It involves thinking, evaluating and reevaluating, rather than the blind adherence to standards of role behavior.

In the sexual and feminist revolutions, the male has been cast as the "enemy." He is held responsible for society's ills. Man is repeatedly told he must change but is rarely told how. Obviously, any significant change in women's roles has a definite and immediate effect on men and their behavior expectations. Some believe strongly that the social changes in sexual roles and behaviors have posed a more severe problem for men than for women. Women have moved out beyond the traditional roles and patterns established for them over the years. The basic problem they face is how to incorporate new opportunities and freedoms into their repertoire of behavior while at the same time retaining those traditional rights and duties they require. On the other hand, men are faced with the necessity of adapting to a new concept of the male role, a role which in many cases involves lessened opportunities and fewer freedoms than were previously theirs simply because they were male.

Being in this underdog position leaves the male with few alternatives: He can fight for the traditional dominance he once held in male-female relationships, or he can totally succumb to every feminist whim. A compromise reaction with revolutionary social changes is a viable choice for the male. He should recognize, accept and understand that the power structure of the male-female relationship has begun to change. He must decide how he will revise some of his attitudes, alter aspects of his behavior in the direction of yielding and dividing his power.

Of particular import to males and females in our society is the quality of relationships between the sexes. Traditional forms of interaction between men and women are no longer viable. In the past, most features of male-female relationships pivoted around the male. This type of relationship is not acceptable to many couples, especially when the female has been able to achieve economical and personal independence. The Women's Bureau of the Department of Labor reports that 60 percent of the women in the labor force are married and that 37 percent of all married women hold jobs.

The sexual revolution has accompanied and lent support to the female liberation movement. K. E. Davis (1971) defines a true sexual revolution as a dramatic change in the attitudes and ethics governing sexual behavior, as well as the behavior itself. The separation of sexual activity from reproductive functions by means of contraception and abortion has become a way of life. This influence coupled with liberated views of female sexual behavior has been still another contribution to changed relationships between men and women. Rubin noted that the sexual attitudes and behavior of men and those of women are converging today. Women expect the sexual freedom that has traditionally been accorded men only. Men, on the other hand, rather than moving in the direction of greater promiscuity, are slowly drifting toward the traditional female norms of expressive, nurturant sexual behavior (I. Rubin, 1971). A significant change in the sexual relationship between men and women has been increased concern of both sexes with the physical pleasure and satisfaction of the female. A. Comfort (1972) asserts that no longer are the needs of women considered subordinate to those of men. Men and women are encouraged to unloosen their inhibitions and permit themselves complete sexual responsiveness, despite lingering remnants of sexual puritanism that have traditionally hampered freedom of sexual expression. Anthropological investigation has revealed that cultures encouraging women to be completely free in their sexual expression produce women whose erotic reactions are as uninhibited and as vigorous as those of their men (Kronhausen and Kronhausen, 1965).

Another effect of the sexual revolution is increased pressure on the males to sexually satisfy the recently verbalized female sexual needs. With dismay many women and feminists have realized that this pressure has produced sexual dysfunctions in their lovers. The male experiences anxiety about his sexual performance and anticipates his mate's making mental comparisons of him with other lovers. In addition, males feel resentment toward women as the source of these anxieties. None of these attitudes favor a satisfying sexual encounter or relationship. A. Comfort (1972) cites that a common cause of impotence is a psychological "turning off" of oneself by apprehension about sexual performance. Kaplan (1974) reports about impotence that the prevalent sexual myths of our culture lead many couples erroneously to feel that a man must function with a certain frequency and regularity, that he must always respond with an instant erection and must always be able to continue coitus for lengthy periods of time. If they are not aware that the sexual response is not under voluntary control, that there are normal fluctuations in sexual interest, or that age and pressures of life may diminish a man's sexual capacity, they may react to a normal temporary diminuation of libido or a transient erective failure with great and unnecessary alarm, which may ultimately lead to serious dysfunctional syndromes. In addition, Kaplan finds that some other highly prevalent sources of sexual anxiety such as fear of sexual failure, the demand for sexual performance, and fear of being rejected by one's partner, can be destructive to sexual satisfaction. In regard to premature ejaculation, W. G. Pomeroy (1972) believes that anxiety is the basic problem in this sexual dysfunction.

The contemporary American male as a lover is caught in a mishmash of contradictions. The masculine stereotype demands that he be sexually virile and attentive, but he is expected to devote most of his psychic and physical energies in the breadwinning capacity. To make love freely and spontaneously, he must acknowledge his sexual partner erotically; yet, his stereotyped view of her gets in the way of real eroticism. McCary (1973) has observed that men who have never learned how to express tenderness, or who are afraid to do so, will often ignore the woman with whom they are involved or make belittling remarks to her. These men want to demonstrate their commitment; but, not knowing how to use the appropriate positive emotions, they use the only emotional expressions they are familiar with—the negative ones.

Another contradiction affecting the sexual relationship between men and women is that the man expects to be the dominant figure in the sexual relationship. But the social and sexual patterns he follows tend to make his female partner the controlling figure. He enjoys bragging about how much he likes women and how full his sex life is, but many of his attitudes toward females reflect more hostility—or at least suspicion—than they do liking. A man may perceive himself as quite a sexy guy, but through some of his actions he betrays a fear and antagonism toward the opposite sex. This situation of an anxious, suspicious male attitude is illustrated through the observations of American men by an English secretary working in New York City: "The basic fact is that they're all babies. . . . They just don't seem to have true masculine qualities. They're always and forever deferring to you. They never make up their own blinkin' minds about where to eat, where to go, what to do. It drives one dotty. . . . They even ask you under the most propitious circumstances if they may kiss you. Fancy a European or an Englishman ever doing that. . . . From all my observations and those of the girls I know here, it is the fault of the American woman. She babies him and wears the pants. It's as absurdly simple as that."[1]

Kaplan (1974) observed that this power dilemma in the male-female relationship was a factor in sexual dysfunction. She states that the power struggle between the sexes may mobilize paranoia in the man if he must always play the successful, adequate role and cannot admit any signs of weakness. He is more likely to avoid sex and reject his wife than to openly share his concern over his sexual problem.

A power struggle between mates is often associated with poor communication between them, and particularly with an inability of the male to express tenderness and affection. This faulty communication has extremely detrimental effects on the sexual relationship. Couples need reciprocal feedback to develop a good sexual interaction and to secure an effective erotic stimulation. The failure of many couples to communicate openly about their sexual feelings and experiences has been cited by authorities in the field as an important factor in the etiology of sexual dysfunction. Kaplan (1974) found that often the lack of communication is not a cause of the dysfunction; rather, it helps to continue a destructive sexual system and escalate an existing problem.

The relationships between men and women have been affected by the questioning and revision of traditional standards of male and female behavior. Since the changes have been rather rapid, many men and women have experienced confused and anxious feelings regarding their own identities. Consequently, these insecurities have an effect on sexual relationships by either bringing about dysfunctions, or in some cases, perpetuating and contributing to already existing sexual problems. It

---

[1]Quoted by Leonard W. Robinson. "English Secretaries Must Have 'Nous.' " *New York Times Magazine* (December 29, 1964).

seems worthwhile at this point to invest our energy and resources in the development of methods of relieving some of the problems that surround the changing male sex role. Immediately, it might be valuable to work on anxiety-inhibiting processes for such males experiencing sexual dysfunctions. On a long-term basis, a source of prevention might be the education of young males as to the expectations and appropriate response behaviors to the changing male roles and sexual behaviors and attitudes.

References

BALSWICK, J. B.
  1970 "The effect of spouse companionship support on employment success," *Journal of Marriage and the Family,* 32, 212–215.
BALWICK, J. B., AND C. W. PEEK
  1971 "The inexpressive male: tragedy of American society," *Family Coordinator,* 20, no. 4, 363–368.
BRENTON, M.
  1966 *The American Male.* New York: Coward-McCann.
COMFORT, A.
  1972 *The Joy of Sex: A Gourmet Guide to Lovemaking.* New York: Crown.
DAVIS, K. E.
  Jan. 1971 "Sex on campus: Is there a revolution?" *Medical Aspects of Human Sexuality,* pp. 128–142.
KAPLAN, H. S.
  1974 *The New Sex Therapy: Active Treatment of Sexual Dysfunctions.* New York: Brunner Mazel.
KRONHAUSEN, P. E., AND E. KRONHAUSEN
  1965 *The Sexually Responsive Women.* New York: Ballantine.
MASTERS, W., AND V. JOHNSON
  1970 *Human Sexual Inadequacy.* Boston: Little, Brown.
MASTERS, W., AND V. JOHNSON
  1970 *Human Sexual Response.* Boston: Little, Brown.
MCCARY, J. L.
  1973 *Human Sexuality.* New York: D. Van Nostrand Co.
MEAD, M.
  1949 *Male and Female: A Study of the Sexes in a Changing World.* New York: Morrow, 1949.
MONTAGU, A.
  1969 *Sex, Man, and Society.* New York: Putnam.
POMEROY, W. G.
  1972 *Dr. Kinsey and the Institute for Sex Research.* New York: Harper & Row.

RUBIN, I.

1971 "New sex findings: some trends and implications," in *The New Sexuality,* ed., H. A. Otto. Palo Alto: Science and Behavior.

STEINMANN, A., AND D. FOX

1974 *The Male Dilemma.* New York: Jason Aronson, Inc.

There Is Nothing Else for It

I am soon going away,
I don't know where I'm going,
but, soon, I am going.

I want to stay.
I want to make a fool of myself,
with you.
I want to be unhappy
for making a fool of myself.

I want to be sorry and sad.
I want another turn,
another chance,
another taste of us,
one more ride on the merry-go-round,
another defeat that feels like a victory.

What is it?
What is it?
Shit,
it's Monday,
that's what it is.
Mondays, like all beginnings,
are dreary and rocky.
But, I got to move on,
and so do you.

Getting older means it hurts a little
where it never hurt before.
And the reserve of energy
is harder to find.
And, in some interior way,
one would rather stay put.

Are you scared?
It would help if you were,
you know that feeling;
ready to fight for what you believe,
but not believing in fighting anymore.

It feels good to say it.
It feels good to say it.
It feels good to say it,
to you.

SIDNEY MILLER

part four

NURTURANCE BY AND FOR MALES

Sharing

Helping

Hugging

NURTURANCE BY AND FOR MALES

Caring

Part 4 of this book is about a "quiet revolution" which is taking place inside a growing number of men in our country. This is not a civil insurrection but an internal growth process, a stretching of sex roles and a daring to be different. One outcome of this growth is nurturance—a caring and concern for women, for children, yes, and even for other men.

"We are oppressed by conditioning which makes us only half-human. . . . We are oppressed by this dependence on women for support, nurturing, love and warm feelings. We want to love, nurture, and support ourselves and other men, as well as women." So reads one of the first formal declarations of the Men's Movement (Berkeley Men's Center Manifesto). Some men are taking this credo seriously; a few men here in these pages disclose their own personal efforts to become more nurturant and caring of others.

Danzig in "Fatherhood and My Rebirth as a Man" relates how he, through his becoming a single parent with full custody of three sons, was "reborn" as a father through the necessity of having to raise his children without a woman's aid. As he described it, it is a lot of work but also sheer joy to discover that fatherhood is a relationship worked out day after day rather than a role given at a birth.

At a different stage in life Haggerson in "Birth Rites: Grandson and Grandfather" shares an analogous experience to Danzig's. By his participating in the home birth of his grandson, Haggerson himself felt reborn, free from his attendant flight behavior at the birth of his seven children many years before.

Males, however, do not have to become fathers or grandfathers to experience the pleasure of caring for children. Lowe in "Male Teachers and Young Children" describes the conditions which often greet the few young men who choose to enter the traditional feminine world of child development and early childhood education. The picture is not all pleasant for these men who defy sexual stereotypes and dare to live in a woman's occupational world so that they can both work with and enjoy young children. As Lowe portrays it, "A reason for needing males in an early childhood educational setting is so children can learn that men can be nurturing, loving, understood, just as women. . . . [But] it is important that he is not coerced into believing that he is an occupational failure, or that he is like a pet rabbit, 'the exceptional male working with young children.' "

Sometimes the object of a man's nurturing is himself. Geof Morgan, a country song writer living in Nashville, muses about the midgets within himself—those warm and caring qualities which are "often discouraged in men, yet are cultivated freely in women." Morgan recognizes, sadly, that he may never be able to bring together in his lifetime his work world and that growing, caring part of himself which is not valued in the business arena.

Nurturance *by* males, however, is easier understood and less suspected than nurturance *for* males by males. Kavaloski shares his "dream for brotherhood" for which men would have to give up their "endless competition, deep distrust and rigid reserve" to share their desires for and fear of intimacy with other men. In his philosophical and historical search for the roots of brotherhood in Western society, Kavaloski uncovers many examples of brotherhood woven into the fabric of community. He finds in these examples that "the ultimate gift of brotherhood is not only self understanding, but the development of one's own humanity." And yet, he also points out the pitfalls and the costs of brotherhood, such as the difficult renunciation of control over others.

Silvestre in "Becoming Brothers and Unbecoming Barriers" attacks perhaps the last bastion of traditional masculinism, the barriers between minority and majority men. Class and racial differences and divergent sexual orientations, according to Silvestre, are insurmountable barriers to the brotherhood of all men. Good intentions, a liberal philosophy and a realization that these barriers are destructive are not enough to bestow brotherhood or to tear down the walls which separate minority men from majority men. The Men's Movement has led some men "to examine their isolation from each other and their lack of brotherliness." This is not enough, however, because to build brotherhood between all men is to build trust and equality between all men. Brotherhood, therefore, "is not a state bestowed along with common parents, membership in a group or attendance at a meeting," but a process by which all the inequalities which now exist between men (and between men and women) are exchanged for trust and equality.

Fatherhood and My Rebirth as a Man

PHILLIP I. DANZIG

When our second son was born, my wife said to me that I would never be as close to the baby as she. Although I could help in feeding, changing and bathing him, I would never experience direct nurturing either in my abdomen or by suckling.

At the time, this hurt. It was not so much the *content* of what she said, because I never had serious wishes for a womb or for lactating, as the *tone* of its context. Why did she stress my biological inability to perform this obviously exclusive role of mothering?

My competitive impulse was to stick up for myself by proclaiming my equally exclusive role in the mysteries of creation. This I resisted; but still, I felt she was probably right. After all, she was a mother and ought to know such things.

Today, four years after a complicated separation in which my wife moved out of the house leaving our three boys to me, the situation is reversed. By virtue of physical and emotional nurturing, I feel closer to my children than I originally wanted, expected or thought possible.

My custodial responsibility is now the primary fact of my life. It supersedes such stormy questions as which parent most strongly wanted the children, who felt more competent to raise them, or who was most responsible for the dissolution of the marriage. It tempers the employ-ment I can have and colors my social life. And it gives me tremendous satisfaction.

How can I explain the complex joy of growing closer to my 17-year-old, helping him plan for college or map out a summer trip to the West Coast? Or my wonder at my intense 14-year-old, who has collected 105 different beer bottles and is always asking me for more? Or my tender feelings for my 9-year-old, so interested in building things and needing special attention in reading?

I wouldn't miss these experiences for the world!

Although I never ignored my children when their mother was living with us, my main emphasis, as with many other men, lay elsewhere. I thought my responsibility to myself was discharged through a career—and my obligations to my family were satisfied by the money I brought home, the "help" I offered to my wife in running the household and by following her suggestions about rearing the kids. This was much more parenting than my father had done; but looking back, it now seems meager. Today I have a more direct, primary and emotional involvement with my children and find that with authentic effort, relationships grow.

CATALYST FOR CHANGE

There were two sets of events which brought me to this acceptance. First, there is my long, steady involvement with some of the social changes of the 1960's, which brought fresh breezes into a sealed-up, 1950's-era marriage. I responded to the aesthetic liberation in popular music, theater, and men's attire. I participated in several peaceful, radical politi-cal protests. I read Marcuse, Chairman Mao, Rollo May and Ernest Becker. I joined a therapy group for couples and, urged by my wife, helped form a men's support (consciousness-raising) group. And I made a few new, younger friends.

These experiences confirmed what I already half knew but had been too timid to realize wholly: We are born without cultural predispositions; we are vastly adaptable; we create our own lifestyles; and we find meaning through discovering ourselves. There is very little biologically preordained about cultural roles, including gender stereotypes.

The second event was more explosive: the splitting of my nuclear family and my acceptance of custody. This allowed me to work out, at intimate scale, some notions of social change, democratic participation, non-directive leadership and mutual accommodation which I had been drawn to previously in radical politics. As my adult responsibilities be-came more personal, I embraced my children as a full-time presence.

COMMITMENT WITH RESPONSIBILITY

For me, this strengthened relationship as father was a by-product of losing the old relationship as husband. Obviously, this need *not* be the impetus for other men. Many couples struggle to achieve balanced parenting roles within stable marriages, and I wish this course had been available to me.

Although my wife and I had wanted to make changes, we were still too bound up in the rewards and delusions of traditional role playing. Sure, I said I wanted to participate more fully in the family, but I did not know how to begin. There was little real incentive, since my wife ran the house quite well. I was lazy and intimidated by her competence in the home. She wanted more from me but seemed vaguely threatened by loss of control in "her" areas. She did not like my buying the "wrong" brands. We just never worked it out.

Starting from a commitment to have custody, the physical aspects have never been much of a problem. Our household routine is now divided into "systems": food, clothing, shelter and social activities. Shopping for food has become a communal effort (and enjoyable). We hit the supermarket and divide up, scurrying around separately to minimize time, but conferring on bargains and preferences. How to choose which box of cookies? Each boy selects his favorite: Peace bought for three dollars.

While I take prime responsibility for *initiating* the cooking, my two older boys do much of the actual work. They take turns setting and clearing the table, though I must do the final clean-up in the kitchen. It is they who have demanded that the youngest do more, and I agree.

Clothes buying is a special pleasure, almost an act of liberation. I now take special pride in knowing the size each child wears. I do not want to impose my taste on them, and they have developed a more realistic attitude toward clothes than I had at their ages. I no longer do the laundry for the two oldest. Although I did not mind the physical work, the sorting tried my patience. My 17-year-old provided the solution: separate hampers, separate laundry days and separate responsibility. If Harry Truman could wash his socks and underwear, why not *my* kids?

After their mother left, each child moved to another room, and I rearranged mine. We have been repainting and plan to buy some new furniture this summer. Each child is responsible for his own room's neatness (not without urging from me, however), and I am responsible for the public areas. Without doubt, my standards are lower than those of many women whose primary work is in the home, and I have had to learn to handle outside criticism. Recently, my 14-year-old has sought responsibility for cleaning public spaces.

Last spring we turned over a new area in the garden for vegetables. Each of us has his own area, but we tend to weed, water and admire at about the same time. Relationships between the boys have been blossoming with the tomatoes. They are getting along with each other better than in the past.

Like many separated parents, both their mother and I take the children (separately) on more activities than formerly. Similarly, I get to do many more of the things I need to do for myself than previously. My social life is important to me, and I know it must be satisfactory. I must have adult companionship for my own sake *and* my children's. I am careful to decide which activities to do with my children, and which to do without them.

I am greatly supported by my men's group, by my association with the women's and the men's movement, and by conferences on men and the male role. I am sustained by the idea that many other men understand the concept of male parenting and are successful in a role for which many are ill-prepared. Somehow, by nurturing their children, they also assist me.

BIRTH PAINS

These past three years I have grown and developed. I see myself differently, at least in part. I am more comfortable with associates, with my children and with myself. Although I have lived through many deeply painful experiences, I have found nurturing friendships.

I have come to see that fatherhood is not a role conferred by a biological act. It is, in fact, for me, not a role at all; it is a relationship. It has become, quite unexpectedly, a basic element in my life. And I have come to welcome it. I believe I have participated in my own rebirth as a man.

Three AM and This Is Crazy

Three AM and this is crazy
but I am full and crazy
and I want words for Dylan
asleep on cushions on the floor,
rolling because it's three AM
and the lights are still on.

Dylan whose body is still whole
after six years of world,
who loves saunas and hot tubs
and splashes of cold water,
who snuggles in bed and on laps,
who moves toward the touches,
toward the warm,
who jumps free into loving bed
asking in clearest plainsong
    "what's this all about,
     this lying on top of each other,"
Dylan who goes to school
to learn that farts are to laugh
and fuck is a word in frustration,
who comes home to lie with me in bath
legs around legs,
penises to explore
while we talk warm talks,
soften to the intimacy
that goes with touch—

    Learn, my son,
    learn the best of me.
    Learn deep to remember
    through the wars
    learn to remember
    somewhere much later
    in the tidal wave confusions
    that touch is love
    and warm is wonder—

Out of nowhere in a peoplefull room
he wants to hug.
Arms reach up. I stop everything,

sink to my knees to hold warm body
press love,
to feel the love in my touch
        in his touch
yielding, surrendering to the flow.
The others will recognize love
or deny love—
no matter.
One moment against a thousand hundreds:
chits against the future,
the bombardment of giggles and cools,
roles and shows.

It comes hard and fast, gentle boy-child.
I have been where you must go,
        death and distortion on every side.
I will pray for you
and that the ground in you
built of the soil of all these times
    these warms
    these laughs
    these yesses
    these wisdoms
that the ground will hold
and not abandon you to the abyss
that splits earth from fire
body from image
pleasure from mind.

Slowly, slowly faith grows in this soil.
The body knows all and somehow
through the hysterical forest
the spastic mountains
the dammed rivers and stifled fires,
somehow through the maze of contortions,
the traps and the snares,
somehow you will flower in your springtime
and leave barren desert behind.

DAVID STEINBERG

Birth Rites:
Grandson and Grandfather

NELSON L. HAGGERSON

Ryan

Even the plants in the room smiled
at the moment he was born, delivered
from Joanna's womb into Patrick's hands.
Daughter Jessica, grandparents, Nelson
and Katie and friends Molly and Jonathan
were caught up in the passion of the
mystery and shouted with joy, along
with Joanna and Patrick at baby's
      first breath!

Ryan he is called, born a prince
fit to become a king.
Born into a setting of love that
served us all communion, he is
also Allison.
Son of Joanna and Patrick
He is Ryan Allison Haggerson.

      Haggerson
      January 3, 1978
      1:25 AM
      nlh

Two years ago I attended a workshop on the rites of birth. An experience I had there—role-playing the birth of a child and then verbally processing the role-playing experience—gave me an unexpected insight into my own behavior as a father of seven children. The particular behavior in question was a form of personal flight during the birth of the child. For all seven children I felt a great need to get away from the pain, away from the blood, away from the birth. Sometimes I fell asleep, sometimes I had to be home to attend to the other children; the first time, the labor was so interminably long that I just had to get out of the hospital for a walk. During those times (1950 to 1964) fathers seemed to be accessories anyhow, especially during the actual birth. The physician and medical persons did all the delivery tasks, the mother had the baby—often while under an anesthetic—and three days later mother and baby were taken home to begin the new routine. I had become proficient at helping once all were home, and I was, in my own mind, a good father. Hence the flight behavior wasn't of concern to me until the advent of a new era, that of natural childbirth and home births. (I realize, of course, that this had happened at other times and places, but it had not been part of my conscious world.) I became aware of the new era through reading and visiting with younger people who were involved in the natural childbirth movement. I had liked the idea; I had intellectually accepted it. However, until I went to the workshop, I had not recognized my earlier fears and attendant flight behavior. So now the question arose in my mind, "Could I now be a father in attendance?" As I processed these thoughts with the psychologist who was conducting the workshop, I began to feel both guilt and frustration: guilt in that I had run so many times, frustration now that both my spouse and I are sterile and I would not be able to test my courage as a father in attendance. The psychologist was quick to suggest that a positive way out of both the guilt and the frustration was to help educate my sons so that they would not have the same fears, or at least help them be more aware of their fears than I was at their births.

Last summer our son and daughter-in-law announced that they were expecting a baby and that they were planning a home delivery. I was delighted! The grandmother-to-be, a public health nurse who works full time with high-risk pregnancies, was considerably less enthusiastic. However, she was outwardly very supportive, helping in any way she could to prepare for the birth.

The mother- and father-to-be checked out the idea with a number of persons, and they quickly found that some people were extremely fearful, some even hostile, of the home birth. Others were very supportive. To maintain their own positive approach to it all, they decided to tell only a few of their plans. Late in the pregnancy they checked with an obstetrician who was willing to deliver the baby at the hospital should it be necessary. That added assurance to them and to us.

My wife and I then began to plan for our vacations to coincide with the expected birth date. As a matter of fact, after talking it over with the parents-to-be, we decided it would be better to be with them after the birth than to go for the birth, only to find that the baby was late and having to return without seeing the baby or the birth. I was still coping with the fear of being there at the birth, even though I could say I wanted to be, so the idea of going a little later was appealing. My spouse seemed to feel the same way. We kidded, however, with lots of people about going to help in the delivery.

As it turned out we arrived two days before the baby was born and were able to stay four days afterwards.

Tuesday morning, January 3, at 12:30 AM our son, Stan, woke us saying, "Jo thinks the baby will be here soon. Will you please join us?" They had both bathed, and he had boiled some water to sterilize a clamp and a syringe. When we got to Jo's room Molly, the lady who lives with them, her son John, and Jo's four-year-old daughter, Jesse, were all in the room. The electric heater had warmed the room (it was zero degrees outside, with snow and ice on the streets), the lamp on the bedside table was lit and a candle on the dresser was burning. The moment we walked in the room, we could see the baby's head emerging. (I ran downstairs and got the sterile clamp and the syringe.) That was a good sign that it was to be a normal birth. I watched Jo's face, Stan's hands and the baby's head, then body. Jo was obviously pushing, but there was no sign of pain on her face—when the baby made the final lunge, Jo smiled in relief. Stan used his gloved hands to help stretch the perineum. Sure enough, it didn't tear. The greatest miracle of all, to me, was that almost immediately after emerging from his mother, the baby began to breathe. There was no slapping, no holding by the feet (both of which I had in my mind as part of the ritual); he just began to breathe. Then he peed, then defecated, then cried. (I couldn't swear to the order of the last three.) Stan used the syringe to suction mucus from his nose and mouth, then placed a sterile clamp near the navel and another several inches away, then cut the cord. Within seconds the baby's face was fondling his mother's breast, and shortly afterwards the baby began suckling. During all of this I did have presence of mind enough to notice my watch. It was 1:24 AM. It had all happened in less than an hour. (Had we planned a trip to the hospital, we would likely have delivered the baby in the car, for it is about a 45-minute drive to the nearest hospital.) By 4:30 the mother, the father, and the grandparents had all held and rocked the baby, and all of the afterbirth had been cleaned up.

At one time during the birth I had looked around the room and noticed that the plants seemed to be smiling along with us. I suspect it was because it was so warm in the room, but then again I don't have much trouble believing that we communicate with plants in some way. At any rate that observation was good enough for the beginning line of a poem I subsequently wrote—"Ryan."

The next day I began to reconstruct the experience, bringing to mind my thoughts and feelings during the birth. I had maintained my calm during the entire birth, sufficiently to observe others, to observe the plants, to remember the conversations. I was not nauseated by the blood or the afterbirth. I had wondered earlier whether I would be. The notion I had carried for many years that pain was necessary was dispelled, as was the mystery of boiling water. The fact that family members, including children, were in the room during the delivery changed my vision of doctors and nurses dressed in green and white being the only appropriate witnesses of a birth. Seeing my son deliver his own child with skill, courage, patience, tenderness relieved me of wondering how in the world I would ever teach my sons how not to be fearful and flee from birth. He taught me. (I must tell my psychologist friend mentioned earlier how this all turned out.) The children, four and eight, took the birth as a matter of fact. Jesse, the baby's four-year-old sister, was concerned that she also have some of her mother's attention. She was soon in her mother's arms.

The eight-year-old boy said to me the next day, "Why isn't Jo up and eating at the table? She has already had her baby."

Three days later at the supper table we were still marvelling at the beauty and normality of the birth. To what human efforts could we attribute the successful delivery? Both Jo and Stan had, almost from the time of conception, planned for the home birth. Jo had exercised daily, eaten a well-balanced diet. They had read as much material as they could about home births; they had discussed every aspect of it. The fact that it was Jo's second baby gave her additional insights. They had really refused to accept negative "what-if" kinds of concerns from others. They didn't tell great-grandmother about their intentions because they were concerned about her excessive worry and fear. I am still not sure how she feels about it, except that she is delighted that the baby is safely here and that Jo is also healthy. They discussed the birth with the children and the other adult in the house, and finally they sought out a physician who was willing to deliver the baby should there be complications and a need to go to the hospital. The physician, in turn, knew of a pediatrician who was willing to examine the baby three days after birth. Finally, and probably most importantly, Jo was truly in touch with her body, her feelings and her intuitions. She "knew" it was going to be all right. She never expressed a doubt. She also believes she would have felt, intuited, and known had a normal birth not been in the making. Furthermore, she recognizes that this is not necessarily the way to go for others.

I must say that being such an integral part of the birth, in view of my earlier fears, is one of the highlights of my life. I learned so much; I felt such joy, experienced such beauty. I might put it this way: This experience at once took much of the mystery out of birth and added infinitely to the mystery of life! My grandson's birth was, in some sense, my own rebirth.

Male Teachers and Young Children

KATHERINE LOWE

*We as Men want to take back our full humanity. We no
longer want to strain to compete to live up to an impossible
oppressive masculine image—strong, silent, cool, handsome,
unemotional, successful, master of women, leader of men,
wealthy, brilliant, athletic and "heavy".... We want to
relate to both women and men in more human ways—with
warmth, sensitivity, emotion and honesty. We want to share
our feelings with one another to break down the walls
and grow closer. We want to be equal with women and end
destructive competitive relationships between men.*[1]

    This quote and the thoughts circling in my mind concerning men as
teachers of young children have been with me since I was first exposed to
concepts concerning Men's Liberation. As I listened to Constantina
Safilios-Rothschild's lecture, "The New Subtle Types of Sex Discrimination in Education," I began to modify her theories of women and their
marginal positions in predominantly male fields and apply the "theories of
marginality" to men who have chosen to enter the traditionally feminine
world of early childhood education. Safilios-Rothschild emphasized the
negative effects of tokenism, and with this in mind I have considered how
the process of *neutralization* could also hold for men as teachers of young
children. Neutralization serves to stifle questioning of existing sex-role
stereotypes which are solidified further if the one token person happens to
be "terrible" and ineffective. There is a chance, then, that the attitudes of
the staff may become even more negative with the presence of the male
than if there were no males present. I knew I had to be cautious as I attempted to apply these conclusions to men as teachers of young children.

[1]Prepared in February 1973 and used by permission of the East Bay Men's
Center.

184

The world *is* male dominated, but perhaps by entering the female-dominated world of early childhood education, a man becomes separated or detached from the patriarchal position he holds in society. In this setting, it would be the women's world that is being threatened. The significant question becomes, do the reactions and responses of women differ from those of men when their world is threatened? Further, are there subtle types of sex discrimination present within an early childhood setting when a man is a colleague?

With these directions in mind, I began to uncover readings which might validate, document, or at least acknowledge my questions concerning the problems of men teachers of young children. This complicated endeavor was to consider the foreseeable problems a male teacher in an early childhood setting may encounter and, at the same time, I was hopeful that within early childhood education it might be shown that the man's special contribution is not in "acting like a man" for the children, but in disproving the idea that men need to act in some special "manly" way. There is an apparent reticence on the part of educational researchers to explore the man who has chosen to contradict sex-role conventions and work with young children. Consequently, the dearth of studies is not surprising. Comparatively, father-child relationships, let alone man-child relationships, have been virtually neglected, in comparison to the voluminous data available on mother-child relations.

This neglect seemingly reflects the sexual stereotypes which have also permeated the educational sphere of our society. Parents and early childhood educators stress the *need* for male involvement and wonder why there are so few men. The problem is that they have failed to examine from a sociological perspective their requests for males. As representatives of society, we have contributed to a social atmosphere which has served to exclude many men from choosing close relationships with children. The social atmosphere has forced men to be "exceptions" when they express and dare to act on needs and desires for emotional involvement with young children (Fein, p. 57). Very few educators or researchers in early childhood education share my concerns about the sociological and psychological implications for the male who has chosen to work with young children. Exceptions are found, especially writers who have a non-sexist perspective. Somewhere the reasons for having men work with young children have, in part, become distorted, and these distortions are revealed within the literature available on men as teachers of young children.

Personally, my allegiances are with a non-sexist approach to early childhood education, a setting in which the child is allowed to develop to his or her fullest potential unhampered by sex-role stereotyping. This view, thus, verges on a discussion of the androgynous model of human well-being. Androgyny basically means that one's sex is not the primary determinant of one's behavior, values or aspirations (Lee, 1976, p. 191). In other words, an androgynous model "suggests that men and women can both work and love, and this may be emerging, as society allows women to explore the reality of competent adulthood and men to touch parts of their emotional lives buried or hidden in 'boys don't cry' and to become caring adults" (Fein, p. 58).

"Emotional Honesty—Simplicity—Directness": In an exploration of men and childhood presented by a "conscious" male, it is stressed that these may be the three paths to a man's buried soul (Fein, p. 61). Men, as well as women, are finding that contact with young children leads them back to themselves, allowing them to integrate their "childlike" selves with their "adult" selves.

I guess I was told so often to stiffen up and be a man when I was little, that I decided there was something wrong with being a child. So I practiced hard to be a man, always afraid that I wouldn't make it, that the scared little boy hiding underneath would pop out at any moment and give me away. Caring for kids has led me to see that I'm like the kids in some ways and I'm different in others because I'm grown-up. Working with children has helped me locate myself as an able, caring adult (Fein, p. 61).

Indeed, a reason for needing males in an early childhood educational setting is so the children can learn that men can be nurturing, loving, understanding, just as women. At least when I envision the role of a man in a nursery school, I think of a man who is contradicting sex-role conventions and is a nurturing figure. However, the distorted reasoning of educators and researchers is exemplified in the following questions directed to me as I attempted to identify problems which may be confronted by male teachers of young children. These questions reveal the "hang-ups" about gender which prevail within the educational sphere.

Why bring men into a classroom to do what women have always done?
What is there about being a man, about being masculine, that can affect the growth and development of a group of young children?
What kind of men do we want?
What is their special thing? (Johnston and Williams, 1970).
In what ways does the influence of a strong male help a child fulfill his or her own being? (Kyselka, 1966).
Do men alter the "tone" of the classroom in more masculine directions? (Lee, 1973).
What effect would male teachers have on the welfare of children in schools? (Lee, 1973).
Do men have a distinct influence on the classroom? Is it positive? (Lee, 1973).
Do male teachers differ from female teachers in their interactions with children? (Lee, Wolinsky, 1973).

Many people involved in early childhood education appear to be primarily concerned with providing a male image for children—especially for boys. Those adopting this perspective feel that having more men will facilitate sex-role identification, especially for boys (Seifert, 1974, p. 299). In this view the presence of males is supposed to accentuate sex-roles among young children (Seifert, p. 299). Clearly, this perspective is in response to the prevalence of homes with no primary male figure and also to what has been labeled "feminized" education. On the other hand, among the emerging literature are those who argue the opposite. This perspective reflects the androgynous view which I presented. "The children will see that even a man can care about them, and in this way a male teacher will obscure sex roles for his classroom of children" (Seifert, 1974, p. 299).

To support my contention that the desirability of having male teachers in the early childhood educational setting at times is distorted, I shall review an open-ended questionnaire which was administered to nursery school teachers in several districts in Manhattan (Chasn, 1974). When questioned with regard to the desirability of having male teachers in an early childhood setting, the teachers appeared to be concerned with the prospect of having a male image for the boys. As in our study, however, the reaction is not that simple. Most of the teachers replied that they wanted a male image to perpetuate male stereotypes. The male teacher would have to be strong, do woodworking and be a super-ego figure—as if females are not (Chasn, 1974). In many ways the desirability for a "real man" reflects a pervasive fear of homosexuality. The pathetic point is that this sample of teachers did not acknowledge that they reflected their prejudice by promoting stereotypes. It is indeed alarming if this sample of nursery school teachers is representative of the general population of nursery school teachers. Since there seems to be a resistance on their part to recognize the implications of stereotyping, perhaps teachers also fail to distinguish between harmony and equality. The questionnaire revealed that teachers believe girls are more passive and boys are more aggressive. Therefore, teachers are encouraging the very behaviors they believe exist. Equality in the classroom appears to be a myth. Sex-role stereotyping becomes analogous to the separate-but-equal myth of segregated Southern schools where teachers also believe there is equality (Chasn, p. 233).

One has to be careful not to imply that teachers' attitudes are solely responsible for sex-role stereotyping, as one must remember that teachers are also products of a sex-role-oriented society. On this note, I have found it useful to review Lee's cultural analysis of sex roles in the schools, in which he eloquently traces the cultural institutionalization of sex roles.

. . . sex role, which was originally a cultural accommodation to a biological reality, ultimately became a cultural reality which required accommodation in its own right. . . . Sex role, then, poses a double threat to the full development of human resources by establishing relatively fixed sex/

function prescriptions irrespective of individual aptitude by assigning
status to people regardless of individual merit (Lee, 1975, p. 335).

Teachers are in a unique position, since they can either counteract
stereotyping or let it continue. However, before change might occur,
teachers must first perceive the different ways in which they characteristically respond to boys and girls. Until teachers acknowledge this initial
step and become aware of how subtle and how pervasive the unequal and
differential treatment of the sexes is, no substantial changes will result.
"Why would teachers change if they believe that they are already treating
children equally?" (Chasn, p. 234).

From a historical viewpoint, one sees that conventional wisdom
advises that the crucial figure in the child's early years is the child's
mother. Partly because of this, the traditional nursery school or child-care
setting has been operated and staffed by women. This view holds that
women through their "innate" nurturing abilities were destined to be with
young children. As a result, men have been socialized away from the field
of early childhood education. Because working with young children is not
congruent with the male sex-role, men who do choose to be with young
children in an educational setting have often been viewed with "humorous skepticism" or, worse yet, suspected of variant behavior (Lee, p. 83).
Variant behavior in this case reveals the fear that men will either be
attracted to young boys or bring harm to "little children." In other words,
they are not men! As a way to shake off the potential stigma of inadequate
masculinity or homosexuality, men characteristically have chosen to prove
their masculine superiority by demonstrating outstanding achievement
and by controlling the field and their female colleagues. Men have ad-
ministrative positions but are not in the classroom (Safilios-Rothschild,
1974, p. 80). Indeed, these widespread attitudes have effectively limited
the number of men who have chosen to enter early childhood education,
but there are also additional reasons why early childhood has remained
sexually segregated. Feminine occupations, such as nursery school teaching or working in a child-care setting are also less "desirable" because of
their low prestige and resulting low pay. One must consider that the less
"desirable" nature of "feminine" occupations is not inherent, "but has
appeared, has been reinforced, consolidated and perpetuated—because
only or primarily women—that is the cheap, 'second rate' labor force, have
been performing them" (Safilios-Rothschild, 1974, p. 79). Therefore, the
"unprofitable" nature of working with children does not harmonize with
traditional male aspirations. One may ask, then, why would a man want to
be liberated, if it only allows him to enter a less "desirable" occupation?
Obviously, the social, political and economic variables all function to limit,
perhaps restrict, the number of men who choose to enter early childhood
education.

What of the man who chooses to be a teacher of young children?

Fortunately, I have been able to locate several articles which consider and explore the problems men may confront when working with young children. According to Kelvin Seifert (1974), the problems a man may encounter can be divided into three areas: (1) the man's behavior with a roomful of children, (2) the children's behavior with him, and (3) his relationship with female colleagues.

The man's behavior with a roomful of children will at times be influenced by the man's memory of his childhood in addition to the children's reaction to him. "I never was allowed to cry when I was little and they shouldn't cry either" (Fasteau, 1974, p. 96).

Children acquire sex-role stereotypes very early, and they are present even within two-year-olds as they first enter school (Etaugh, 1975). The male teacher is disproving the child's sex-role stereotypes, since *he* is their teacher. Because of this, the children may be expressing degrees of surprise, disbelief, mistrust (Seifert, 1974, p. 299). A man may have to endure more initial rejection than a female teacher. The adjustment period may not be easy, and it will be compounded if the man begins to doubt his ability to do such "feminine" work. If the man is not "together" and begins to have negative feelings about his work, the initial testing period will be especially painful.

It appears to be realistic to expect men to have the "biggest" problems in terms of their relationship with the staff. The extent of prejudice has not been systematically studied, but most men entering the field experience it. "Status inconsistency" describes men who are teaching young children. Their "status" is inconsistent with what is generally expected of men. As the staff forms impressions of the male among their midst, they will likely be extending from the basic premise that the man is in an occupation that is usually considered feminine work.

The initial process will be to try to understand his *reasons* for working with young children. By nature, the subtleties of sex discrimination are not usually confronted or examined, thus limiting one's ability to admit their presence. For this reason, it is easier for the staff to consider their man an "exception" to the rule. This becomes a dilemma for men who are working with young children. If a man is considered an "exception," the staff is able to argue that most men do not like working with children but our "man" is different" (Seifert, 1974, p. 71). If the man insists he is a "real man," this may unconsciously imply that he is incompetent, because men are not "supposed" to be skilled at working with young children. This in itself explains why men teachers of young children often end up taking minor roles in the classroom. As a means to legitimize their presence, men do accept minor roles, and this seems to perpetuate the male image. Whichever explanation is adhered to by the staff and the man, it interferes with the opportunity for men and women to demonstrate the falseness of sex-role stereotypes.

As Barbara Simmons (1976) stressed within her discussion of

stereotyping, if a man is present, he should be helping to break down stereotypes, not to perpetuate them (p. 195).

Is he the fix-it man? Is he in charge of the work bench? Is his job to take the active boys outside to work off steam? Is he relieved of messy clean-up tasks and bathroom supervision? Is he preparing to become principal or director because "men are so much better at managing"? (Simmons, 1976, p. 1975).

It appears that people continue to have investments in traditional sex-role steretypes. At least, in many instances, it is difficult for people to admit that they may be perpetuating sex-role stereotyping through their relationships with children and with each other; but, for any person who is sensitized to the subtleties of sex discrimination the problems become "real, noticeable and painful" (Seifert, 1974, p. 300).

Thus far, research related to male teachers of young children has primarily focused upon the examination of behavior processes to see whether men actually interact any differently than women teachers with young children. For example, Lee and Wolinsky observed that "male teachers were very approving toward boys, while female teachers were slightly more approving toward girls. Female teachers moreover were inclined to be more disapproving toward boys than girls, while the opposite held for approvals" (Lee and Wolinsky, 1973). It is suggested that now one can begin to identify and investigate selected outcomes which bear a logical relationship to what teachers are actually doing (Lee, 1973). However, if these findings are going to support any change, researchers must inquire about what may cause these behaviors. This can be accomplished only through recognizing that the dynamics of the classroom must also be examined. Areas to be examined are the man's feelings about working with children, the children's relationship with him and the man's relationship with the staff. Then it may become apparent that men teachers of young children and the problems which are often experienced as "personality conflicts" are a manifestation of social forces larger than the individual persons involved (Seifert, 1974, p. 299).

It is also important to recognize that evaluations of programs involving males can also become distorted. I was caught off guard when I uncovered this "proud" response.

There have been no complaints from the children's parents. The male and female teachers get along beautifully. The women teachers, as surrogate mothers, welcome the male authority. And most important, the children love the men (Stogner, p. 58).

Whether or not a male teacher is consciously troubled by sex-role stereotyping, he must function in a world full of behaviors judged by sex-role distinctions. It is important that he is not coerced into believing that he is an occupational failure, or that he is like a pet rabbit, "the exceptional male working with young children" (Seifert, 1974, p. 72). Much of the recent publicity given to the need for more male teachers in early childhood education suggests that women teachers feel men can do "things that she can't" (Lee, 1976, p. 190). Again I emphasize that within early childhood education, the man's special contribution is not in "acting like a man" for the children, but in disproving the idea that men need to act in some special "manly" way.

There are many special burdens which men teaching young children will most likely encounter. Through the examination of the dynamics of early childhood education, it becomes even clearer why less than 2 percent of the teachers grade three and below are men (NEA, 1972, in Lee, p. 190). Seifert (1974) predicts that "it should not surprise anyone if further research finds that male child care workers tend to prefer part-time positions, rather than full-time ones, and that once in the classroom, they tend to play relatively minor teaching roles" (p. 73). This is frightening, but it will be validated if enthusiasts of early childhood education prefer men to take these roles.

The study of men as teachers of young children does merit and require further inquiry. The available evidence suggests that it is time to move away from concentrating on the differences between the sexes and recognize that the range of differences *among* men or women is as great as the differences *between* men and women (Cuffaro, 1975, p. 477). There is the need, rather, to emphasize human qualities. Men teachers must be examined and understood in connection with our sexist social, political and economic attitudes and also in relationship to the role behaviors which exist within our social framework, especially the early childhood educational milieu.

References

BURTT, MERILYN
Nov. 1965 "The Effect of a Man Teacher." *Young Children,* pp. 93–7.
CHASN, BARBARA
Jan. 1974 "Sex-role Stereotyping and Pre-kindergarten Teachers." *Elementary School Journal,* pp. 220–35.
CUFFARO, HARRIET K.
Sept. 1975 "Re-evaluating Basic Premises: Curricula Free of Sexism." *Young Children,* pp. 469–78.
ELLENBURG, F. C.
Winter 1975 "Elementary Teachers: Male or Female?" *Journal of Teacher Education,* pp. 329–34.
ETAUGH, CLAIRE, GENE COLLINS, AND ARLENE GERSON
Mar. 1975 "Reinforcement of Sex-typed Behaviors in Two-Year-Old Children in a Nursery School Setting." *Developmental Psychology,* p. 255.

FASTEAU, MARC F.
1974 *The Male Machine.* New York: McGraw-Hill.

FEIN, ROBERT A.
1974 "Men and Young Children." In *Men and Masculinity,* ed. by Joseph Pleck and Jack Sawyer. Englewood Cliffs, N.J.: Prentice-Hall.

HARRIS, CHARLES M., AND SUE W. SMITH
Feb. 1976 "Man Teacher-Woman Teacher: Does It Matter?" *Elementary School Journal,* pp. 285–88.

JOHNSTON, JOHN
Dec. 1970 "A Symposium: Men in Young Children's Lives." *Childhood Education,* pp. 144–47.

KYSELKA, WILLIAM
Jan. 1966 "Young Men in a Nursery School." *Childhood Education,* pp. 293–99.

LEE, PATRICK C.
Sept. 1973 "Male and Female Teachers in Elementary Schools: An Ecological Analysis." *Teachers College Record,* pp. 79–98.

——— Winter 1975 "A Cultural Analysis of Sex Role in the School." *Journal of Teacher Education,* pp. 335–39.

——— Feb. 1976 "Reinventing Sex Roles in the Early Childhood Setting." *Childhood Education,* pp. 187–91.

LEE, PATRICK C., AND ANNE LUCAS WOLINSKY
Aug. 1973 "Male Teachers of Young Children: A Preliminary Empirical Study." *Young Children,* pp. 342–52.

McLEOD, BERNADINE
Jan. 1967 "Don't Call it Women's Work." *Education,* pp. 301–2.

MENDELSON, ANNA
June 1972 "A Young Man around the Class." *Young Children,* pp. 281–83.

MURGATROYD, RAYMOND
Nov. 1955 "A Man among Six-Year-Olds." *Childhood Education,* pp. 132–35.

Newsweek
Feb. 9, 1976 Education: "New Hands in Finger Paint," p. 45.

SAFILIOS-ROTHSCHILD, CONSTANTINA
1974 *Women and Social Policy.* Englewood Cliffs, N.J.: Prentice-Hall.

——— Feb. 1976 "The New Subtleties (Subtle Types) of Sex Discimination in Education." Guest Lecturer. Mills College.

SCIARRA, DOROTHY JUNE
Jan. 1972 "What to Do until the Male Man Comes." *Childhood Education,* pp. 190–91.

SEIFERT, KELVIN

1974 "Some Problems of Men in Child Care Center Work." In *Men and Masculinity,* ed. by Joseph Pleck and Jack Sawyer. Englewood Cliffs, N.J.: Prentice-Hall.

———

Summer 1974 "Getting Men to Teach Preschool." *Contemporary Education,* pp. 299–301.

SIMMONS, BARBARA

Feb. 1976 "Teachers, Be(a)Ware of Sex Stereotyping." *Childhood Education,* pp. 192–95.

SPRUNG, BARBARA

Nov. 1975 "Opening Options for Children: A Non-sexist Approach to Early Childhood Education." *Young Children.*

STEIN, RUTHE

Oct. 13, 1976 "They Want to Be Full-Time Fathers." *San Francisco Chronicle,* p. 15.

STOGNER, ROBBIE BELL

Nov. 1973 "Can Men Do the Job?" *Day Care and Early Education,* pp. 10–14.

SUGAWARA, ALAN I., J. PHILIP O'NEILL, AND CRAIG EDELBROCK

June 1976 "Sex and Power of Preschool Teachers and Children's Sex-Role Preferences." *Home Economics Research Journal,* pp. 243–47.

VAIRO, PHILIP D.

Feb./March 1969 "Wanted: 20,000 Male First-Grade School Teachers." *Education,* pp. 222–24.

WILLIAMS, BRUCE

Dec. 1970 "A Symposium: Men in Young Children's Lives." *Childhood Education,* pp. 139–44.

WOLINKSY, ANNIE P.

1974 "Male and Female Teachers in Early Childhood Settings." Dissertation, Teachers College, Columbia University.

The Midgets Within Me

GEOF MORGAN

Most of my time is spent writing songs.

I have built a one-room building separate from my house, where it is not unusual for me to sit from one to ten hours a day as I search my mind for just the right combination of words. It is important for me to be alone when I write because, for the most part, my writing has become a private search, a steady pushing, a constant probing of myself.

I write for a living. So, sometimes when I think a feeling is personal only to myself, I find that I connect with people who feel the same way. Since I write for a living, sometimes my inward searching is relaxed in favor of the money-making aspect of my business. But still, I never fail to sit down each day and chase the elation that I feel when I touch an inward part of me.

Writing is where I gather my strength. It is a quiet place where I accept myself completely. When I feel crazy, writing makes me sane. When I feel worthless and empty, writing makes me feel full again. The silence, the listening to myself, lets me hear what I think, what I feel. When I write, I slowly begin to trust myself again. I hear my best friend. I hear myself.

But I am human, too. I need the approval of others of what I write. I am lucky to have a few people who believe in what I do. They help me through the periods when my career and my success falters.

In the last few years I have met men who are involved with similar searches within their own lives and careers. I have met many of them through men's conferences that have taken place over the last few years. Some that I have met are in the music business. By talking with them I have begun to feel that my dilemmas are not mine alone.

I want to make it clear how important my personal growth is to me. One of my songs states that I carry midgets within myself; they are an unencouraged part of me that is protected in my writing. These midgets seem to be the qualities that are often discouraged in men, yet are cultivated freely in women.

Feelings of gentleness, nurturing, sensitivity, and spontaneity toward the feelings of others: As an artist, I know that it is important to maintain those qualities for my art, but on the street I am expected to suck in my gut and keep those feelings to myself.

So here I am in this emotional dilemma. I am allowed to be myself when I write; yet I have to put on a mask to present myself to others. It is important to my writing that I be silly, playful, and gentle so the spark of what I write can come out. It can be let loose to go where it wants without other parts of my personality getting in the way. For dealing with people in the industry, even when I am not feeling it, I must act confident, strong, powerful, and successul. These are the qualities that are taken seriously in the music business.

It gets confusing and frustrating when I forget which character I am in. My songs are an important part of what I must hold on to in this confusion as I try to deal with and understand the other side of myself that I am afraid I will lose without the safety of my studio and my music.

The values in the male-dominated music industry are the usual ones: financial reward, fame, power, and success. It is difficult for me *not* to judge my songs based on those values. I do not want to be naive and say that there are no better songs than any other, or that there is no importance in my craft, but there are values other than the money generated by a song. It is a constant struggle for me to keep the proper perspective.

I should mention that I also have quite a few commercial songs within myself. That is a part of me that I do not want to deny. Some of my childishness, and silly writing, leaves me with a simple idea for a catchy hook line that would be good in a "Top 40" hit. I often feel embarrassed about some of those songs, but I must remember that they too are a part of that special feeling that I have. This is another dilemma that I must constantly deal with. Artistic songs, commercial songs, personal songs, and exploratory songs, they all have a place in me. Sometimes I will sit down and be amazed at the junk that I write, but it is all in myself and I love every part of it, or at least I want to love it.

There are highs and lows, but that is part of the process—and that is what my writing is for me, a process. The songs all have a place, a time, and a meaning. They are all from that part of me that I value so much.

Finding outside support for my commercial material is not too difficult. Record companies, publishers, and lounges all like to have hit songs. But it is not as easy to find audiences for some of my other work, so I write commercially. If you ever listen to AM radio, you know there is a big market there.

At the publishing company I write for, there is a strong sense of ambition: a sense of growing to a more powerful position in the industry, the excitement of being up and coming. Everyone is pushing to get more songs recorded, to find good commercial ideas, to gain prestige in the business.

Often, with all the hustling around, it will take me a few days to overcome the feelings of depression that I get when I am around the business, even when I jump into it for only a few hours at a time.

In the hustling situation, my career growth is all that matters. Most of the men and women in the business put all their energy into this part of their lives, too. I often wonder whether they assume that their personal growth and relationships have to wait until they are finished with the "real" business. Their priorities are so obvious.

Respect and support come from how much power you have in the business, and from little else. Feelings outside of a song do not have any immediate cash value, so they tend to be non-existent. Anger at a competitor is okay, elation in success is all right, but all other forms of emotion are not allowed to exist. Emotions get in the way of hustle; they slow it down and make everyone nervous. The people seem to say, "Got problems, boy? Go see your minister or your therapist. Come back when you are feeling better."

I am not this way. I have never used money as my measure of success, nor decided to give up my personal growth. These attitudes are supported by those who understand me, but all too often they put me at odds with the people in the music industry.

The primary problem is that most people in the business feel that success comes first. I have often felt uncomfortable when someone who had been advising me ended a statement with, "If you want to have success in this world, you will want to have *it* more than anything in this world."

I squirm in the following silence. Then I wonder what must be wrong with me. I do not hunger with all my soul for the bright lights. I try not to stay too long in my thoughts, though, for fear that I may lose support of someone who can help me keep paying the rent. Still, it has become obvious to me that most men put more time into the business than I do.

It is a familiar fantasy to want to become rich and famous. As a teenager, I dreamed of the lives of heroes and stars. I wanted that lifestyle. It has taken me some time and a whole lot of painful searching to discover that expanding other parts of myself would be more beneficial to me, but the fantasy is not totally gone.

On a smaller scale the fantasy may happen, but dealing with it, trying to see its value to me and what I could offer others with that power is becoming more settled in my head. It is funny how a stomach can still yearn for foods that it no longer trusts.

There is a lot of business that is not taken care of because I find it unsatisfying. I no longer see myself completely as a projectile on the course to the target of success. I can leave a situation that is unfulfilling and still have next month's rent in my pocket. Consequently, my progress has been slow; and watching others moving more rapidly, getting more songs recorded, and getting more articles written about them hurts my ego. I continually need to reassure myself that I know what I am doing and that it is right for me.

I must continually tell myself that I have chosen not to run that race. This is not easy to do.

But I make a living at music, and that is positive. I put enough energy into the industry to make it possible for me to continue to write, and that keeps me going after those midgets within me.

I feel that my life is on two tracks. One track is my singer-songwriter-star track. The other is my personal growth track. I am not sure how the two tracks will continue, but right now I do not mind riding them both even though sometimes the split makes me feel shaky.

I have a fantasy that someday the two tracks will merge down the line and begin to feed into each other. They say that a fantasy that comes true is a vision. For right now, I will continue to work for that vision.

Midget in Me

If you don't feed a colt enough in his first year
He'll never grow to all he could, he won't see as
*   clear*
Stunted and uncertain, slow on his feet
Kinda like that midget in me

I was raised on logic and workin' with my hands
Use your head to get ahead, it's the training of a
*   man*
But hearts go unattended in this society
So now there's a midget in me

Refrain:

A twisted, beat-up, little man, breathing thinner air
A poor weaker part of me I didn't know was there
And I'm not sure he'll make it now I've set him free
That frightened midget in me

I've felt and still feel anger when looking for the
*   blame*
I've wasted walls and angry songs while cursin' lists
*   of names*
But now that I've found him I can't turn like I don't
*   see*
That hungry midget in me

I hear that being human is just like joining hands
And not this separation into woman, into man
So maybe what's been missing is my femininity
And it's a gentle midget in me

GEOF MORGAN

Men and the Dream of Brotherhood

VINCENT KAVALOSKI

"Why aren't I enough?" she said. "You are enough for me. I don't want anybody else but you. Why isn't it the same with you?"

"Having you, I can live all my life without anybody else, any other sheer intimacy. But to make it complete, really happy, I wanted eternal union with a man too: another kind of love," he said.

"I don't believe it," she said. "It's an obstinacy, a theory, a perversity."

"Well—" he said.

"You can't have two kinds of love. Why should you!"

"It seems as if I can't," he said. "Yet I wanted it."
(from *Women In Love*, D. H. LAWRENCE)

Brotherhood, I write the word and must pause, feeling the familiar waves of longing and hope—and finally deep despair, rising within me once again. I think of hundreds of men joining hands and singing joyously together last summer at the Men's Conference in State College, Pennsylvania, voices merging in a mighty affirmation of brotherhood, old and new. I think of my men's group at its best, supporting one another's emerging humanness and new-found freedom; relentlessly challenging the old depths in which our minds have been anchored so long; and finally, talking and laughing away the hurts and doubts, that like wind and rain inevitably accompany this struggle to grow, to break out of the seed-shells we have called our lives for too long.

I know now the promise of what is possible for us: men supporting men. Yet, that very promise stands as an ever-present, tragic indictment of our collective reality. We have built a world where men's primary relation-

Grateful acknowledgment is made for use of the quotation from *Women in Love* by D. H. Lawrence. Copyright 1920, 1922 by D. H. Lawrence, copyright renewed 1948, 1940 by Frieda Lawrence. Reprinted by permission of Viking Penguin, Inc.

ship toward one another is founded upon endless competition, deep distrust and rigid reserve. Intimate and abiding friendships between men are rare. Rarer still is the wider day-to-day sense of fraternity at work and in one's community: the unspoken sense of my brothers struggling to realize a common, shared humanity.

Why? Why are we unloving brothers to one another? Why is it so difficult for us to be open, close, and vulnerable with each other? Are we hiding from each other? Could it be that in the face of my brother pressed close to my own I see something I fear?

Have you ever seen your friend asleep—and found out how he looks? What is the face of your friend anyway? It is your own face in a rough and imperfect mirror.[1]

The Masculine Mystique

The contemporary literature of Men's Liberation (and for that matter, Women's Liberation) relies almost exclusively upon the concept of *sex roles* in order to explain this and the other types of cultural oppression which men and women suffer in our society.[2]

This role-theory approach to men's (and women's) oppression does have its usefulness. The key concept of *role* with its implicit connection with actors and acting seems straightforwardly accurate in certain situations. The "pick-up" bar, for example, functions as a place where men admittedly try out their favorite "approaches" and "come ons" to solicit women. The only other situation I know of which even remotely approaches the artificiality of the "pick-up" bar is the academic convention where young "up-and-coming" professors and graduate students compete at meetings to appear to be "tough-minded" professionals, and then afterward in the bars, to be "hard-drinking," "good-guys." The repressed anxiety over the quality of one's "performance," the sense of an "audience" and the question of "success" or "failure" all have direct analogues with the theater; and the very quotation markes I am forced to put around these cliches indicate the exaggerated and stereotypical role-playing nature of the behavior. However, unlike legitimate drama, what is involved here is really a feeble form of self-deception: Under the guise of doing something else, we are really acting in a way calculated to extract a reward from them, namely, "getting laid" or "getting tenure."

Of course, for some men the entire world is experienced on the

---

[1]F. Nietzsche, "Thus Spake Zarathustra" in *The Portable Nietzsche,* ed. and transl. by Walter Kaufmann (Viking Press: New York, 1954), p. 168.

[2]Mark Fasteau, *The Male Machine,* pp. 3, 7, 10; Warren Farrell, *The Liberated Man,* p. 31 and *supra*; Joseph Pleck and Jack Sawyer, eds., *Men and Masculinity,* pp. 7, 24, 134, 172.

model of a pick-up bar or a professional convention: Every waking hour is devoted to "getting laid" or "getting ahead"—or both. But I wonder whether this exaggerated role-playing model really applies to most men in most areas of their lives? Are we always acting a role in bed with our lovers, when walking with our children and in our day-to-day relations with one another? Is human life, then, nothing but the duplicity of many actors on a stage? And who am *I* beneath this masculine role? Is there even a face beneath the mask?

My intention in challenging these assumptions of role theory is *not* to argue that "things are not really as bad as they seem." Things may be *worse* than they seem. We men have collectively built a world of oppression so rigid and encompassing that genuine human life sometimes seems possible only in opposition to it. However, the structure of this oppression of, and by, men is not adequately accounted for by role-theory approaches.

More specifically, this explanation, even in its most plausible applications, appears simply to push the problem back a step: Where do these sex roles come from? From the socialization of children by parents and teachers and other adults, it is replied. But this is really just equivalent to saying we learn roles from people who already have these roles. Where do they in turn get them? No matter how far back we push the question, role theory can give no response other than its original question-begging answer. This is so because it has eschewed philosophical-historical inquiry for the sake of a narrowly sociological one. In the remainder of this paper, therefore, I will investigate the problem through a reinstatement of these categories of understanding.

The Mystic Roots of Brotherhood

The dream of brotherhood runs deep in the culture of the West. The oldest and most widespread literary document of the ancient world, the Mesopotamian Epic of Gilgamesh, tells the story of two men who through a terrible struggle become convenanted brothers and together explore the dark mysteries of love and death.[3] It is a profound and enthralling

---

[3]From "The Epic of Gilgamesh," trans. by E. A. Speiser, in James B. Pritchard, ed., *The Ancient Near East: An Anthology of Texts and Pictures* (copyright © 1958 by Princeton University Press; Princeton Paperback 1964), p. 40. Reprinted by permission of Princeton University Press. Pritchard places the date of the original Akkadian work at the turn of the second millenium. G. S. Kirk, in his *Myth: Its Meaning and Functions in Ancient and Other Cultures* (Cambridge U. Press: London, 1978) concurs and adds that it was "probably the most familiar" of all Mesopotamian literary works (p. 134). Indeed, it performed for the ancient Mesopotamian cultures the same educative functions that the *Iliad* and the *Odyssey* performed for the Myceneans. An eminently readable version is N. K. Sandars's *The Epic of Gilgamesh* (Penguin Books: London, 1960).

narrative which poses, over 5000 years ago, at the very dawn of human consciousness, the complex archetype of male friendship, rent with all its contradictions.

The Epic tells the story of giant Gilgamesh, king of the ancient Sumerian city of Urak, whose "unbridled arrogance" causes him to act abominably toward his own people, sleeping with all the wives and young girls and pitilessly overworking the men. The people prevail upon the goddess Aruru, who in some sense made Gilgamesh, to create his double, and to "let them contend that Urak may have peace."[4] This amazing creature, named Enkidu, resembles Gilgamesh except for his thick covering of shaggy hair, his horns and his habit of running wild on the steppe with the animals. Gilgamesh is informed of his existence by a hunter and has a temple prostitute sent to lure him to Urak. In a beautifully erotic scene, she "pulls off her clothing, laying bare her ripeness" and "for six days and seven nights Enkidu comes forth mating with the lass."[5] The animals who were formerly his companions draw away from him forever: Eros has decisively separated him from Nature. In return, he receives the gifts of Culture: He gains "wisdom, broader understanding" and, most significantly, "a yearning for a friend." He and the girl depart for Urak in order "to change the old order."[6]

Meanwhile Gilgamesh has a prophetic dream of a strong comrade to whom "he is drawn as to a woman."[7] When Enkidu arrives in Urak, the people recognize that "he is like Gilgamesh to a hair" and induce him to challenge the king, who is presumably on his way to yet further debaucheries. A tremendous wrestling match then ensues between the two powerful protagonists which shakes walls and shatters doorposts.[8] Finally, Enkidu recognizes Gilgamesh's kingship, and the two become fast friends and comrades-in-arms.

Then begins a series of heroic adventures wherein the two companions, drawing strength from each other, vanquish the monster Humbaba and slay the Bull of Heaven. Gilgamesh's motivation in all this is to gain an "eternal name," thereby challenging the very death and finitude which the gods have decreed for men. Finally, some of the gods become jealous and decide Enkidu must die as a lesson and punishment to Gilgamesh. On his deathbed Enkidu realizes this and yet laments his own death because it means final separation from his beloved friend:

[4]Pritchard, p. 41.

[5]Ibid., p. 43.

[6]Ibid., p. 44.

[7]Ibid., p. 46.

[8]Ibid., p. 50.

Must I, by the spirit of the dead
Sit down, at the spirit's door
Never again (to behold) my
Dear brother with mine eyes?[9]

Gilgamesh, in turn, is inconsolably grief-stricken:

He who went with me
Underwent all hardships—
Enkidu, whom I love dearly,
Who with me underwent all hardships—
Has now gone to the fate of mankind!
Day and night I have wept over him . . .
Since his passing I have not found life.[10]

The implication is clear: In brotherhood there is life; outside of it, only a living death. Gilgamesh tears off his clothes and roams the steppe half-mad with grief, "storming like a lioness deprived of her whelps,"[11] He thus begins to actually resemble Enkidu before he became civilized by the temple prostitute: In some mysterious way Gilgamesh thus has taken on the persona of his lost brother.

The remainder of the epic relates his search for the plant which brings immortality, the frustration of his hopes and his eventual resignation to human finitude and temporality.

The story is usually interpreted by scholars as dealing with the theme of "man's search for an understanding of death" or, alternatively, as an exploration of the polarity of Nature (represented by Enkidu in his wild state) and Culture (represented by the civilized albeit decadent Gilgamesh). Both these philosophical motifs are present and are crucial to understanding the story; yet it is the theme of the close relationship between Gilgamesh and Enkidu which dominates the narrative. Moreover, it is this theme which unites and gives social significance to the other two motifs.

From this point of view, Enkidu's initial wildness, coupled with his otherwise close resemblance to Gilgamesh, expresses the sense in which the brother-friend represents what Jung calls our Shadow, the dark repressed, instinctual (or "natural") side of ourselves. The wrestling match could be seen, then, as the struggle to understand that hidden part of ourselves, a struggle for self-understanding. It is precisely in this sense

[9]Ibid., p. 56.

[10]Ibid., p. 63.

[11]Ibid., p. 61.

that Nietzsche suggests that the "face of your friend . . . is your own face in a rough and imperfect mirror."[12]

Yet Enkidu is more than just a projection of Gilgamesh or an alter ego; he is also an individual in his own right, an Other. Thus the fury of the wrestling match portrays the tension involved in entering into genuine friendship: The brother is an Other, and despite the deep reflection he gives you of yourself, he can never be fully assimilated to the Self. This is underlined by Enkidu's death: Though Gilgamesh experiences it as the loss of his own living spirit, he eventually learns to go on without his brother.

What is perfectly clear is that the convenanted frienship between the two men has humanized each of them, and that therefore the ultimate gift of brotherhood is not only self-understanding but the development of one's own humanity.

Yet the picture is clouded by the subtle inequality of the two: Though convenanted brothers, it is still Gilgamesh who is "king" and Enkidu who is "younger brother." The disparity seems to rest on—or at least be reinforced by—the fact that Enkidu was unable to overcome Gilgamesh in the wrestling bout. Hence, in their subsequent adventures it is Gilgamesh who initiates and leads and ultimately gains the honor. Moreover, these adventures themselves, while directed against "evil" figures, are, nevertheless, acts of aggression. To this extent the epic appears to support Lionel Tiger's troubling thesis that male bonding inhibits violence within the group only by directing it outward against others.[13] Thus the problem of aggression, power and hierarchy is first posed within the cultural context of male friendship, a problem which haunts its cultural evolution for the next 5000 years.

The Greek Source

The dream of fraternity runs parallel to the history of political life in the West. Indeed, the ancient Greeks believed that the very life of the *polis*, or city, rested upon the fraternity of the male citizens. Politics was what transpired amongst friends: The heated discussions, speeches and elections to public life all took place amongst a group of men who lived and met with each other face to face. The heart of Athens and the other Hellenic city-states was always the *agora*, the marketplace where Socrates, the sophists, and the other citizens gathered for endless discussion and debate. Aristotle states, as a non-controversial thesis, that it is friendship [*philia*] which "holds the state together," and the "lawgivers apparently

---

[12]Nietzsche, p. 168.

[13]Lionel Tiger, *Men in Groups* (Vintage Books: New York, 1969), p. 241.

devote more attention to it than to justice."[14] More specifically, he notes that Athenian democracy is founded on "the association of brothers," that is, on fraternal bonds among men who are "equal and decent."[15] Without friendship there could be no justice.

There was, however, a darker side to this picture. The fraternity which governed the city and provided the artistic, philosophical and social vitality of the culture included *only* mature male citizens: It excluded women, children, slaves and servants, foreigners and non-property-owners. We see, then, that the bonds of association which constituted the fraternity were built, at least in part, on the *exclusion* of most of the people of the city: A privileged "we" defined dialectically against a lesser "they."

Secondly, the *arete,* or excellence, to which these male citizens collectively aspired, and which thus functioned to bind them together, was its very core *eristic,* that is, founded upon competition: Friend struggled relentlessly against friend in an attempt to push each other to greater heights of accomplishment. The Olympic games are perhaps the most obvious example of this. But even dramatists and poets engaged in the *contest,* and the plays of Aeschylus, Sophocles and Euripides are remembered largely because they won prizes at the biannual competitions in Athens. The sophists became the most prominent teachers because they taught the art of successful disputation or argument. Even Socrates, though he practiced a cooperative dialectic with his young students, was not above using his keen logical mind to vanquish the orators and sophists such as Thrasymachus in the *Republic* who challenged him.

The very concept of competition entails an implicit hierarchy: Individuals compete against one another in a particular skill in order to establish who is better, that is, "higher" in it. This brings out the fundamental tension within the Greek experience of fraternity which was also in the Gilgamesh Epic, one which, bequeathed to us through our historical connection with the Greeks and Mesopotamians, continues to haunt our relations with one another. Are all the "brothers" of the fraternity equal? There is a sense in which their all being citizens gives them equal privileges and duties. However, this presumed equality becomes the very basis for the contest and the introduction of hierarchy: Who among you is the *best* of what? That is, within the group of presumed equals, the individual's need for identity seems to demand differentiation through the ranking of merit.

With Plato the introduction of hierarchy becomes even more explicit. His *Republic* consists, in essence, of three separate fraternities arranged in

---

[14]Aristotle, *Nichomachean Ethics,* transl. with introduction and notes by Martin Ostwald (Bobbs-Merrill: Indianapolis, 1962), p. 215.

[15]Aristotle, pp. 235–36.

a strict ordering: Guardians, Auxiliaries and Craftsmen. The Guardians rule, moreover, by virtue of their superior rationality: They are the "philosopher-kings." Plato, following the notion that "the *polis* is the individual writ large," then applies this idea of the "rule of reason" to the individual citizen, arguing for the necessity of subordinating the lower parts of a person's soul, namely, the emotions and desires, to this "higher" faculty:[16] "Otherwise there must surely be a sort of civil strife among the three elements, whereby they usurp and encroach upon one another's functions . . ."[17] Plato is assuming that without the hierarchical control of the emotions and desires by reason, there will ensue confusion and disorder: "a soul maddened by the tryanny of passion and lust."[18] Indeed, justice, the central concept of the *Republic*, even comes to be defined within this schema: "Justice is produced in the soul, like health in the body, by establishing the elements concerned in their natural relations of control and subordination . . ."[19]

We see, then, in the Greek experience, at the very source of our Western culture, the inextricable entanglement of the ideas of fraternity and the good man with deep-rooted assumptions about hierarchy, patriarchy, control, competition and the untrustworthy, chaotic nature of the emotions. Somehow our own struggle for liberation must learn to understand this historical legacy better, for it lurks even today like a dark presence beneath the surface of our own lives as men.

Mutual Aid in the Middle Ages

In his important but little-known book *Mutual Aid*, the Russian revolutionist and humanist Peter Kropotkin brilliantly documents the historical manifestations of human solidarity in the form of non-hierarchical institutions. These mutual-aid institutions—the tribe, the village communities, the guilds, the medieval cities—demonstrate (thought Kropotkin) the existence of an instinct of cooperation and mutual aid.[20] One of his most powerful and moving discussions centers on the emergence of the "free cities" of Western Europe between the twelfth and fourteenth centuries. Kropotkin argues that these cities, and the fresh breath of freedom which they represented, were organized around guilds and brotherhoods.

[16]Plato, *The Republic,* ed. and transl. by F. M. Cornford (Oxford U. Press: New York, 1954), pp. 65, 137.

[17]Plato, p. 142.

[18]Ibid., p. 304.

[19]Ibid., p. 145.

[20]Peter Kropotkin, *Mutual Aid* (Extending Horizon Books: Boston, 1914), p. xiii.

[The Guild] was an association for mutual support in all circumstances and in all accidents of life, "by deed and advise", and it was an organization for maintaining justice—with this difference from the State, that on all these occasions a humane, a brotherly element was introduced instead of the formal element which is the essential characteristic of State interference. Even when appearing before the guild tribunal, the guild brother answered before men who knew him well and had stood by him before in their daily work, at the common meal, in the performance of their brotherly duties: men who were his equals and brethren indeed.[21]

In Kropotkin's account three things appeared in every brotherhood, no matter what its overt purpose: (1) The members treated each as, and named each other as, brothers—all were equal; (2) they claimed self-jurisdiction and self-governance for themselves and fought the attempts of petty war lords, clergy and kings to control them; (3) they took oaths of mutual support: "If a brother's house is burned, or he has lost his ship, or has suffered on a pilgrim's voyage, all the brethren must come to his aid; if a brother falls dangerously ill, two brethren must keep watch by his bed til he is out of danger, and if he dies they must bury him.... After his death they must provide for his children, if necessary ..."[22]

Despite Kropotkin's glowing accounts of these brotherhoods, they appear to contain at least lingering traces of the specters discussed earlier, namely, *exclusivity* and *hierarchy*. In the first place, the guilds were selective, often (but not always) barring women and serfs, and sometimes engaged in rivalries and even feuds amongst themselves. As to the second specter, while the brethren were equal under their laws and tribunals, there is some question as to social pecking orders. Certainly the craft guilds, for example, distinguished between masters, journeymen and various grades of apprentices.

Nevertheless, the guilds represent one of the brighter periods in the history of fraternity, and their gradual eclipse by centralized state authority starting in the fifteenth century was definitely a tragic loss for mankind. The male associations current today, such as college fraternities and fraternal organizations—Elks, Shriners, Moose, Chipmunks—divorced as they are from the focus of common work, and devoid of equality and self-governance, must be considered as sadly degenerate forms.

Modern Images of Fraternity

Among modern writers, perhaps Nietzsche, D. H. Lawrence and Thomas Mann provide us with the most striking and revealing images of male friendship. Nietzsche's conception of agonistic or strifeful friendship harks back to the Greeks:

[21]Ibid., p. 176.
[22]Ibid., p. 172.

If one wants to have a friend one must also want to wage war for him: and to wage war, one must capable of being an enemy.

In a friend one should still honor the enemy. Can you go close to your friend without going over to him?

In a friend one should have one's best enemy. You should be closest to him with your heart when you resist him. [23]

Similarly, in D. H. Lawrence's *Women in Love,* a novel which really is about *men* in love, the moment of most intense intimacy between Birkin and Gerald occurs while they are wrestling:

So they wrestled swiftly, rapturously, intent and mindless at last, two essential white figures working into a tighter, closer oneness of struggle, with a strange octopus-like knotting and flashing of limbs in the subdued light of the room; a tense white knot of flesh gripped in silence between the walls of old brown books. Now and again came a sharp gasp of breath, or a sound like a sigh, then the strange sound of flesh escaping under flesh. Often, in the white interlaced knot of violent living being that swayed silently, there was no head to be seen, only the swift, light limbs, the solid white backs, the physical junction of two bodies clinched into oneness. [24]

At the conclusion of this powerful mystical struggle—reminiscent of that between Gilgamesh and Enkidu—Gerald and Birkin have the only genuinely deep, open and honest exchange in the book. The experience has caused them to suspend—at least momentarily—their self-control, reserve and masculine ambivalence.

Thoreau, in an essay on friendship, makes this quality of reserve explicit:

There are some things a man never speaks of, which are much finer kept silent about. To the highest communications we only lend a silent ear. Our finest relation are not simply kept silent about, but buried under a positive depth of silence, never to be revealed. [25]

Thomas Mann gives us a powerful image of this very "depth of silence" in *Death in Venice* in the strange and demonic love which flames up between an old man and a young boy. Although it is perhaps one of the most consuming passions ever portrayed in literature, at least on the part

[23]Nietzsche, p. 168.

[24]D. H. Lawrence, *Women in Love* (Modern Library: New York, 1920), p. 308.

[25]Henry David Thoreau, *A Week on the Concord and Merrimack Rivers,* (Riverside Press, Cambridge, Mass., 1901), p. 385.

of Aschenbach, the old man, no words are ever spoken between them:

> There can be no relation more strange, more critical, than that between two beings who know each other with their eyes, who meet daily, yes, even hourly, eye each other in a fixed regard, and yet by some whim or freak of convention feel constrained to act like strangers. Uneasiness rules between them, unslaked curiosity, a hysterical desire to give rein to their suppressed impulse to recognize and address each other; even, actually, a sort of strained but mutual regard. For one human being instinctively feels respect and love for another human being so long as he does not know him well enough to judge him; and that he does not, the craving he feels is evidence. [26]

While our own male friendships are probably not as stark and dramatic as those portrayed by these authors, nevertheless I think these images suggest some of the contradictory elements implicit in our experience. The *desire for*— and at the same time, *fear of*—intimacy is usually connected with the ambivalent reserve and self-possession with which we conduct ourselves together.

It is possible that there is genuine value in the ritual of silence as Thoreau and Mann describe it. Sometimes a quiet look, a nod, or just some deep attention is more eloquently communicative than any possible effervescence of words. Etched indelibly in my memory is a scene from last year which brought this home to me. Returning to State College, Pennsylvania from Madison I ended up in Altoona at an all-night diner. It was a kind of working-class mutual-aid institution all its own. Policemen just off duty, milk-truck drivers about to start their morning run, night-shift workers on break, even the Greyhound bus driver, all gathered there at 4 AM to hear and joke good-naturedly with each other. The remarkable part was the matter-of-fact way everyone helped out: getting each other coffee, busing dishes, handing down the fresh orders. Most importantly, in the general banter and congeniality I could sense an unspoken fraternity of men nurturing and supporting each other in the best way they knew how.

Men and Technocracy

The tradition of *agonistic* (or strifeful) friendship portrayed by Lawrence, Nietzsche and the Greeks, too, has a direct legacy, but with this difference: *Our* competitiveness with one another, especially at work and in school, seems to lack the mutuality of challenge toward a common

---

[26]From *Death in Venice and Seven Other Stories,* by Thomas Mann, trans. by H. T. Lowe-Porter, copyright 1966 by Alfred A. Knopf, Inc., p. 50.

arete, or excellence. We seek not so much to bring out each other's maximum potential, as to "do each other in" and "get ahead" by any means whatsoever. This seems directly related to the nature of our work situations. Most of us work in and for large, centralized and rigidly hierarchical institutions which are ultimately accountable to capital. Thus communication reduces to communiques. Unlike the brotherhoods and guilds, this top-down structure promotes an atmosphere of distrust and endless competition for the next rung of the ladder. The formal apparatus of bureaucracy replaces the informal face-to-face dialogue as the basis of decision making; *mediated* interchanges, those mediated by hierarchical roles and rules, replace the *immediate* interchange of free and equal brothers; institutional control replaces fraternal persuasion as the *modus operandi.* [27]

The Ethos of Being-toward-Control

Plato was more insightful than we realize when he claimed that the individual was simply the state writ small. For we can recognize in ourselves the hierarchical beings bred by hierarchical society. Even Plato's "rule of reason" is still in charge at the peak of the pyramid.

This rationality is not the wide-ranging, probing philosophical reason that the Greeks advocated, but rather its mongoloid half-brother, "calculative reason," the narrow technical reason of puzzle solving and canny planning. This "reason" which attempts to control our bodies and feelings, and which inhibits us with one another, is a purely instrumentalist faculty, concerned with ever-improved means to unexamined ends. It drives us frequently to an experience of our lives as *performance:* Sex as performance ("how was it?"), work as performance ("did the boss like it?") and—in this age of instant intimacy and T-Groups—even honesty as a performance. [28] Thus we are driven to constantly subjugate everything else to this blind faculty ironically called reason: Through it we seek to control our bodies, moving them mechanically and joylessly about this business; we try to control our feelings, bottling them up inside ourselves; and we even seek to control our children, our lovers, and the people around us.

We are not, luckily, always successful in controlling all these aspects; but the very constancy of the attempt, the ever vigilant orientation *toward* control is itself enough to alter fundamentally our experience of

---

[27]I develop this theme in "The Imperialism of the Mind: Technical Reason and the Problem of Scale."

[28]Jack Wikse brilliantly develops this theme in *About Possession: The Self as Private Property* (Penn. State Press: State College, 1977).

people and nature. We are being controlled by our own need to control. A woman becomes a sex object designed to satisfy our lust; a colleague becomes a competition object to be out-flanked; a beautiful landscape becomes a "cost-effective" site for a billboard.[29] The experience of "being-toward-control" is one of enervating rigidity, strained calculation and relentless manipulation. Television and alcohol alone seem to bring some measure of relief because they take us away from ourselves: They release us temporarily from being-toward-control. Or do they? One thing is certain: Being-toward-control, considered as the core of masculine consciousness, mutilates the personhood of those around us and plunges us into a nightmarish desert of our own making. For if our very being constitutes itself as being-toward-control, and thus our experience of others is always of possible or actual *objects,* how can we ever find each other as authentic *persons,* as human beings?

Thus it is that a brotherhood of liberation can only be founded upon the renunciation of *control* as a way of life.

Giving Up Control

The prospect of actually giving up being-toward-control is terrifying. Will I then be "out of control," wildly flailing down life's darkened corridors? Will I, perhaps, become controlled by men who refuse themselves to give it up? Will my life collapse into *anarchy* without the rigid control of my calculative reason?

Beneath these fears of self-dissolution lurks the cultural legacy of Plato's hierarchy assumption: Without the strict subordination of our other faculties to the "rule of reason," anarchy will result.[30]

Ironically, the inner meaning of *anarchy,* the very thing we—and Plato—most fear would ensue from the overthrow of control shows this the most clearly. *An Archos* means literally "without a first or ruling principle." This could imply no principles whatsoever—which is the implication Plato seems to assume. *Or,* it could imply many principles, of more or less equal power, working harmoniously together. Within the individual it would mean a balanced integration of all of one's faculties—feelings, desires, rationality, and so forth, all functioning together without, however, one dominating to control the others. In the political sphere, it would mean the elimination of centralized top-down government, and the inauguration of direct, decentralized democracy. In each case it stands for the overthrow of the ancient structures of domination and control which have

[29]Max Horkheimer develops this theme in *The Eclipse of Reason* (New York: Seabury Press, 1974).

[30]Plato, pp. 140–43.

for too long prevented us from looking deeply into the faces of our brothers and sisters and made us afraid of the image we discern dimly therein. Only when we summon the resolution to take this step, beyond control and self-possession, and into the realm of mutual trust and the mutual creation of a new social order will we begin to understand the reflection we see. "And now the real drama of human life can unfold, in all its beauty, harmony, creativity and joy."[31] Walt Whitman, who described himself as the "poet of comrades," expressed this timeless vision over a century ago:

Come, I will make the continent indissoluble,
I will make the most splendid race the sun ever shone upon,
I will make divine magnetic lands,
    With the love of comrades,
        With the life-long love of comrades.

I will plant companionship thick as trees along all the rivers of America, and
    along the shores of the great lakes, and all over the prairies,
I will make inseparable cities with their arms about each other's necks.
    By the love of comrades,
        By the manly love of comrades.[32]

---

[31]Murray Bookchin, *Post-Scarcity Anarchism* (Ramparts Press: San Francisco, 1971), p. 169.

[32]Reprinted from *Leaves of Grass* by Walt Whitman, edited by Harold W. Blodgett and Sculley Bradley. Copyright © 1965 by New York University. Reprinted by permission of New York University Press.

It's Sad You Won't Believe Me

I wanted you to be my friend, I wanted to be yours,
It's hard to take the risks involved to open up the doors,
To share each other's feelings was all I ever asked,
It's hard to have relationships you know are going to last,

And it's sad you won't believe me when I say I understand,
It's sad you won't believe I really care.

It's true that I've been hurt a lot, it's true that you've been too,
If we could hang together I know we'd make it through,
But you won't accept the caring and the good I have to give,
You've chosen to be lonely and that's the way you'll live,

And it's sad you won't believe me when I say I understand,
It's sad you won't believe I really care.

It's time for me to go my friend, to travel my own way,
Perhaps we'll see each other in a better light one day,
I'll never know the secrets and the questions on your mind,
Perhaps you'll find the answers in another part of time.

It's so sad you won't believe me when I say I understand,
It's so sad you won't believe I really care.

It's sad you won't believe me when I say I understand,
It's sad you won't believe I really care,
It's sad you won't believe . . .
                              I
                                    care.

Words and music by BILL FOULKE
Copyright © 1980 by Bill Foulke.
Used by permission.

Becoming Brothers
and Unbecoming Barriers

TONY SILVESTRE

That the content and structure of intimate relationships between people is significantly affected by social factors is a sociological truism. Students in beginning sociology courses are taught about changing family functions and their effect on wife-husband and parent-children relationships. Sociologists reassure us that the family is not dying, but rather is changing, and while some family functions are becoming less important, others are developing.

During the past hundred years, sociologists have been preoccupied with wife-husband, parent-child and lover-lover relationships. This preoccupation is understandable, since the change in the meaning of these relationships has been so dramatic and well publicized.

Much less attention has been paid to relationships that appear to be losing importance, such as relationships between godparent and child, cousin and cousin, and siblings. Attention to brotherhood, for instance, has focused on studies of the order of birth and of the intellectual or criminal activity of twins, and certainly not on their developing affectional ties, support or communications networks.

Sibling relationships are more and more ignored, since decreasing family size, increased mobility, and the growth of welfare services have all worked to lessen the amount of interaction as well as dependence on family members. As production of goods shifted from the home and the neighborhood to distant factories and as success in one's calling necessitated greater specialization, family work and the post-adolescent ties they can foster has diminished. What families alive today can we compare to the Brontes, the Mozarts or the James gang? Only the very rich who can regulate their occupations and for whom distance is a mere inconvenience see the extended family as an everyday reality.

Relationships between blood brothers are reduced to formalized exchanges such as participating in family celebrations, reasonable financial or material support and some social interaction. To be friends with your brother is to be in an exceptional relationship. Brothers are not expected to be confidants or intimates.

Certainly brotherhood has always embraced more bonds than simply those based on lineage. Males in tribal societies have often identified all members as brothers, as do men today in religious groups, fraternal and professional organizations and social clubs. However, even these ties are reduced to little more than trivialized rituals of brotherhood—fraternity-house beer parties, Wednesday night bowling and Sunday morning kisses of peace.

It can be argued that male sex-role strictures during this century make more intimate relationships unlikely. Disclosure of intimate emotional and intellectual sensibilities among men is uncommon; in fact, it is discouraged. Except for anger, men do not learn the ethics of emotionability or the skills for development and refinement of emotional expression.

The men's movement, informed by feminism, leads men to examine their isolation from each other and their lack of brotherliness. Although most men know their isolation and their embarrassment when dealing intensely with other men outside of ritualistic camaraderie, articulating it is itself a problem.

Without adult experiences of brotherhood, without models for fashioning brotherly ties and without artistic or scholarly explorations of brotherliness, men lack a common language and shared values.

If we look back to other ages when brotherhood had important meanings we can, at least, begin to understand where we must go. Western folklore and art abound with portrayals of intimacy between men.

The most positive albeit sketchy portrayal of love between two men is the biblical story of David and Jonathan. "And it came to pass, when he had made an end of speaking to Saul, the soul of Jonathan was knit with the soul of David and Jonathan loved him as his own soul" (First Kings 18:1). Jonathan's love for David leads him twice to save David from the wrath of the king and finally to give up any claim to the throne of Israel, clearing the way for David's ascension. On Jonathan's death, David grieved, "I mourn for thee, my brother Jonathan, exceedingly beautiful, and amiable to me above the love of women. As the mother loveth her only son so did I love thee" (Second Kings 1:26). Unfortunately, the story-tellers were more careful to preserve in detail the memory of their battles and not their love, and so we know little more about their relationship.

The stories of Achilles and Patrilocus and of Gilgamesh and Enkidu also evidence strong love commitments between men in other cultures but leave us without a complete picture of the values, circumstances, rights and responsibilities of brotherhood.

Contemporary portraits of male relationships are no more complete. Redford and Newman offhandedly face death together, Marty and Angie share frustrations and a beer and the boys are urged to do it for the Gimper. The lack of substance in these characters, their cosmetic reality merely reflects the lack of meaningful content in our ideas about brother-hood. The relationships between the "brothers" of the sixties and seven-ties are as unreal and shallow as the marital relationships of the fifties between Dezi and Lucy, Ozzie and Harriet, and, of course, Gracie and George.

A second body of folklore to examine includes those stories of relationships that fail or face serious difficulties. Understanding where relationships falter will help us pinpoint the necessary and crucial ele-ments for establishing bonds among men.

Detailed portraits of unsuccessful relationships or relationships that weakened and later grew stronger are relatively numerous. Many of the many famous biblical characters were involved in such relationships.

The Process

The stories of Cain and Abel, Esau and Jacob, Joseph and his brothers, and Jesus and his disciples all contain lessons about brotherhood.

In all these stories, male relationships go through periods of weaken-ing and strengthening. It is clear that brotherhood is a process and not a state that is bestowed along with common parents, membership in a group or attendance at a meeting. The fact of the existence of a relationship is not enough to guaranteee its development or dependability. Cain killed Abel, Jacob tricked Esau and Judas betrayed Jesus. On the other hand, betrayal need not present an insurmountable barrier. The relationships of Jacob and Esau and Joseph and his brothers developed in dramatic ways and proceeded to a fuller blossoming. After spending years in the country-side marrying, producing children, and gathering wealth, Jacob returns home. Fearing Esau's revenge, Jacob sent emissaries and gifts ahead of his entourage. It is not clear whether such precautions were necessary. "Esau ran to meet him, embraced him, fell on his neck and kissed him. And they wept" (Genesis 33:4). Brotherliness can grow stronger in time and withstand the disruptions of deceit and the competition for prestige and wealth.

Most men, however, do not understand this *process* of developing healthy emotions or the ethics of emotionality. Both are necessary and important as a basis for affective relationships. Men who are often naive about their feelings will be overcome with affection and closeness to other men. They assume that these feelings are evidence of a powerful relationship when, in fact, the emotions may simply be one-sided, a sign of relief from suppression or simply an infatuation. For example, these feelings are rampant at the end of men's movement conferences. Men often leave with a pocketful of phone numbers and addresses which most will be too embarrassed to use. The feelings at the conferences are genuine and good, but they are not the makings of brotherliness; they are rather the awakenings of feelings too long suppressed.

Certainly, the movement from sentiments of admiration must be regulated by the needs and assets of the persons involved. Again, folklore contains lessons for us.

TRUST

All the betrayals from Cain and Abel to Shakespeare's Brutus and Caesar were possible because trust existed. Abel willingly and without protection went into the fields with Cain. Esau, even after being tricked once by Jacob with a bowl of lentils, did not stay close to Isaac's death-bed, thereby allowing Jacob's impersonation. For good or for evil, a brother must have trust and be trusted. Such faithfulness, of course, does not develop in full blossom at a potluck dinner. Among blood brothers it develops over a lifetime, reinforced by family and peer expectations. Men who choose others as their brothers face greater difficulty, since they may not share a common history and environment. At the same time, they may have less time to develop trust.

It is noteworthy that the three creatures in the innermost circle of Dante's hell are men who betrayed their brotherly trust, namely Judas, Brutus, and Cassius. In each case, the brotherhood that was betrayed was one chosen, not a happenstance of birth. Although Cain killed Abel with his own hands, his punishment was exile, while Judas, who *chose* brotherhood with Jesus, hung himself. To betray brotherly trust is to remove oneself from the human community. Cain went into exile, "A fugitive and a wanderer shall you be on the earth." Judas hung himself "outside of the city gates." To betray one's brother brands a person untrustworthy. The betrayer who knows the cheap price of his loyalty will never believe that the loyalty of others to him is stronger or more dependable. The betrayer can never have a brother. He is always in exile, always isolated, always wary. It becomes clear that trust relationships entered into willingly demand as much if not more nurturing, commitment and responsibility than blood relationships.

Stories from history tell us that one cannot assume brotherhood because of formal ties or other circumstances. We cannot assume that men we offend through our ignorance and arrogance will receive us because we "mean well." Our internal and personal progress is a cause for our rejoicing; yet we cannot expect that it excites everyone. Realizing the destructiveness of our racism, for instance, leads to personal growth. However, before it can lead to stronger ties with Third World men, we must take action. We must give reason for trusting us. We are naive to think that our loudly declared good intentions are enough to alter our history. To have a dominant status in society means always to assume that one's class-based view of the world is the true one. Consequently, one assumes that sophistication is white, strength is male, courage is heterosexual, and beauty is youth. Confronting these assumptions is an everyday experience for minority persons. Those in dominant positions must realize that status barriers in our society are real and affect everyone, not just "bigots." Good intentions or a liberal philosophy or a sharp mind may lead to a realization that these barriers are destructive, but that realization alone is not enough to break through them.

POWER

People with powerful status often assume that trust can be established in the face of status differences and that one's recognition of the power structure allows one to transcend it. What is not understood, however, is that the barrier has resulted in lost communication, ignorance and insensitivity. Until these issues are addressed, barriers remain.

In all the brother stories already cited, one finds consistent violation of the primogeniture customs, the rules of power transfer. In the sacrifice of Cain, the elder son is rejected and supplanted by the younger Abel's more pleasing sacrifice. Jacob the heel-grabber tricked his older twin into selling his birthright and losing the blessing of the first born. Joseph's dreams, which so infuriated his brothers, described this younger sibling in a position of power over the others. Judas, who exercised considerable power in his control of the purse strings of the followers of Jesus, was often superseded in affection by John and in confidence by Simon and James.

The younger receive the blessings while the older lose their traditional rights. For understanding relationships between brothers, position, title, wealth and power must be recognized and their effects studied. The folktale characters escaped the destructiveness of status and class differences by surrendering their advantages. Jonathan gave up his claim to Saul's throne in the face of David's ability. Jude knelt before Joseph. Jacob got the elder son's blessing. To achieve brotherhood means to go beyond everyday power-based modes of relating. To achieve brotherhood with men made unequal by social roles and statuses, it is necessary to destroy the inequality. It is necessary for the socially dominant person to give up his prerogative, his place, his precedence. Not to do so maintains the traditional ties which are not brotherly by their nature.

White men cannot usually understand why blacks are not participating in the men's movement. One often hears the question, "Why don't more blacks see value in the men's movement?" The question should be, "What is there about me and my movement that makes it irrelevant to blacks?"

Powerful people in any society assume the correctness of their perspective and see little necessity for examination of it. Whites may invite a black to a meeting and ask him what his people want or how to attract other black men to the movement. A few workshops are proposed and a committee set up, yet the basic position of arrogance and power is not seen. If white men are interested in the world of blacks, they would then study it as diligently as they study those things they need for success in their own careers. They would then understand their self-importance and presumptiveness in granting a black an audience with them in white space, in white time and in white terms.

KNOWLEDGE

Building a trusting and equitable relationship depends on a growth in cognitive and affective knowledge among the people involved. The Old Baltimore catechism taught that before one could serve, one had to love God and before one could love God, one had to know God. Knowing other men means observing them, sharing with them, and revealing oneself to them, in a creative and sensitive way. Communication, however, can be blocked even by our language.

Language not only reflects the power structure but helps maintain it. At the national meeting of the Gay Academic Union in 1973, a number of street transvestites demanded to be heard. Although they managed to gain the floor for a few minutes, they were not treated in a respectful and serious way. Since their issues were not couched in academic language, they were greeted with groans. The rules of the bureaucracy were eventually enforced, and they were parliamentarily removed. The system worked, and embarrassing questions were left unanswered.

Subtler methods are available. Most men's conferences offer workshops and discussions for "special interest groups" as if racism, classism, homophobia and ageism are not important or crucial for everyone.

If the men's movement is to generate brotherhood in all men, it must create meeting space for all men to come together and know each other, instead of assemblies of white, straight, middle-class men with separate space for "others."

A common language and space are essential but not sufficient for effective communication; appropriate content is necessary.

Middle-class men in our society know the rules of bureaucracy. They assume that other men will also conform. Men make secure predictions about the strategies, politics and beliefs of their colleagues in business, government and the universities, but they do not learn the rules of emotive and affective relationships. If men are to become brothers, they must recognize and understand the importance of this deficiency. Men are taught to be self-assured about their perspectives, to take it for granted that their view of reality is sufficient.

If men are to become brothers, they must learn to listen and to respect others not for what they do but for who they are.

Trust based on knowledge is essential for brotherhood. It reduces the risk of destructive competition, since men will not need a contest to prove themselves.

Trust between men allows for differences and disagreements. When men know that they are respected and loved, they need not fear their brothers. Anger, even vigorous disagreement, is not an attack on the person. This is important for feminist men who are trying to overcome their need to dominate and to direct. Such men often avoid confrontation but in doing so neglect to deal with the difference that these confrontations represent.

For most men, experiencing warmth and affection from other men is a new and relieving experience. Conflicts may be perceived as threats to these newly formed affective ties. It is not easily understood that men who disagree can also support each other while they struggle with issues. Anger need not signal a desire to annihilate. It may be a call to listen.

Status and class separations impede communication, and the lack of knowledge that results makes trust and equity unlikely. When barriers are analyzed and all men begin to understand their blindness, men will seriously be able to begin to find brotherliness.

PART TWO

Trust, equity and knowledge are necessary components for brotherhood. However, translating these values into actions becomes problematic in the face of some barriers. A history of hostility, embarrassment or fear can so preoccupy people that even attempting to know others becomes unlikely. For most men sexual orientation is an impassable barrier.

Becoming intimate with a homosexual for most straight men is a near impossibility, yet to hope that gay and straight men become brothers is not unrealistic. If sex roles are to change, if we are to move toward a more androgynous society, such brotherhood is essential. However, in our homophobic society, same-sex behaviors constitute "unnatural" relationships. Acceptance will not be achieved easily. Sexual orientation is for some men an insurmountable barrier in the move toward brotherhood. In fact, many of the relational patterns between these men and gay men are the same as the patterns between members of dominant groups and minority members.

At a recent men's conference, the issue of gay and straight brother relationships was a topic of discussion. An analysis of the conference dynamics will make clear some of the results of the barriers raised.

One discussion began with a presentation by a straight-identified panel member, who described his discomfort with the gay issue because of gay men's sexual activity in public places such as men's rooms.

Certainly short-term, anonymous, sexual encounters are an important concern for all men, as is sexual and affectional behavior in public places. If solicitation for sex were the issue, that too is not solely a homosexual issue. Limiting identification of these issues with the gay community perpetuates the old stereotype of gays as uncontrollable and promiscuous molesters. If tearoom behavior in itself is such a concern to some men and creates barriers to brotherhood for them, one might suggest that they read Laud Humphrey's major work on the subject, "Tea-Room Trade." He makes the point very clearly that most tearoom devotees behave, fantasize, self-label and are socially labeled as straight or bisexual. To have raised the issue in the terms it was raised was to reveal an ignorance and insensitivity that said to gays in the room that the panelist was not concerned enough with barriers to brotherhood to have studied the issue earnestly.

Within the first ten minutes of this particular discussion, patterns of dominant-minority interaction emerged. It was assumed that the arguments presented by a gay represented the views of all gays. The differences that arose among gays at the discussion did nothing to weaken that assumption. Apparently, some people were not understanding that no homosexual represents all homosexuals, just as no black represents all blacks, just as no heterosexual represents all heterosexuals.

A number of men in the room were quick to present their liberal credentials. "Everyone should do their own thing; people could fuck dogs for all I care." Another quickly joined in with, "I have never had sex with another guy, but I think gays deserve the same rights as anyone else." Both men identified people according to the use of their genitals. They ignored or were not aware of gay political identity, affection between men or sex-role behavior. Liberals persist in defining the gay issue in terms of orgasms while ignoring its relevancy and significance to sexual identity and economic and political concerns of all people.

As can be imagined, the session energized considerably. One man, upset with the display of gay anger, asked that everyone calm down and share ideas. He went on to describe his belief that all men are the same and that the only reason men are gay is because they have had bad experiences with women.

When the pandemonium ended, a very well-meaning man turned to some gays and asked that he be helped to learn about gays. He went on to describe how homosexuality is not talked about and how most straight-identified people need to be taught.

It was clear that most of the straight-identified men in the room had never heard about Susan Saxe, Troy Perry or George Weinberg, had never read books or newspapers about gays, had never invited speakers to their meetings and had never seriously thought about the issues. It was clear that most of the men were not embarrassed by their ignorance, and even clearer was the fact that only several of the men had ever taken any actions in support of the political and economic rights for gays. Furthermore, most could not understand that perhaps the gays attending this discussion on becoming brothers had their own expectations for the meeting and were not thrilled about the prospects of giving a mini-introductory course on homosexuality. Instead of working toward brotherhood, the gays were expected to educate, as if the personal education of some straights should be their prime concern. Those who wanted to be taught refused responsibility for their ignorance and acted as if a change in their intellectual beliefs was beneficial for gays. They did not see that to change their homophobic attitudes would be beneficial and necessary for their own growth.

Before there can be trust or equality, there must be knowledge. Obviously, some barriers perpetuate ignorance, and the victims of the ignorance are often held responsible.

The theme is familiar and repeated for subject people. Minority people must earn their rights. They should use their money to attend functions in order to justify themselves, to make clear grievances (in a reasonable way), to earn respect and to gain support. Very often the major result of this effort is the education and enlightenment of those in power. Such an experience often provides useful insights into powerful people's own needs. One cannot expect, however, that enlightenment will lead to action on behalf of the minority or on behalf of society.

The conference ended on a sadly ironic note. Most of the men sat or stood in a circle, hugging each other, holding hands and singing the song "Men Supporting Men," which begins, "We've all come together to find another way, a road that leads much straighter to a brighter day." Straighter! Most men were even insensitive to this last affront. Homophobia keeps many men apart through suspicions and fear. In order to achieve brotherhood, the issues of affectional and sexual ties among all men must be faced. Homophobia denies the commonality of brotherhood and will always keep men apart unless it is acknowledged and confronted.

Being a "model man" in our society is a dehumanizing and impossible task. He is supposed to be silent, isolated, willful and unemotional, and such men do exist. When men understand and accept their feelings for each other, they will develop a new model of manliness, a more humane one.

The rules of behavior between men are socially established. Men can touch, but only quickly and with force. Men may share time alone only if involved in a game. Men can share problems, but not intimate ones. The lines are drawn to exclude any display of tenderness, caring or passion. These exclusions make close relationships between men unlikely. One may go out with the boys, but suspicions grow if it becomes one special boy; the men who make up one's circle should be interchangeable. If there is a ranking or a preference, it is to be based on having more things in common, not on special feelings. For the stereotypical male, a friend who can joke, drink, hold certain views, and mind his own business can be his brother.

Certainly these restraints on male relationships, fostered by homophobia, inhibit the kind of human growth that only friendship can nurture. Overcoming fears and ignorance about sexual orientation and sexual minorities will have social repercussions beyond any personal liberation. Many of our educational and economic systems depend on a particular kind of competition and alienation among workers. It is interesting that sex discrimination in employment segregates men and women and fosters competition between members of the same sex. Women who do have "men's jobs" are often accused of becoming desexed. Men who have traditionally "female jobs" are immediately assumed to be less than male. Therefore segregation in employment is fostered and reinforced. Those who are able to break through the barriers and withstand the stigmatization become discreditable. The segregation, as well as the fears generated by homophobia, appears necessary if a spirit of competition is to be successfully fostered.

All people, from students to factory workers to politicians, are expected to work alone and to work more successfully than their status-mates. Grades and promotions depend on one's success at the game. Obviously, such competition must be impersonal. One must be able to analyze one's competition objectively and, at the same time, not reveal any personal weakness. Personal disclosure is dangerous. Homophobia supports competition by restraining intimacy and communication among workers. It is difficult to create and maintain solidarity with persons whose bodies you are expected to find repulsive and whose innermost frustrations and hopes remain hidden.

Developing brotherhood among straights and gays will help reduce the dichotomies fostered by sex-role stereotyping. Many men, in attempting to overcome learned sex-role behavior, have devoted themselves to personal growth and have eschewed politics which they consider masculinist. Increased awareness of gay issues should make it clear that the personal and the political are not at separate ends of the same spectrum. Intimate relations of gays are intruded upon by public agencies, and so one's jobs, insurance, credit, and credibility, one's children and one's reputation are all affected because of the most personal behavior. For gays, one's affection is political business.

Denying the political significance of changes in personal relationships actually reinforces traditional sex-roles. After all, it perpetuates the belief that personal growth and political action are incompatible and that the traditional categories of instrumental activity and expressive activity are valid albeit not necessarily genitally related.

This notion, though allowing for genital variation in these two pursuits, limits human behavior to two exclusive expressions: public participation and personal intimacy.

Revolutionaries who protested in the face of insurmountable opposition continue to protest. They certainly knew enough to realize the futility of their effort. Yet they protested. They realized that their own integrity and dignity demanded action. What compromise can substitute for human dignity? To be oblivious to the suffering of people around us, to ignore the daily assaults on our honor can only diminish us. If we are to gain and hold our self-respect, we must protest the outrages generated by homophobia. If we ignore the political oppression facing sexual minorities, we support that oppression. Our silence indicts us. We cannot give them the comfort of our silence again.

Freeing men from fear of emotional intimacy will allow men to begin developing emotional sensibilities. At present, men know the rituals, ethics and uses of anger. Most men have a Thomistic sensibility in the area of violence as a response to insult. Other emotional activity has not been in any sense as thoroughly analyzed among men. The expression of feelings will lead to a development of an ethic for men that will make the development and maintenance of all personal relationships possible. At present, the novelty of emotional expression is overpowering for many men. The feeling of hugging is more important than the person hugged. As a result, many men are still isolated by their need for gratification. More intimate experiences will teach men about crushes, rejection and sensibility. Brotherhood needs this sharing.

Removing the barrier raised by sexual and affectional relationships is necessary not only so that gay-identified men will be more willing to participate in the men's movement but so that all men can become free from the social restraints on their development. Fear of being called a queer, of having one's masculinity questioned, is the greatest single hindrance in overcoming male sex-role demands. The questions of homophobia are central to all men's concerns. It has been the club used to keep workers from exploring their feelings of alienation and the goals of success they are expected to internalize. Until men are secure in their own masculinity, the men's movement is too dangerous. There can only be security when the issue of sexuality is confronted fully, honestly and at all levels.

Julian

Julian, do you know I had to go, I had to find myself another way,
I think about you often and I know that we will meet again someday,
But for now we'll live apart in silence and in memories we've earned,
Sorrow is a part of life but nothing is forever I have learned.

I wish you Joy, I wish you Love.

Julian, you're my friend, you told me so and I believe that it is true,
Your kindness and your understanding more than once had helped to see
* me through,*
Your eyes are full of rainbows, but there's gentle sadness in your
* heart I know,*
But there's hope in every morning and the pains of life will not disrupt
* the flow.*

I wish you Joy, I wish you Love.

I think sometimes I let you down, I never gave you all the things you
*   gave to me,*
It doesn't take a mystic now to realize that sometimes even blind men see,
Teddy bears aren't just for kids to keep away the loneliness of night,
I did the best I could to make you feel your life would somehow be
* all right.*

I wish you Joy, I wish you Love.

Relationships like ours are hard to have where some refuse to understand,
They never realize that love is something to be shared by everyone who can,
You and I were lucky that we had the time to open up and share,
A special kind of joy that comes to only those who take the risk to care.

I wish you Joy, I wish you Love.

Julian, now I miss you but I know that somehow you will know just what
*   to do,*
And you will find another friend, and chances are that I will find
*   another too,*
But for now we'll live apart in silence and in memories we've earned,
Sorrow is a part of life but nothing is forever I have learned.

I wish you Joy, I wish you Love.

I wish you Joy, I wish you Love.

Words and music by BILL FOULKE
Copyright © 1980 by Bill Foulke.
Used by permission.

part five

RESOURCES FOR CHANGE IN MALES

A Men's Support Group,
State College,
Pennsylvania, 1976

Men's Conference,
New Jersey, 1975

An Opportunity to Share

RESOURCES FOR CHANGE IN MALES

Getting the Message Across in Song

As a group, men are having very difficult times and paying high costs for traditional masculinity. Nevertheless, men who wish to reorient their lives and their environment away from sexism do have some resources at their disposal. It may be true that men in some geographical locations have fewer of these resources available to them than do others. Yet, some of the means discussed in papers within this section are everywhere ready and free for the using. Pleck's paper suggests one resource to be the anti-sexist Men's Movement which has developed during the last half of the 1970's both in North America and Western Europe. According to Pleck, participation in the Men's Movement at least may help men learn how to express the full range of their emotions and to validate themselves as men, two tasks which most men expect women to do for them. This will release men not only from their dependence on women in these matters but also from men's resentment and need to control women, which usually arise from men fearing that their women will withhold this validation.

Workshops for fathers and would-be-fathers are offered as resources for some males by Rypma and Kolarik in their paper, "A Training Project for Fathers." The main assumption of these authors is that males *can adapt* to a rich variety of behaviors and attitudes and that therefore an experiential workshop on fathering or similar experiences can change some men's attitudes and behavior and improve their repertoire of skills. A number of case studies are presented in which fathers improve their interpersonal skills and gain confidence in parenting without returning to patriarchal customs, which have been the only models some of them may have known.

Consciousness-raising (CR) groups are another resource for men who wish to confront their own sexism and that in society as well. Creane outlines a number of basic guidelines which he has found helpful for starting and maintaining consciousness-raising groups for men. Many of these suggestions will be especially helpful for those men who wish to initiate such a group whenever they cannot locate CR groups in their geographical region.

Since homophobia is a major factor in the maintenance of traditional male roles and sexism, those means which might be used to reduce homophobia are also resources. Morin and Nungesser in their article, "Can Homophobia Be Cured?" explore some methods which have been used to reduce homophobia, particularly among therapists. Morin and Nungesser hold that the reduction of homophobia results not only in a reduction of male-dominant attitudes but in higher self-esteem for the person whose attitudes toward homosexuality have been changed.

Finally, research is another resource upon which intervention and change may be built. Research on black males, however, is practically non-existent, according to Staples, a black sociologist. More could be done to help black males who have very high mortality rates, for instance, if we knew more about black males' socialization, their attitudes toward family planning, their sexuality and their ideas of masculinity. More, therefore, could be done to help black males free themselves from stereotypic roles if more studies were made on black males.

Men's Power with Women, Other Men, and Society: A Men's Movement Analysis

JOSEPH H. PLECK

My aim in this paper is to analyze men's power from the perspective afforded by the emerging anti-sexist men's movement. In the last several years, an anti-sexist men's movement has appeared in North America and in the Western European countries. While it is not so widely known as the women's movement, the men's movement has generated a variety of books, publications, and organizations[1] and is now an established

[1] See, for example, Deborah David and Robert Brannon, eds., *The Forty-Nine Percent Majority: Readings on the Male Role* (Reading, Mass.: Addison-Wesley, 1975); Warren Farrell, *The Liberated Man* (New York: Bantam Books, 1975); Marc Feigen Fasteau, *The Male Machine* (New York: McGraw-Hill, 1974); Jack Nichols, *Men's Liberation: A New Definition of Masculinity* (Baltimore: Penguin, 1975); John Petras, ed., *Sex: Male/Gender: Masculine* (Port Washington, N.J.: Alfred, 1975); Joseph H. Pleck and Jack Sawyer, eds., *Men and Masculinity* (Englewood Cliffs, N.J.: Prentice-Hall, 1974). See also the *Man's Awareness Network (MAN) Newsletter,* a regularly updated directory of men's movement activities, organizations, and publications, prepared by a rotating group of men's centers (c/o Knoxville, Tenn. 37916); the Men's Studies Collection, Charles Hayden Humanities Library, Massachusetts Institute of Technology, Cambridge, Mass. 02139.

presence. The present and future political relationship between the women's movement and the men's movement raises complex questions which I do not deal with here, though they are clearly important ones. Instead, here I present my own view of the contribution which the men's movement and men's analysis make to a feminist understanding of men and power, and of men's power over women, particularly in relation to the power that men often perceive women have over them. Then I will analyze two other power relationships men are implicated in—men's power with other men, and men's power in society generally—and suggest how these two other power relationships interact with men's power over women.

Men's Power over Women, and Women's Power over Men

It is becoming increasingly recognized that one of the most funda-mental questions raised by the women's movement is not a question about women at all, but rather a question about men: Why do men oppress women? There are two general kinds of answers to this question. The first is that men want power over women because it is in their rational self-interest to have it, to have the concrete benefits and privileges that power over women provides them. Having power, it is rational to want to keep it. The second kind of answer is that men want to have power over women because of deep-lying psychological needs in male personality. These two views are not mutually exclusive, and there is certainly ample evidence for both. The final analysis of men's oppression of women will have to give attention equally to its rational and irrational sources.

I will concentrate my attention here on the psychological sources of men's needs for power over women. Let us consider first the most common and commonsense psychological analysis of men's need to domi-nate women, which takes as its starting point the male child's early experience with women. The male child, the argument goes, perceives his mother and his predominantly female elementary school teachers as dominating and controlling. These relationships *do* in reality contain elements of domination and control, probably exacerbated by the restric-tion of women's opportunities to exercise power in most other areas. As a result, men feel a lifelong psychological need to free themselves from or prevent their being dominated by women. The argument is, in effect, that men oppress women as adults because they experienced women as op-pressing them as children.

According to this analysis, the process operates in a vicious circle. In each generation, adult men restrict women from having power in almost all domains of social life except childrearing. As a result, male children feel powerless and dominated, grow up needing to restrict women's power, and thus the cycle repeats itself. It follows from this analysis that the way to break the vicious circle is to make it possible for women to exercise power outside of parenting and parent-like roles and to get men to do their half share of parenting.

There may be a kernel of truth in this "mother domination" theory of sexism for some men, and the social changes in the organization of child care that this theory suggests are certainly desirable. As a general explanation of men's needs to dominate women, however, this theory has been quite overworked. This theory holds women themselves, rather than men, ultimately responsible for the oppression of women—in William Ryan's phrase, "blaming the victim" of oppression for her own oppression.[2] The film *One Flew over the Cuckoo's Nest* presents an extreme example of how women's supposed domination of men is used to justify sexism. This film portrays the archetypal struggle between a female figure depicted as domineering and castrating and a rebellious male hero (played by Jack Nicholson) who refuses to be emasculated by her. This struggle escalates to a climactic scene in which Nicholson throws her on the floor and nearly strangles her to death—a scene that was accompanied by wild cheering from the audience when I saw the film. For this performance, Jack Nicholson won the Academy Award as the best actor of the year, an indication of how successful the film is in seducing its audience to accept this act of sexual violence as legitimate and even heroic. The hidden moral message of the film is that because women dominate men, the most extreme forms of sexual violence are not only permissible for men but, indeed, are morally obligatory.

To account for men's needs for power over women, it is ultimately more useful to examine some other ways that men feel women have power over them than fear of maternal domination.[3] There are two forms of power that men perceive women as holding over them which derive more

[2]William Ryan, *Blaming the Victim* (New York: Pantheon, 1970).

[3]In addition to the mother domination theory, there are two other psychological theories relating aspects of the early mother-child relationship in men's sexism. The first can be called the "mother identification" theory, which holds that men develop a "feminine" psychological identification because of their early attachment to their mothers and that men fear this internal feminine part of themselves, seeking to control it by controlling those who actually are feminine, i.e., women. The second can be called the "mother socialization" theory, holding that since boys' fathers are relatively absent as sex-role models, the major route by which boys learn masculinity is through their mothers' rewarding masculine behavior, and especially through their mothers' punishing feminine behavior. Thus, males associate women with punishment and pressure to be masculine. Interestingly, these two theories are in direct contradiction, since the former holds that men fear women because women make men feminine, and the latter holds that men fear women because women make men masculine. These theories are discussed at greater length in Joseph H. Pleck, "Men's Traditional Attitudes toward

directly from traditional definitions of adult male and female roles, and which have implications which are far more compatible with a feminist perspective.

The first power that men perceive women have over them is *expressive power*, the power to express emotions. It is well known that in traditional male-female relationships, women are supposed to express their needs for achievement only vicariously through the achievements of men. It is not so widely recognized, however, that this dependency of women on men's achievement has a converse. In traditional male-female relationships, men experience their emotions vicariously through women. Many men have learned to depend on women to help them express their emotions, indeed, to express their emotions for them. At an ultimate level, many men are unable to feel emotionally alive except through relationships with women. A particularly dramatic example occurs in an earlier Jack Nicholson film, *Carnal Knowledge*. Art Garfunkel, at one point early in his romance with Candy Bergen, tells Nicholson that she makes him aware of thoughts he "never even knew he had." Although Nicholson is sleeping with Bergen and Garfunkel is not, Nicholson feels tremendously deprived in comparison when he hears this. In a dramatic scene, Nicholson then goes to her and angrily demands, "You tell him his thoughts, now you tell me *my* thoughts!" When women withhold and refuse to exercise this expressive power for men's benefit, many men, like Nicholson in the film, feel abject and try all the harder to get women to play their traditional expressive role.

A second form of power that men attribute to women is *masculinity-validating* power. In traditional masculinity, to experience oneself as masculine requires that women play their prescribed role of doing the things that make men feel masculine. Another scene from *Carnal Knowledge* provides a pointed illustration. In the closing scene of the movie, Nicholson has hired a call girl whom he has rehearsed and coached in a script telling him how strong and manly he is, in order to get him sexually aroused. Nicholson seems to be in control, but when the girl makes a mistake in her role, his desperate reprimands show just how dependent he is on her playing out the masculinity-validating script he has created. It is clear that what he is looking for in this encounter is not so much sexual gratification as it is validation of himself as a man—which only women can give him. As with women's expressive power, when women refuse to exercise their masculinity-validating power for men, many men feel lost and bereft and frantically attempt to force women back into their accustomed role.

Women: Conceptual Issues in Research," in *The Psychology of Women: New Directions in Research,* ed. Julia Sherman and Florence Denmark (New York: Psychological Dimensions, in press).

As suggested before, men's need for power over women derives both from men's pragmatic self-interest and from men's psychological needs. It would be a mistake to overemphasize men's psychological needs as the sources of their needs to control women, in comparison with simple rational self-interest. However, if we are looking for the psychological sources of men's needs for power over women, their perception that women have expressive power and masculinity-validating power over them is critical to analyze. These powers are the two resources women possess which men fear women will withhold, and whose threatened or actual loss leads men to such frantic attempts to reassert power over women.

Men's dependence on women's power to express men's emotions and to validate men's masculinity has placed heavy burdens on women. By and large, these are not powers over men that women have wanted to hold. These are powers that men have themselves handed over to women by defining the male role as being emotionally cool and inexpressive and as being ultimately validated by heterosexual success.

There is reason to think that over the course of recent history—as male friendship has declined, and as dating and marriage have occurred more universally and at younger ages—the demands on men to be emotionally inexpressive and to prove masculinity through relating to women have become stronger. As a result, men have given women increasingly more expressive power and more masculinity-validating power over them, and they have become increasingly dependent on women for emotional and sex-role validation. In the context of this increased dependency on women's power, the emergence of the women's movement now, with women asserting their right not to play these roles for men, has hit men with a special force.

It is in this context that the men's movement and men's groups place so much emphasis on men learning to express and experience their emotions with each other, and on men learning how to validate themselves and each other as persons, instead of needing women to validate them emotionally and as men. When men realize that they can develop in themselves the power to experience themselves emotionally and to validate themselves as persons, they will not feel the dependency on women which has led in the past to so much male fear, resentment, and need to control women. Then men will be emotionally more free to negotiate the pragmatic realignment of power between the sexes that is underway in our society.

Men's Power with Other Men

After considering men's power over women in relation to the power men perceive women have over them, let us consider men's power over women in a second context: the context of men's power relationships with other men. In recent years, we have come to understand that relations between men and women are governed by a sexual politics that exists outside individual men's and women's needs and choices. It has taken us much longer to recognize that there is a systematic sexual politics of male-male relationships as well. Under patriarchy, men's relationships with other men cannot help but be shaped and patterned by patriarchal norms, though they are less obvious than the norms governing male-female relationships. A society could not have the kinds of power dynamics that exist between women and men in our society without certain kinds of systematic power dynamics operating among men as well.

One dramatic example illustrating this connection occurs in Marge Piercy's novel *Small Changes.* In a flashback scene, a male character goes along with several friends to gang-rape a woman. When his turn comes, he is impotent, whereupon the other men grab him, pulling down his pants to rape *him.* This scene powerfully conveys one form of the relationship between male-female and male-male sexual politics. The point is that men do not just happily bond together to oppress women. In addition to hierarchy over women, men create hierarchies and rankings among themselves according to criteria of "masculinity." Men at each rank of masculinity compete with each other, with whatever resources they have, for the differential payoffs that patriarchy allows men.

Men in different societies choose different grounds on which to rank each other. Many societies use the simple facts of age and physical strength to stratify men. The most bizarre and extreme form of patriarchal stratification occurs in those societies which have literally created a class of eunuchs. Our society, reflecting its own particular preoccupations, stratifies men according to physical strength and athletic ability in the early years; later in life it focuses on success with women and ability to make money.

In our society, one of the most critical rankings among men deriving from patriarchal sexual politics is the division between gay and straight men. This division has powerful negative consequences for gay men and gives straight men privilege. In addition, this division has a larger symbolic meaning: Our society uses the male heterosexual-homosexual dichotomy as a central symbol for *all* the rankings of masculinity, for the division on *any* grounds between males who are "real men" and have power and males who are not. Any kind of powerlessness or refusal to compete becomes imbued with the imagery of homosexuality. In the men's movement documentary film *Men's Lives,*[4] a high school male who studies modern dance says that others often think he is gay because he is a dancer. When asked why, he gives three reasons: because dancers are "free and loose," because they are "not big like football players," and

[4] Available from New Day Films, P.O. Box 615, Franklin Lakes, N.J. 07417.

because "you're not trying to kill anybody." The patriarchal connection: If you are not trying to kill other men, you must be gay.

Another dramatic example of men's use of homosexual derogations as weapons in their power struggle with each other comes from a document which provides one of the richest case studies of the politics of male-male relationships yet to appear: Woodward and Bernstein's *The Final Days*. Ehrlichman jokes that Kissinger is queer, Kissinger calls an unnamed colleague a psychopathic homosexual, and Haig jokes that Nixon and Rebozo are having a homosexual relationship. From the highest ranks of male power to the lowest, the gay-straight division is a central symbol of all the forms of ranking and power relationships which men put on each other.

The relationships between the patriarchal stratification and competition which men experience with each other and men's patriarchal domination of women are complex. Let us briefly consider several points of interconnection between them. First, women are used as *symbols of success* in men's competition with each other. It is sometimes thought that competition for women is the ultimate source of men's competition with each other. For example, in *Totem and Taboo* Freud presented a mythical reconstruction of the origin of society based on sons' sexual competition with fathers, leading to their murdering the fathers. In this view, if women did not exist, men would not have anything to compete for with each other. There is considerable reason, however, to see women not as the ultimate source of male-male competition but as symbols in a male contest whose real roots lie much deeper.

The film *Paper Chase* provides an interesting example. This film combines the story of a small group of male law students in their first year of law school with a heterosexual love story between one of the students (played by Timothy Bottoms) and the professor's daughter. As the film develops, it becomes clear that the real business is the struggle within the group of male law students for survival, success, and the professor's blessing—a patriarchal struggle in which several of the less successful are driven out of school and one even attempts suicide. When Timothy Bottoms gets the professor's daughter at the end, she is simply another one of the rewards he has won by doing better than the other males in her father's class. Indeed, she appears to be a direct part of the patriarchal blessing her father has bestowed on Bottoms.

Second, women often play a *mediating* role in the patriarchal struggle among men. Women get men together with each other and provide the social lubrication necessary to smooth over men's inability to relate to each other non-competitively. This function has been expressed in many myths, as, for example, in the folk tales included in the Grimm brothers' collection about groups of brothers whose younger sister reunites and reconciles them with the king-father, who had previously banished and tried to kill them. A more modern myth, illustrated in James Dickey's *Deliverance,* is that when men get beyond the bounds of civilization, which really means beyond the bounds of the civilizing effects of women, men rape and murder each other.[5]

A third function women play in male-male sexual politics is that relationships with women provide men a *refuge* from the dangers and stresses of relating to other males. Traditional relationships with women have provided men a safe place in which they can recuperate from the stresses they have absorbed in their daily struggle with other men, and in which they can express their needs without fearing that these needs will be used against them. If women begin to compete with men and have power in their own right, men are threatened by the loss of this refuge.

Finally, a fourth function of women in males' patriarchal competition with each other is to reduce the stress of competition by serving as an *underclass.* As Elizabeth Janeway has written in *Between Myth and Morning,*[6] under patriarchy women represent the lowest status, a status to which men can fall only under the most exceptional circumstances, if at all. Competition among men is serious, but its intensity is mitigated by the fact that there is a lowest possible level to which men cannot fall. One reason men fear women's liberation, writes Janeway, is that the liberation of women will take away this unique underclass status of women. Men will now risk falling lower than ever before, into a new underclass composed of the weak of both sexes. Thus, women's liberation means that the stakes of patriarchal failure for men are higher than they have been before, and that it is even more important for men not to lose.

Thus, men's patriarchal competition with each other makes use of women as symbols of success, as mediators, as refuges, and as an underclass. In each of these roles, women are dominated by men in ways that derive directly from men's struggle with each other. Men need to deal with the sexual politics of their relationships with each other if they are to deal fully with the sexual politics of their relationships with women.

Ultimately, we have to understand that patriarchy has two halves which are intimately related to each other. Patriarchy is a *dual* system, a system in which men oppress women, and in which men oppress themselves and each other. At one level, challenging one part of patriarchy inherently leads to challenging the other. This is one way to interpret why the idea of women's liberation so soon led to the idea of men's liberation, which in my view ultimately means freeing men from the patriarchal sexual

[5]Carolyn G. Heilbrun, "The Masculine Wilderness of the American Novel," *Saturday Review* 41 (January 29, 1972), 41–44.

[6]Elizabeth Janeway, *Between Myth and Morning* (Boston: Little, Brown, 1975); see also Elizabeth Janeway, "The Weak Are the Second Sex," *Atlantic Monthly* (December, 1973), 91–104.

dynamics they now experience with each other. Because the patriarchal sexual dynamics of male-male relationships are less obvious than those of male-female relationships, however, men face a real danger: While the patriarchal oppression of women may be lessened as a result of the women's movement, the patriarchal oppression of men may be untouched. The real danger for men posed by the attack that the women's movement is making on patriarchy is not that this attack will go too far, but that it will not go far enough. Ultimately, men cannot go any further in relating to women as equals than they have been able to go in relating to other men as equals—an equality which has been so deeply disturbing, which has generated so many psychological as well as literal casualties, and which has left so many unresolved issues of competition and frustrated love.

Men's Power in Society

Let us now consider men's power over women in a third and final context, the context of men's power in the larger society. At one level, men's social identity is defined by the power they have over women and the power they can compete for against other men. At another level, most men have very little power over their own lives. How can we understand this paradox?

The major demand to which men must accede in contemporary society is that they play their required role in the economy. However, this role is not intrinsically satisfying. Social researcher Daniel Yankelovich[7] has suggested that about 80 percent of U.S. male workers experience their jobs as intrinsically meaningless and onerous. They experience their jobs and themselves as worthwhile only through priding themselves on the hard work and personal sacrifice they are making to be breadwinners for their families. Accepting these hardships reaffirms their role as family providers and therefore as true men.

Linking the breadwinner role to masculinity in this way has several consequences for men. Men can get psychological payoffs from their jobs which these jobs never provide in themselves. By training men to accept payment for their work in feelings of masculinity rather than in feelings of satisfaction, men will not demand that their jobs be made more meaningful, and as a result jobs can be designed for the more important goal of generating profits. Further, the connection between work and masculinity makes men accept unemployment as their personal failing as males, rather than analyze and change the profit-based economy whose inevitable dislocations make them unemployed or unemployable.

Most critical for our analysis here, men's role in the economy and the

---

[7]Daniel Yankelovich, "The Meaning of Work," in *The Worker and the Job*, ed. Jerome Rosow (Englewood Cliffs, N.J.: Prentice-Hall, 1974).

ways men are motivated to play it have at least two negative effects on women. First, the husband's job makes many direct and indirect demands on wives. In fact, it is often hard to distinguish whether the wife is dominated more by the husband or by the husband's job. Sociologist Ralph Turner writes: "Because the husband must adjust to the demands of his occupation and the family in turn must accommodate to his demands on behalf of his occupational obligations, the husband appears to dominate his wife and children. But as an agent of economic institutions, he perceives himself as controlled rather than as controlling."[8]

Second, linking the breadwinner role to masculinity in order to motivate men to work means that women must not be allowed to hold paid jobs. For the majority of men who accept dehumanizing jobs only because having a job validates their role as family breadwinner, their wives' taking paid jobs takes away from them the major and often only way they have of experiencing themselves as having worth. Yankelovich suggests that the frustration and discontent of this group of men, whose wives are increasingly joining the paid labor force, is emerging as a major social problem. What these men do to sabotage women's paid jobs is deplorable, but I believe that it is quite within the bounds of a feminist analysis of contemporary society to see these men as victims as well as victimizers.

One long-range perspective on the historical evolution of the family is that from an earlier stage in which both wife and husband were directly economically productive in the household economic unit, the husband's economic role has evolved so that now it is under the control of forces entirely outside the family. In order to increase productivity, the goal in the design of this new male work role is to increase men's commitment and loyalty to work and to reduce those ties to the family that might compete with it. Men's jobs are increasingly structured as if men had no direct roles or responsibilities in the family—indeed, as if they did not have families at all. Paradoxically, at the same time that men's responsibilities in the family are reduced to facilitate more efficient performance of their work role, the increasing dehumanization of work means that the satisfaction which jobs give men is, to an increasing degree, *only* the satisfaction of fulfilling the family breadwinner role. That is, on the one hand, men's ties to the family have to be broken down to facilitate industrial work discipline; and on the other hand, men's sense of responsibility to the family has to be increased, but shaped into a purely economic form, to provide the motivation for men to work at all. Essential to this process is the transformation of the wife's economic role to providing supportive services, both physical and psychological, to keep him on the job, and to take over the family responsibilities which his expanded work role will no longer allow him to fulfill himself. The wife is then bound to her husband

[8]Ralph Turner, *Family Interaction* (New York: John Wiley, 1968), p. 282.

by her economic dependency on him, and the husband in turn is bound to his job by his family's economic dependence on him.

A final example from the film *Men's Lives* illustrates some of these points. In one of the most powerful scenes in the film, a worker in a rubber plant resignedly describes how his bosses are concerned, in his words, with "pacifying" him to get the maximum output from him, not with satisfying his needs. He then takes back this analysis, saying that he is only a worker and therefore cannot really understand what is happening to him. Next, he is asked whether he wants his wife to take a paid job to reduce the pressure he feels in trying to support his family. In marked contrast to his earlier passive resignation, he proudly asserts that he will never allow her to work, and that in particular he will never scrub the floors after he comes home from his own job. (He correctly perceives that if his wife did take a paid job, he would be under pressure to do some housework.) In this scene, the man expresses and then denies an awareness of his exploitation as a worker. Central to his coping with and repressing his incipient awareness of his exploitation is his false consciousness of his superiority and privilege over women. Not scrubbing floors is a real privilege, and deciding whether or not his wife will have paid work is a real power, but the consciousness of power over his own life that such privilege and power give this man is false. The relative privilege that men get from sexism, and more importantly the false consciousness of privilege men get from sexism, plays a critical role in reconciling men to their subordination in the larger political economy. This analysis does not imply that men's sexism will go away if men gain control over their own lives, or that men do not have to deal with their sexism until they gain this control. I disagree with both. Rather, my point is that we cannot fully understand men's sexism or men's subordination in the larger society unless we understand how deeply they are related.

To summarize, a feminist understanding of men's power over women, why men have needed it, and what is involved in changing it, is enriched by examining men's power in a broader context. To understand men's power over women, we have to understand the ways in which men feel women have power over them, men's power relationships with other men, and the powerlessness of most men in the larger society. Rectifying men's power relationship with women will inevitably both stimulate and benefit from the rectification of these other power relationships.

The I Love Me Song

I am as strong a person as anyone can be.
You'll have to have a lot of strength to be as strong as me.
I'm strong because I love you and will until I die.
And stronger 'cause the one that I love most of all is I.

I am the highest flier that ever hit the sky.
I can soar above the clouds and I don't even try.
High above the buildings and out over the sea.
Every body way down there wants to be with me.

You know I am so beautiful, I can't believe it quite.
How in this world of error anything could be so right.
The essence of perfection, how lucky can I be,
To be such close acquaintance with anyone like me.

I'll tell you a little secret, just between me and you.
I know that I am pretty great, but you can be great too.
All it takes is believin', try it and you'll see.
Just close your eyes, let your spirits rise, and sing along with me . . .

I am the strongest person when I work with you.
When we work together there's no telling what we'll do.
True strength comes in numbers—put it to the test.
When we work together is when I love me best.

Words and music by WILLIE SORDILL © 1980

A Training Project for Fathers

CRAIG BLAINE RYPMA
AND
GEORGE MICHAEL KOLARIK

Fathering is a focused behavior that can be critically analyzed in much the same way as other focused behaviors, for example, suckling, aggressiveness, procreation. It is assumed that much behavior can be considered the interaction of biological influences and social learning. Thus, as in much behavior, fathering may have biological foundations; mothering has traditionally been distinguished from parenting behavior in general and, as such, has been examined in its various biological and social ramifications. Thus fathering may not be unique. If fathering does have a strong biological component, we therefore can conclude that it is subject to predictable biological laws. An examination of the biological roots of humankind reveals that what may distinguish our species in the phylogenetic progression is an incommensurable degree of adaptability bolstered by superior intelligence. The essential purpose of "A Training Project for Fathers" is to enhance the father's ability to adapt to a richer and more wholesome understanding of the biological, sociological and psychological forces which collectively define his behavior and his paternal attitudes.

This thesis could not have been strongly supported a few years ago.

With the body of research on fathers growing, the need for new ideas, new methodologies and new understanding of the complex interaction between man and child forbids further delay. Following the fall of the Roman Empire, and with the advent of popular Christianity, colonization, the institution of child labor laws, compulsory education, mass transportation, and the Industrial Revolution, the father's role has diminished and his effectiveness as a parent has decreased. He has been forced to adapt outside of the family, and the adaptability within the family may now be of paramount importance if the molecular family structure is to continue.

Those in the profession of restructuring broken families, and more specifically broken, maladaptive personalities, have begun to search for methods to counteract this degenerative process. Furthermore, the difficulty of recruiting for research purposes fathers who are locked into a social system that they have unawaringly evolved from is extreme. It is a system that elicits the very behaviors that support their demise. Therefore, research in this area has been very difficult.

If the father's dilemma were viewed more optimistically, his predicament may be regarded as simply the result of social destruction. Thus, it might be foolish to attempt to regain the social atmosphere of a past epoch in which the position of the father was more eminent. The challenge appears to be to understand the present without overlooking its biological foundations. Intelligent behavior, buttressed by adaptability to changing conditions, is the epitome of humankind's resources. "A Training Project for Fathers" is based on this philosophy.

As a preliminary step in testing this hypothesis, the following experimental workshop was devised. A program based on "A Training Project for Fathers" was well advertised, with 3,000 individuals and 100 organizations being contacted. Our goal was to attract both men and women, of all ages, interested in what is popularly termed *fathering*. Newsletters describing the workshop were sent to day-care centers, mental health organizations, medical practitioners, hospitals, rest homes, schools (both elementary and secondary), universities, newspapers, and radio stations. Until the day that the workshop was to begin, however, no men had volunteered to participate. Eighteen women had enrolled expressing an interest to better understand their primary roles as family caretakers. The women ranged in age from 25 to 37. They were middle class, Caucasian, both single and married. To our surprise, at the initial meeting the workshop consisted of 12 women and 15 men. The males ranged in age from an 18-year-old laconic single male "just getting myself ready for my future role as a father," to a grizzled grandfather of ten who expressed a desire to "learn what I had done wrong" with his children so he would not make the same mistakes with his grandchildren.

The Presentation

The workshop format of lecture and discussion progressed from initial considerations of prehistoric, biblical and historical roles of the father to more topical issues relating to the father's role in relation to the adolescent, specific problems faced by step-fathers, fathers dealing with the drug culture, and "expectant" fathers. The general attitudes toward fathering that were elaborated in the early part of the course could be used later to fortify the elements discussed under the practical considerations section. The discussion and presentation progressed from the theoretical to a more practical application of fathering behavior. Interwoven through the presentation were three distinct components: a comprehensive view of the historical evolution of the father role; the sociological, psychological, and biological considerations of paternal behavior; and problems that fathers may encounter, with subsequent potential solutions.

Our objective in regard to the history of the father was to trace the development of the father role anthropologically and historically. Generally speaking, the conception of the prehistoric father is a natural starting point in understanding the evolution of paternal functions. We felt that fathering behavior has naturally been reflected throughout history in the arts, literature and religion of the time. Thus, for example, we examined the concept of the father in relation to theological development; that is, we examined the significance of his role according to various dogmas, culminating with the advent of Christianity and the debut of the importance of the mother-child unit (Madonna). Progressing, we then analyzed the similiarities of the father role in different cultures in an attempt to discover some common denominators amongst fathers in general. We hypothesized that similarities across cultures imply a genetic antecedent, whereas differences in paternal patterns may be the result of social learning. Lastly, we directed our historical overview to the American father's heritage; and finally, the role of the father in contemporary U.S. society was contemplated.

With respect to sociological considerations, our goal was to examine the interaction of the father's attitudes and his society. We viewed our pluralistic society as one containing numerous socializing agents. Selecting from among these, we felt that we could not disregard the influence of the feminist movement, our country's heavy industrialization, the drug culture, and lastly and very importantly, the media's influence in the perception of the father's role. It seemed reasonable to assume that the country's most serious social problems (drugs, divorce, crime) could stem in part from the father's possible alienation from society's basic institution—the family.

The psychological component of our effort examined the various patterns of fathering on certain facets of the father's own social and

personal adjustment. This area included an analysis of sex-role development and the paternal basis of certain psychopathologies. We probed the
effect the mother's role had on the father's behavior and vice versa. In
addition, the effects of paternal deprivation and paternal absence were
explored in terms of age of onset and maternal attitudes toward the
father's divestment.

The conclusion of this part of the workshop was a description of the
biological aspects of fathering behavior in humans as well as in other
species.

As the aforementioned components were developed, we hoped not
only to increase men's and women's understanding of the father's role but
also to cultivate the use of behavior techniques and communications skills
that might be effective in dealing with problems that fathers might encounter. At the conclusion of the project, both the male and female
participants had begun to rethink their roles. In our discussion of the
importance of fatherhood, adaptation was stressed by setting an atmosphere that allowed for the realization that men could share fully the
responsibilities and joys of parenthood without necessarily returning to
patriarchal customs. The men had begun to realize their capacity for
parenthood.

An Objective Measure

Consistent with the experimental notion of the workshop, a pilot
assessment of parental attitudes was attempted. Statistical data may be
irrelevant due to design, sample size, and the necessity of non-parametric
analysis. Subjectively, it was determined a priori that a change of five
points in either direction of a scale might be realistically significant. A
prediction of the direction of the attitude change was not considered
because the authors were only looking for the impact of the workshop on
these measures. Nevertheless, some interesting subjective interpretations can be inferred from the data.

An objective test (the Q4 version of the Parental Attitude Research
Instrument, Schluderman and Schluderman, 1976) was administered
both before and after the workshop. The test consists of 20 scales of five
items each, resulting in one hundred items. The subject is asked to indicate
whether he "strongly agrees," "mildly agrees," "mildly disagrees," or
"strongly disagrees" with the attitude expressed by that idea. The test-
retest reliabilities of this comprehensive survey of fathering attitudes
ranged from 0.57 to 0.75. Thus, test-retest reliability appeared adequate
for further analysis. Furthermore, previous studies have shown that
neither differences in marital status nor in the amount of experience in the
father's role differentiates paternal attitudes toward childrearing on the
PARI scales.

For example, a 33-year-old Caucasian father of two children, ages four and seven, reported that he took the class to better understand effective childrearing techniques. This individual changed most significantly on the scale "Breaking the Will." This scale consists of questions such as "A child should never be taught to fear adults" and "You can't make a child behave by cracking down on him." This is a scale that attempts to measure the degree to which a father imposes his disposition on his children. Although purely speculative, it appeared that this subject decreased on this scale as he gained from the workshop confidence and definition as to what fathering means for him. That is, as more effective behavioral skills and communications techniques were gained through the duration of the eight weeks, the individual reported that he was able to examine his own attitudes. Consequently, he might have shifted these attitudes from an emphasis on imposing control to one which facilitated his child's own self-control.

A 54-year-old father of ten whose purpose for taking the course was to gain a richer understanding of what was meant by "father psychology" changed most on the scale "Ascendency of the Husband." This scale consisted of items such as "The father has no right to demand that the whole family must do what he knows is best" and "There should not be a boss in the family, and the father should not boss the family around." This scale purportedly measures the father's attitudes about his family's deference to his familial position. This subject's score increased from the pre- to the post-measure presumably because of realization of the importance of the father on certain facets of his child's social and personal development. Perhaps discussion on the concept of paternal deprivation accomplished this positive shift.

The 28-year-old father (of a nine-month-old son) anxious for support in his newly acquired paternal role changed in a positive direction on the scale "Deception," accompanied by a lower score on the scales "Harsh Punishment" and "Change Orientation." The scale "Deception" measures a particular form of behavioral control with questions such as "Deceiving a child is very often necessary for his or her own good" and "Often you have to fool children to get them to do what they should without a big fuss." The scale "Harsh Punishment" likewise measures the father's attitude toward behavioral control by means of questions such as "It is no use trying to make a child behave by slapping the child immediately for getting into mischief" and "If small children refuse to obey, parents should not whip them for it." It would appear that this subject had begun to rethink his attitudes toward his child's socialization. The negative shift on the scale "Change Orientation" further supports this hypothesis. This scale measures the father's inclination to support his own behavior as opposed to his control of the child's behavior.

All other male members of the workshop class changed similarly. As the class provided a theoretical foundation, the subjects apparently gained confidence in their ability to grow and adapt. Consequently, this produced self-reported constructive modifications in their behavior toward their families and, most importantly, toward their children.

The Biological Approach

Complex behaviors such as the father-child interaction are best understood by analyzing biological and environmental elements. The authors feel that men in general have a biological tendency to father. The combination of this biological propensity with environmental factors shapes a learned response for both the father and the child, a nature-nurture phenomena.

Researchers of paternal behavior have customarily focused their attention in a social-psychological direction. Cognizant of this conceptual ellipsis, in an earlier publication, one of the authors (Rypma, 1976) implies that paternal behavior is partly the result of inheritable biological forces. This postulation bridges the hiatus where scientific theory slides into speculation. The strength of biology as one cause of human behavior is found in the following material.

As humans evolved from tree-dwelling to terrestrial creatures, they were compelled to compete with other carnivorous animals. In addition, the growing intelligence and expanding cranial capacity of early humans resulted in a longer development, both before and after parturition. Awkward pregnancy and a helpless infancy increased the vulnerability of the mother and the baby. This was especially significant when quickness and aggressiveness were called for by the primitive environment. Equipped innately for the demands of survival, the father's role was to protect, to nurture, and to provide for a relatively helpless family. With the development of modern culture this role diminished, leaving behind its vestiges in the absence of as threatening an environment. Other empirical data support this thesis. Comparative psychologists have pointed out that in the development of certain behaviors in animals, there are critical periods involved. That is to say, during some definite stage in development there is a period during which the animal is particularly susceptible to certain experiences. Stolz et al. (1954) suggest that there is such a period in relation to the father's entry into the psychological development of the child. However, Greenburg and Morris (1974) suggest that fathers develop a feeling of preoccupation, absorption, and interest in their newborn within the first three days after birth and often earlier. It is hypothesized that this very early bonding is basic and innate even though there likely is an interaction between this potential and cultural arena. Meredith (1975) refers to a further physiological consideration concerning the paternal response and reports that adult mammals of both sexes have a fundamental attraction and fostering instinct for anything shaped like an infant (round, small and big eyed). This has been termed the *cute* response. It means that whenever an adult human or animal sees something small, round and cute, he becomes predisposed to treat the creature gently and kindly. In addition, if the general theory of evolution can be accepted as valid, then the behavior of man is the most highly developed of all animal behavior. As such, examples of paternal behavior in lower animals may give further dimension to the biological arguments (examples are summarized by Rypma, supra). Additionally, there is emerging literature which implies paternal physiology. Etkin (1964) suggests that paternal behavior may be influenced by endocrine secretions. For example, if the hormone prolactin is injected into capons or roosters, they begin to show parental behavior. Fisher (1964) injected testosterone into the center of the brain of male rats; these rats responded with forms of maternal behavior. These behaviors were elicited only by testosterone. They did not occur either when these sites were injected with other chemicals or when they were stimulated by electricity. Erhardt (1975) presents data which imply that prenatal exposure to high levels of the male hormone androgen affects psychosexual differentiation in the genetic female in terms of an increased physical energy level and a low interest in maternal caretaking. On the other hand, genetic males with a similar prenatal exposure likewise have a normal male psychosexual differentiation with a possible increased energy expenditure level.

Estrogen and progesterone may effect assertiveness in genetic males. Erhardt additionally reports that this relationship of hormones and behavior is independent of the genetic sex. It can be produced experimentally contrary to the animals' genetic sex.

Examinations of paternal behavior and its hormonal etiology become more complex as one ascends the phylogenetic ladder. Biological and environmental factors become more intricately interwoven and more difficult to differentiate with regard to any particular behavior. Thus, it is not surprising that the evidence of the hormonal effects on paternal behavior is still rather speculative and fragmentary.

According to Rypma (1976) evidence suggests a biological proclivity to father. It may be a biological part of being human.

The workshop "A Training Project for Fathers" explored the biological antecedents of paternal behavior and the sociological forces that deny or enhance a father's sharing in the growth of his child.

Concluding Remarks

Investigators involved in understanding family dynamics have characteristically focused their attention in a social-psychological direction. They have been successful in defining some of the social and psychological forces that may result in crime, divorce, and the like. Their view, however, may have been blurred by overlooking one of the most fundamental resources for understanding behavior: our basic biological functions—the foundations of life itself.

It seems reasonable that we should, therefore, examine our biology. This reveals that adaptability and intellectual capacity are, at least, partly due to a normal evolutionary success. Identification of where the father stands today and mobilization of our basic resources to deal with the father's present condition are called for.

At the end of the eight-week course, the members of the group had integrated the various components of the workshop. They reported a realization that through a better understanding of the sociological, psychological and biological aspects of fathering, they had developed a greater capacity to be more comfortable and confident with the task of fathering. Analysis of this project lends support to this approach.

In conclusion, many questions about the nature of fathering have yet to be answered. Consistent, systematic investigation may yield the development of adequate concepts and the emergence of a multi-faceted definition of the paternal response. This will enable a more systematic appraisal of fatherhood, providing human developmentalists, psychologists, teachers, and practitioners the opportunity to disseminate to the public a more holistic conception of fathering.

Consciousness-Raising Groups for Men

JAMES CREANE

Consciousness raising (CR) is a different approach from traditional politics where one reads, discusses and tries to implement the principles one has decided upon. In CR groups for men, a person discovers common problems and common solutions from our everyday experience of being a man in this society. CR, then, is using direct experience to discover the necessary individual, social, and political changes that must be made. In this sense the personal is political. Without a commitment to social and political change the personal, in my judgment, remains only the personal. In short, the goal is to have our actions in both public and private life reflect our values and commitments.

CR groups decide for themselves what topics they want to discuss and in what order. Each person decides what he wants to share or withhold at a particular moment in the group—more on this later. However, you can learn a great deal about yourself and your group by observing what and when you and/or the group feels comfortable sharing on a particular topic.

The basic guidelines for CR are few and simple.

1. The group decides on the day and length of time for the group's

meetings. Most of the groups I have been in, or have facilitated, have lasted three to four hours. Some groups meet three to four hours but leave open the option to stay longer if there is interest and energy. Stable membership is also important to build trust and for continuity.

2. The group decides on a topic for discussion usually a week in advance. Topics range from fathers and sons, money and relationships, unemployment, sexual performance, child care, and housework to male-male friendships, power and authority in male-male relationships, and power and authority in male-female relationships. In fact, this book can be used as a resource for topic selection.

3. The group decides on the next meeting place. This is most commonly done by rotating the meetings in each member's apartment or house. The advantage to this arrangement, besides rotating responsibility, is that the group can get an additional sense of the person by seeing his living space. Also, the group can observe the impact of different environments on the intensity of the group's involvement.

4. The group usually sits in a circle, which generally helps to promote involvement and to increase communication. Each person speaks, or declines the opportunity by passing. Each person speaks without interruption except to answer short questions to clarify a statement. The group can begin with any member and continues around the circle. A member who passes can elect to speak later.

5. Either a second "go-around" or open interaction can be used to explore common themes from individual members' expriences. The group then analyzes the social sources of those experiences.

Some additional guidelines on common problems and concerns:

1. *Confidentiality.* Most groups adopt a rule of strict confidentiality in order to facilitate open and honest sharing in the group. Even if you have some positive comments about a group member, tell it to that person rather than to someone outside the group. Some groups do allow a member to tell others what he said about *himself* in the group.

2. *Size of the group.* Seven to ten is usually a good number. It allows for enough variety of experience to make the sharing and

analysis more useful, without having the group so large as to preclude intimacy and involvement.

3. *New members.* Because it is difficult to assimilate and integrate new members, my own preference is not to admit new members after the first month unless the group feels it is stagnating or becoming too homogeneous. I also think that when a group gets down to five or less members, it may have fewer hassles if it merges with another group in a similar situation.

4. *A member wants to drop out.* This most often happens when a person is undergoing the pain of changing. Very often some attention and encouragement from the group will be enough to encourage him to stay. If not, the person's decision must be respected.

5. *Accuracy and validity.* Each member's statements about his experience are assumed to be accurate and valid whether or not they seem that way to you. This acceptance is especially important in the beginning of a group, when people are anxious. As long as a person is speaking from his direct experience, what he says must be assumed to be true for him. His perceptions and viewpoint, and yours, may change as the group develops.

6. *Friendships outside the group.* These are great provided they don't sabotage the group. I have seen too many alliances formed outside the group that directly affected what went on in the group. Some of my most intimate friendships were formed from my CR group; but in the same way that we never discussed the weather, we never talked about the group while we were in it.

7. *Communication.* "I" statements are generally most productive. Some examples: "I felt really depressed after my wife left me" or "My sense is that all of us who have spoken about being divorced have expressed feelings of both guilt and failure" or "I get very angry at Harry when I sense that he rejects the group's encouragement and support" or "I hear what you are saying, but my experience has been different" or "I sense that you are feeling down tonight."

   "I" statements can be, and too often are, subverted from their original purpose. Properly used, "I" statements encourage trust, honesty and acceptance. They also make it easier for another to hear what you are saying without feeling defensive; but they can also be used to conceal judgmental attitudes, criticism, unsolicited advice, blame, and interpretations of someone else's experience. When used this way they are likely to generate confusion, suspicion, anger, hostility and sometimes outright rage. Some examples of disguised abusive statements: "I feel the reason Harry is so depressed about his divorce is that he has very strong feelings of attachment to his mother. I feel he would be much better off if he would give them up." "I feel that you are really a cruel person." "In my experience, you are a cruel, selfish man." "I hear what you are saying, but I feel you aren't making sense."

8. *Punctuality.* This is an issue for the group to decide. My own observation is that the problem arises most often after the group has been meeting for a while and the initial sense of discovery and elation has died down. Perhaps a tardy member is reconsidering the degree of his commitment to the group, and the group needs to discuss this.

9. *Decision making.* Since CR is committed to democratic decision making, the way in which the group makes its decisions is very important. Sometimes, because of our concern that every member have an equal opportunity to influence the group's decision, simple decisions can be agonizing. This process, nonetheless, can be an important educational experience for men, since it raises important questions: cooperation versus competition, negotiating versus win or lose, and who does what to attain and exercise power and influence. My suggestion is to try to include the preferences of as many members as possible, and to try to structure future activities to include the interests of the minority. An awareness of structure and alternatives is an important part of decision making.

10. *Rejecting a member.* This obviously is a painful and difficult decision for a group, but it is a decision that must occasionally be dealt with. Sometimes a person is not emotionally ready for a CR group or is so disruptive of the CR process that a group feels it must reject a person for its own survival. Since CR is a voluntary association and since it is clearly not a therapy group with a trained leader, it has the right to reject a person. However, it is the group's responsibility to make sure that it is rejecting the person for his behavior and its impact on the group, not for a group stereotype such as "John will never change."

11. *The learning process.* Consciousness raising (CR) is part education and part resocialization. From its educational aspects we discover new values. We then support and encourage each

other to internalize and enact these new values in our behavior (resocialization). Since we learn most intensively when we are *slightly* anxious, a group needs to be aware of this fact. I believe a group can choose its topics and exercises so that sufficient anxiety is generated to enhance learning but not so much that people feel threatened.

12. *Goals and direction.* A group needs to occasionally evaluate its accomplishments and to choose and define its future direction. Each member can say what he feels he has learned, in what areas he is dissatisfied and the direction he would like the group to take. Differing expectations will have to be negotiated.

13. *The unlucky problem.* "I like my group but I want them to be more politically aware, or more open, or whatever." I've been through this one myself with one CR group. The more I argued, entreated and pleaded, the more the group resisted. The group finally told me not to try to impose my values and needs on them, and to accept them for who they were. I listened, considered, and left. Sometimes the only response is to look for, or to start, another group.

14. *The homogeneity question.* How many young or old, single or married, rich or poor is it desirable to include in the group? My own preference is to have as wide a mixture as possible, since I believe that a wide mixture enriches the group's range of experience, but it does preclude intensive concentration on a single, often pressing, concern. Hence, single people or married people or older people often form a single-interest group to deal with their preoccupations and problems. A common problem or situation also forms a bond which helps to generate interest and involvement.

Options and Variations

1. Ideas tell you where to look. If the group has little experience with the ideas of the men's movement and the women's movement, TV is a great way to begin. All the group needs are some pads and some pencils. Each member writes down his observations and shares them at the end of a program. The basic idea is to compare roles men and women are shown in with ones they are not shown in. Look for patterns rather than exceptions. Watching some soap operas and then some male action shows is a useful way to see how the behavior of men and women is presented differently.

2. Doing some physical contact exercises such as the trust exercise, hugging, or massage is useful for four reasons. The exercises

   a. Help men get over their fear of being seen as homosexual or feminine.
   b. Build trust within the group.
   c. Help men to learn how to nurture other men, something men badly need to do so that we can stop confining women in this role.
   d. Feel good.

   Bernard Gunther's *Sense Relaxation Below Your Mind* (Pocket Books) is a good resource for physical exercises.

3. Begin the group with a short go-around with each member saying what he feels like saying about his week. This provides a good opportunity to share what changes a person has made, as well as his victories and defeats in fighting sexism.

4. Role playing and role reversal: I know of no better way to become conscious of how someone feels in a socially assigned role than to role play it. The more you can get into your role, the more you will learn. I never felt I could portray a woman until I tried, when I found I could do it well. Some possible combinations: man and woman on a date, father disciplining a son, employer giving orders to worker, husband criticizing a wife's housework, gay man trying to tell a straight man about his fears, and a man trying to be supportive to another man. Situations with power and control imbalances, such as a divorce proceeding, are generally illuminating.

5. Meet with another men's group or a woman's group. Attend conferences and men's centers, and do some reading. New information or ideas help to keep a group from becoming inbred and stale as well as contribute to the CR process. Groups can become stagnant and be afraid to admit it.

6. Tape record part of a group session, and then play it back and discuss it.

7. Use non-verbal techniques. Sitting in silence for a half hour and watching each other's non-verbal communication is a quick way to become aware of how much communication is non-verbal.

8. Individual members can ask for an entire evening, or part of an evening, to deal with an urgent problem.

9. The group can decide to cook supper or spend a weekend together.

10. Bring in an experienced facilitator and get some feedback.

No list of suggestions and guidelines can be long enough to cover every problem that any group of people can have when they form a CR group. Even if that were possible, I don't have the experience to provide such a list. So, my final suggestion is that you get about ten people together, exchange addresses and telephone numbers, choose a topic and begin. (See Table I, Ideal Development of a CR Group, for topics.)

Model of the Ideal Development of a CR Group

These sequences are schematic and arbitrary—not every individual or every group will follow the same sequence exactly nor in the same order. I include them here so that group members can use them to identify their interests and concerns. I believe there is a rough relationship between each numbered stage in the first three sequences. I have listed the sequences in the order of the increasing need for trust and commitment.

TABLE I
Ideal Development of a CR Group

I. Individual Member

1. Sharing feelings about self and life.

2. Opening up—learning to trust other group members.

3. Sharing experiences—moving from the comparatively safe past to a recent experience that is more difficult to share.

4. Participating in analysis.

5. Taking responsibility for changing situations based on new values.

6. Becoming political—coming out of the closet and going public.

7. Participating in evaluation of and commitment to group's goals.

8. Participating in group's political actions.

9. Having commitment to movement; deciding to stay or leave the group.

II. Group Process

1. Listening only.

2. Building trust.

3. Stressing commonality of feelings and problems.

4. Analyzing social origins of problems.

5. Providing support and feedback for members' goals.

6. Beginning group evaluation and criticism.

7. Normative pressures within group—new values tend to become standards.

8. Taking group action and evaluating impact of action.

9. Disbanding group or continuing as support group to affirm validity of group's values.

III. Levels of CR Group Development

1. Commitment to group.

2. Involvement and concern with group members.

3. Building primariness in the group trust, openness, sense of *we*.

4. Developing sufficient sense of *we* to allow constructive criticism and feedback.

5. Willingness of individual and group to take responsibility for immediate situation.

6. Awareness that there are no personal solutions for social problems.

7. Commitment to changing social structure through political action.

IV. Consciousness Raising and Political Aspects of Group

1. Group decision making—on-going process.

2. Resocialization—support for new values.

3. Building common ideology.

4. Abstracting and forming theory: outside reading, conferences, meetings with other groups.

5. Commitment to movement.

6. Political action.

V. As Opposed to Support Groups or Therapy Groups

1. Opening up—sharing feelings about life and self.

2. Concern and support from group for individual psychological problems and distress. Personal change.

3. No analysis of social structure. No social change.

Men Supporting Men

We've all come together to find another way
A road that leads more clearly to a brighter day
Where we can be just who we are, to love and laugh and cry
And there's only one way to make it, 'cause it's an uphill climb.

Chorus:

Arm in arm, hand in hand, walkin' side by side
Tearin' down the walls to look in each other's eyes
To find a place where it's okay for a different kind of friend
A world we'll build together with men supporting men.

We've felt the walls since we were born, that keep us all apart
We're here to share the doors we've discovered with our hearts
There've been times I've felt alone, the road is so unclear
But I can see a light in every face that's here

(Chorus)

Men are taught competing and survival of the fit
But a different world is coming, the torch is being lit
Free to give and share our strength with each woman, child and man
We're not there, but it's not far, we can see it from where we stand

(Chorus)

GEOF MORGAN

Can Homophobia Be Cured?

STEPHEN F. MORIN
AND
LONNIE NUNGESSER

Changing attitudes toward homosexuality and homosexuals are a personal and social concern for millions of Americans today. Millions of men and women are trying to educate the public about homosexuality in order to discredit belief systems based upon myths and stereotypes. In contrast, the anti-homophile groups led by homophobics perpetuate the negative attitudes toward homosexuals which have served for centuries to oppress them. Gay-oriented mental health professionals comprise another group concerned with overcoming homophobia. They see that overcoming homophobia is central to the development of male-male intimacy and self-esteem in men of all sexualities. As an individual personality dynamic, homophobia refers to "the irrational, persistent fear or dread of homosexuals."[1] It is very important to clarify the dynamics of homophobia among homosexuals themselves, which becomes self-hatred resulting

[1]MacDonald, G. J. The relationship between sex-role stereotypes, attitudes toward women, and male homosexuality in a non-clinical sample of homosexual men. Paper presented at the meeting of the Canadian Psychological Association, Toronto, 1976.

from the internalization of others' irrational fears,[2] or negative attitudes.[3]

Several writers have suggested that homophobia is a major factor in the maintenance of traditional male roles.[4] In American society, sex roles are among the most important standards of behavior; and sex-inappropriate behavior is one of the most severely punished infractions of our social code. Any study of the relationship between male homophobia and the male sex role must consider issues of discreditability and social stigma.[5] For example, being gay is strongly associated with the violation of sex-role stereotypes in American society because it is commonly believed that gay men do not fit the cultural criteria for masculinity. Further, research on attitudes toward male homosexuality and beliefs concerning the male role reveal that the "typical male homosexual" is seen to be quite different from the "typical male heterosexual" in consistently negative ways.[6] A number of studies have found that the need to maintain a double standard between men and women is a basic component of homophobia.[7] Homosexuality has also been associated with the belief that men are more potent than women.[8] Thus, according to the traditional male sex role, the homosexual is labeled a traitor, a violator and a threat.

MALE ROLE AND HOMOPHOBIA

The acquisition of sex-typed behavior is a functional component of the socialization of children in a predominantly heterosexual society. Sex typing in children is an integral part of their socialization, and its effect is evidenced at a surprisingly early age. For example, research has demonstrated that boys display a preference for "masculine" toys by the age of

[2]Morin, S. F., and Garfinkle, E. M. Male homophobia. *Journal of Social Issues*, 1978. 34, 29-47.

[3]Nungeser, L. G. Homophobia and male homosexuals: a multi-dimensional measurement of beliefs, attitudes and behaviors. Stanford University Press, 1978.

[4]Lehne, G. K. Homophobia among men. In D. David and R. Bramon, (eds.) *The Forty-nine Percent Majority: Readings on the Male Sex Role.* New York: Addison-Wesley, 1975.

[5]Goffman, E. *Stigma.* Englewood Cliffs, N.J.: Prentice-Hall, 1963.

[6]Karr, R. Homosexual labeling: an experimental analysis. Unpublished dissertation, University of Washington, 1975.

[7]MacDonald, A. P., and Games, R. G. Some characteristics of those who hold positive and negative attitudes toward homosexuals. *Journal of Homosexuality*, 1974, *1*, 9-28.

[8]Ibid.

four to six, while girls, although they are less sex-typed at the preschool age,[9] display preference for "feminine" articles at the same age.[10] By definition, sex typing is the acquisition of *role* behaviors appropriate to a child's ascribed gender. According to one study on the sex typing of males, boys generally ascribe their role not in terms of desired masculine attributes, but in terms of the avoidance of "anything . . . that the parent or other people regard as 'sissy.' "[11] Such bi-polar views of the social sex roles prevent any behavior that might be considered undesirable or inappropriate.[12]

As a result of the socialization process, heterosexual and homosexual men learn that homosexuality represents a failure to live up to accepted masculine norms: for example, competitiveness with men; absence of emotional expression, particularly in the presence of other men; and sexual potency with women.[13] Therefore, for homosexual men, the outcome of internalizing traditional male norms results in a feeling of failure, guilt, and negative identity.[14]

Recent research shows that heterosexual people perceive homosexual men as less masculine than heterosexual men. In a survey of readers of *Psychology Today* 70 percent of the heterosexual respondents reported that they believe homosexual men to be "not fully masculine."[15] That study also revealed that homosexual men were much more likely than heterosexual men to rate themselves "less masculine than average" (40 percent versus 7 percent). Furthermore, homosexual men rate themselves "more feminine than average" to a greater degree than heterosexual men (36 percent versus 19 percent).

[9]Maccoby, E., and Jacklin, C. *The Psychology of Sex Differences.* Stanford University Press, 1974.

[10]Sears, R. Development of gender role. In F. Beach (ed.), *Sex and Behavior.* New York: John Wiley, 1965, pp. 133-163.

[11]Hartly, R. E. Sex-role pressures and the socialization of the male child. *Psychological Reports,* 1959, 5, 457-468.

[12]Kagen, J. Acquisition and significance of sex typing and sex-role identity. In M. L. Hoffman and L. W. Hoffman (eds.), *Review of Child Development Research,* vol. 1. New York: Russell Sage Foundation, 1964. Kohlberg, L. A. Cognitive-developmental analysis of children's sex-role concepts and attitudes. In E. E. Maccoby (eds.), *The Development of Sex Differences.* Stanford University Press, 1966.

[13]Fasteau, M. F. *The Male Machine.* New York: Delta, 1976.

[14]Altman, D. *Homosexual Oppression and Liberation.* New York: Avon, 1973.

[15]Tavris, C. Men and women report their views on masculinity. *Psychology Today,* 1977, *10* (8), 34.

In the Karr (1975) study, a sample of one hundred men rated the "typical male homosexual" on an evaluative factor as less good, less honest, less fair, less positive, less valuable, less stable, less intellectual, less friendly, and less clean, as well as more shallow and unhealthy than the "typical male heterosexual." On a masculinity factor, homosexuals were rated as more delicate, more passive, more womanly, smaller, softer, and more yielding than heterosexual men. These data indicate that the male role is a distinct and powerful one, and that gay men are seen to deviate from this role in significant ways. It is apparent from these findings that the fear of being labeled a homosexual can operate as a powerful force in keeping men within the boundaries of their traditional roles.

In support of this concept is the Karr (1975) study. Karr arranged an Asch-type experiment in which one experimental confederate was labeled as a homosexual by a second confederate in the experimental condition; he was not labeled in the neutral condition. Participants performed a non-verbal communication task, and then were asked to rate the other members of their group, including the confederates, on a number of dimensions. On a masculinity factor, the homosexually labeled confederate was rated as significantly less masculine, smaller, weaker, softer, more passive, more yielding, more delicate and less powerful than he was rated when not labeled. In this context many gay men have described their own self-concept as neither stereotypically masculine or feminine, but rather as more typically *androgynous,* that is, expressive of characteristics of both sexes.

In principle, the concept of androgyny assumes that an individual is both masculine and feminine, both instrumental and expressive, both agential and communal and that it is even possible for an individual to blend these complementary modalities in a single act: for example, being able to fire an employee if the circumstances warrant it, but doing so with sensitivity for the human emotion that such an act inevitably produces.[16]

Sandra Bem (1976) designed a study to look more closely at the specific processes that might be responsible for an individual's behavioral restriction. On the one hand, it is possible that the sex-typed individual fails to engage in the cross-sex behavior simply because it does not occur to him or her or because he or she does not feel sufficiently skilled at it. In other words, it is possible that cross-sex behavior is not motivationally problematic for the sex-typed individual and that he or she would willingly engage in such behavior if the situation were structured to encourage it.

On the other hand, it seems more likely that cross-sex behavior is motivationally problematic for the sex-typed individual and that he or she

---

[16]Bem, S. The measurement of psychological androgyny. *Journal of Consulting and Clinical Psychology,* 1974, *42,* 155-162.

actively avoids it as a result. This avoidance could emerge either because sex-typed individuals are motivated to maintain a self-image as masculine or feminine or because they are motivated to present a public image of masculinity or femininity to those around them. In either case, the individuals actively prefer sex-appropriate activities and resist sex-inappropriate activities, even in situations where those preferences could incur some costs; Bem's study indicates these individuals experience discomfort and temporary loss of self-esteem if they are actually required to perform cross-sex behavior.[17]

As homosexuals internalize the normative point of view regarding sex roles and sexuality, they also learn that they are disqualified according to it; and, they nearly always have control of the information that could serve to discredit them. As such, homosexuals are discreditable. They have a social stigma.

According to Goffman (1954) the third stage of learning for the stigmatized person is *passing*. He learns to manage the information about his "failing," making sure nothing he says or does will give him away. The fears of rejection upon self-disclosure cause many gay men and women to grow up "passing" in isolation, while many grow old isolated in their closets. The psychological dangers of passing can be devastating. Ultimately, the message is the same: It is a negative self-statement about one's own right or worthiness to gain social acceptance.

How, you may ask, does a homosexual "pass" as a heterosexual? He typically would dress in masculine attire such as faded denims and a flannel shirt, while closely monitoring voice inflections, body movements, and other self-expressive behaviors which might be construed to be a departure from the proscribed social male sex role. Learning to control one's expressive behaviors is at the heart of passing, or remaining in the closet. Gay-oriented mental health professionals currently cite the reclaiming of self-expression as one of the most common needs of their clients. For example, two feelings which males have commonly learned to control through suppression of self-monitoring are anger and erotic-affectional feelings.

Considering individual differences in the self-control of expressive behavior, Mark Snyder has developed a scale to measure those individual differences. According to Snyder, the ideal self-monitor is a person who, out of concern for social appropriateness, is particularly sensitive to the expression and self-presentation of others in social situations. He then uses those cues as guidelines for monitoring and managing his own self-presentation and expressive behavior. The homosexual male who felt his sexuality was potentially socially inappropriate would be a very restrictive

[17]Bem, S., and Lenney, E. Sex typing and the avoidance of cross-sex behavior. *Journal of Personality and Social Psychology,* 1976, *33* (1), 48-54.

self-monitor along that particular dimension. In contrast, the homosexual who felt positive about his or her sexuality would have little concern for the appropriateness of his or her presentation.

Currently studies are underway at Stanford University, where Sandra Bem, and one of the authors, is administering the *Bem Sex Role Inventory* (BSRI) to selected samples of gay/homosexual males. This paper and pencil measurement designed by Sandra Bem (1974) distinguishes between sex-typed and androgynous individuals. In addition, the study is administering the Snyder Self-Monitoring Scale, a questionnaire which measures individual differences in self-expressive behavior.

Therefore, according to the normative and heterosexist point of view, a bi-polar conceptualization of the social sex-roles, male-male *sexual* behavior and male homosexuals are viewed as typically un-masculine. For example, the statement "only women sleep with men" subscribes to the normative and heterosexist point of view, as well as the bi-polar view of the social sex roles. Homophobia thus appears to be extremely functional in the maintenance of the traditional male role. The fear of being labeled homosexual serves to keep men within the confines of what the culture defines as sex-appropriate behavior. It interferes with the development of intimacy between all men. Consequently, it also limits options and deprives men of the potentially rewarding experiences of learning from and being close to one another.

MEASURING HOMOPHOBIA

While homophobia is a relatively new area of study, there have been some attempts to measure and analyze it. Important personality correlates have been revealed, but the studies have generally relied upon unidimensional assessment techniques that are not standardized, are lacking in psychometric data, and/or are not sensitive to sexual orientation.

Perhaps the first empirical study of homophobia was conducted by Smith (1971), who suggested that homophobic individuals may be status conscious, authoritarian and sexually rigid. Another attempt to measure homophobia used a Likert scale; Dunbar, Brown and Amoroso (1973) found moderate correlations between homophobia and (a) negative attitudes toward a variety of hetero*sexual* practices, (b) guilt about an individual's own sexual impulses, (c) a constricted view of male-appropriate behaviors, and (d) a willingness to perceive as homosexual any male exhibiting "feminine" characteristics (as defined by the subject). General cross-cultural similarities in these attitudes have also been demonstrated.[18]

[18]Brown, M., and Amoroso, D. M. Attitudes toward homosexuality among West Indian male and female college students. *Journal of Social Psychology*, 1975, *97* (2), 163-168.

A major criticism of the aforementioned homophobia measurements is that they fail to consider the multidimensionality of homophobia. There are varying degrees as well as varying attitudes and types of homophobia, determined by sexual preference. For example, the predominantly heterosexual (college-age) male will have internalized and not challenged many of his attitudes toward homosexuals and homosexuality, while the predominantly homosexual male will probably have challenged many of the negative attitudes based upon myths and stereotypes.

Two studies have considered this. In the most current study, one of the authors is developing an instrument which will provide a distinction between positive and negative identities in homosexual males. The *Nungesser Homosexual Attitudes Inventory* (NHAI) has three independent scales and serves as a measure of positive attitudes toward the fact of one's own homosexuality, toward homosexuality and other male homosexuals, and toward the knowledge of one's homosexuality. The NHAI contains a list of 34 attitudinal statements selected from an 84-item pool, which will be administered to samples of gay/homosexual males. Individual items reflect concerns such as feelings of fear or discomfort with one's own sexual impulses and fear or worry about disclosure of one's own sex-role violation. Other items relate to the legal rights of homosexuals. Items are rated on a six-point Likert scale from Strongly Disagree (1) to Strongly Agree (7). Another study which considers the multi-dimensionality of homophobia was conducted by Millham, Miguel and Kellogg (1976); they obtained six meaningful factors from analysis of a 38-item pool. They labeled these factors as (1) or (a) Repressive-Dangerous, (2) or (b) Personal Anxiety, (3) or (c) Preference for Female or Male Homosexuals, (4) or (d) Cross-sexed Mannerisms, (5) or (e) Moral Reprobation, and (6) or (f) Preference for Male over Female Homosexuals. The subjects were 795 male and female heterosexual undergraduates enrolled in the introductory psychology classes at the University of Houston. Homosexuals were requested to eliminate themselves discreetly by recording meaningless identification codes on the answer sheet. A major finding of this study was that having a male or a female homosexual friend or relative resulted in significantly lower personal anxiety, less advocation of repression, and lower moral reprobation scores in describing both male and female homosexual targets. Both of these studies represent the multi-dimensionality of male homophobia, and they provide some insight into the curability of homophobia.

SYMPTOMS AND CURES

The more popular measurement studies mentioned in the preceding section have operationally defined homophobia as beliefs and attitudes. Homophobia, however, has been symptomatically demonstrated through social distancing experiments,[19] and it is emotionally manifested as a fear response to male-male intimacy. Other symptoms range from feelings of guilt, worthlessness and failure to sex-role rigidity. The range of degrees and kinds of homophobic symptoms contributes to the difficulty in measuring it.

Our methods of curing homophobia must consider the unique interaction between the symptoms of homophobia and its causes. For example, changing a homophobic behavior such as placing a physical distance between an individual and a male homosexual may result in changing the negative attitude by resolving cognitive dissonance through systematic desensitization. In this way, treating the symptom may lead directly to changing the attitude and possibly curing the cause. This interaction between symptoms and cause is the interaction between behavior and attitude; this results in a change of attitude and/or a cure of the cause of homophobia.

There is a great deal of controversy over the extent to which attitudes toward homosexuality can be changed. It has been suggested that many middle class heterosexual (college-age) males have not adopted firm attitudinal decisions about alternative lifestyles.[20] It would appear that for the vast majority of people, beliefs about homosexuals are simply an unchallenged part of their socialization experiences. However, this is a complex issue related to the variety and intensity of the motivations supporting homophobic beliefs.[21]

Few people have systematically tried to change other people's attitudes toward homosexuality, but in those few cases where it has been attempted, change has been surprisingly rapid and rather extensive. Morin (1974) reported dramatic changes in attitudes resulting from a single course on homosexuality offered to graduate and undergraduate students in psychology.[22] Consistent with Weinberg's (1972) predictions, improvements in attitudes toward homosexuality showed a significant positive correlation with independent measures of the student's own self-esteem. Subsequent research has indicated that exposure to as little as one article can significantly change a person's reported attitudes toward homosexuality in either a positive or a negative direction, depending on the content of the article. The relative ease with which homophobic attitudes can be altered has come as a surprise; however, it is important to note that these are changes of surface attitudes and have not been subjected to tests of behavioral validation.

Sex education in the United States does not seem to have eased the

[19]Morin and Garfinkle. Male homophobia.

[20]Lumby, M. E. Homophobia: The quest for a valid scale. *Journal of Homosexuality, 2* (1), 39-47.

[21]Morin and Garfinkle. Male homophobia.

public's prejudiced attitudes toward homosexuals. Of the respondents in the Levitt and Klasses (1974) sample who had received sex education (27 percent), only 40 percent had homosexuality even mentioned in that training. Of that 40 percent, two thirds were told that homosexuality was always wrong, and only 1.5 percent were told that it was not wrong at all. If sex education is to have any impact on attitudes toward homosexuals, it would appear that significant changes will have to be made both in the curriculum and in the attitudes of the sex educators.

One type of behavioral change in attitudes toward homosexuality has been noted by the present authors in training psychotherapists to work with gay clients. Part of the training process has involved providing experiences in which individual therapists may begin to challenge their own homphobic attitudes. For example, when all the male therapists went on an excursion to several gay bars, many men reported significant changes in their perception and attitudes. Typical observations were "I felt like such an outsider, there were so many of them and so few of us," "I initially felt uncomfortable watching two men dance . . . but later, after a few drinks, it didn't upset me at all," and "During the night, I moved from feeling like a voyeur to feeling like a participant."

Many of the men had to deal with being asked to dance. Most said yes, but some said no. For most, it was a major decision. Few men reported receiving sexual advances, and many expressed disappointment and surprise that they were ignored. Some expressed the recognition that being looked at as a sex object was not a totally pleasant experience. Most reported, with some amazement, an appreciation of what women must experience in heterosexual bars. Many of the women in the training classes have been overwhelmed by the men's lack of insight into women's experiences.

At the end of the evening of bar-going, it was not unusual for the men to embrace when saying goodnight. Almost all reported that this single venture into the gay subculture broke down more of their homophobic attitudes than did all of their reading and discussion on the subject. Similar changes in attitudes have been reported in the experience of men's groups.[23]

Close personal interaction with gay men of similar social status appears to be a crucial experience in altering homophobic attitudes and behavior. Furthermore, people consistently report feeling better about themselves as their homophobic attitudes decrease.

Research on the environmental factors which enhance the development of positive attitudes toward homosexuals and homosexuality is being

[22]Morin, S. F. Educational programs as a means of changing attitudes toward gay people. *Homosexual Counseling Journal,* 1974, *1* (4), 160-165.

[23]Clark, Don. *Loving Someone Gay.* Millbrae, California: Celestial Arts, 1977.

conducted by one of the authors. Nungesser (1978) has developed the *E*nvironmental *F*actors *I*nventory (EFI) in order to examine the relationship between attitudes toward homosexuality in individual gay/homosexual males, and the attitudes toward homosexuals and homosexuality expressed by (1) the individual's current significant other (that is, family, straight friends, gay friends, colleagues) and (2) the individual's previous exposure to attitudes toward homosexuals and homosexuality and sexuality in general, as expressed by influential socialization agents (that is, family, state, church and school).

In addition, gay-oriented mental health professionals provide some helpful methods for changing attitudes toward homosexuals and homosexuality. They often assist their clients in identifying and breaking down their negative stereotypes of gay/homosexual men and gay/homosexual lifestyles, replacing those negative attitudes with a recognition of individual values, and in seeing homosexuality as a sexual preference congruent with many personality characteristics.

Frequently, there are certain behavioral or environmental changes recommended by the therapists. For example, they encourage the development of a social support system, consisting of several gay/homosexual males and lesbian women whom the client respects, and most importantly, whom the client recognizes as valuing homosexuality. Research provides support for this suggestion, as it has been demonstrated that identification with a group whose attitudes are similar to the individual's desired attitude expressions (his actions rather than his potentiality) will lead to the internalization of those attitudes; consequently, the new reference group will provide an affirmational environment for its new member.[24]

In short, one can change attitudes when they are causing conflicts. Many people never question their socialized values and beliefs regarding homosexuality and male homosexuals, however, and thus continue to perpetuate the belief systems upon which homophobia is based. Negative attitudes toward homosexuality and male homosexuals is a pervasive phenomenon. It is a personal concern for millions of gay/homosexual males and lesbian women, and it becomes a political concern for basic human rights and dignity.

There are considerable benefits to be realized from the internalization of positive attitudes and values toward homosexuality and male homosexuals. Research has demonstrated that having positive attitudes and values toward homosexuality will result in a higher self-esteem, a reduction of male dominance in the same sex role, and an increase in male-male intimacy.

The conflict between the male sex role and homosexuality could best

[24]Bem, Daryl. *Beliefs, Attitudes and Human Affairs.* Monterey, California: Brooks/Cole, 1970.

be resolved by rejecting the dimorphic definition of the social sex roles and sexualities. It would appear that as the men's "consciousness-focusing" movement progresses, those who desire more intimate and more rewarding relationships, both with other men and with women, are also going to have to challenge their own male homophobia. The irrational fear of closeness to other men and of the label "homosexual" has been a long-standing dynamic which has kept many men imprisoned in their traditional roles. Acceptance and appreciation of gay/homosexual males within the men's movement is essential because they have a vital part to play in the development of new definitions of the male role.

Research on the Black Male: A Resource for Change

ROBERT STAPLES

Any study of the black male should be global and chronological in character. This means investigating the multidimensional aspects of his life as it evolves from birth to death. By global I also means that, in addition to the socio-psychological factors influencing black male behavior, one should investigate economic and health factors. A logical point at which to start is birth. A little-known and poorly publicized fact is the low sex ratio of births to black women. Although national data on this phenomenon is difficult to come by, local samples indicate the ratio at birth is a low as 60 male births to every 100 female births. Since the male sperm is responsible for the gender of the child, one needs to find out what socio-psychological or epidemiological factors are operative in creating such an unusually low sex ratio in births to black women.

Central to the understanding of the black male sex role is an investigation of the process of socializing black males into their gender identity. The literature is full of assumptions, but little proof, about how black males are reared in their families. A dominant, but unproven, theory is that the content of the male role is not adequately conveyed to them because of absent or weak father figures. Others have contended that black mothers raised their sons to be docile in manner because of the risks to life and limb to which an aggressive black male would be exposed. Another prominent presumption is that black mothers have traditionally favored female children over male children. All these hypotheses should be carefully tested by an examination of socialization processes in the black family and how they shape sex-role identity.

No study of the black male would be complete without an exploration of the period of youth. The problems of this group are enormous and increasingly growing more severe. In a sense, youth have been divorced from what little progress blacks have made as a group. On all social indicators, they are worse than other age or racial cohorts. In the area of education, black youth have the highest drop-out rate of all sex-race groups, the highest mortality rate (with homicide and suicide as leading causes of death), commit the majority of the crimes of violence and have the highest rate of unemployment of any group in the nation. If its problems are not dealt with, this group represents soical dynamite, both for the black community and the society at large. It is also during youth that the concept of maculinity is formed. Important here is the differential influence of mechanisms and agents of socialization: the peer group, the parents, the schools or the mass media.

Within the youth period, ages 16 to 24, attitudes are formed toward futuristic lifestyles and roles. Hence, it is necessary to assess how young black males see themselves, if at all, in the role of husband and/or father. Are these roles subordinated to the more glamorous and mass-media-portrayed ones of the free-wheeling bachelor and superstud? What is the ranking of role priorities among black youth, and what forces in their environment create and encourage it? Further investigation is needed of the self-concept of black youth, their levels of self-esteem, and how it is maintained or eroded by social factors such as educational success or failure, family background, rates of employment, and so forth.

One might consider using the panel approach, interviewing black males of different age groups at the same point in time. While such an approach may generally be inferior to a well-conducted longitudinal study, it can provide data on the differences within and between subgroups of black males. Other factors should be controlled, such as socio-economic status, region, urban-rural environments, and family background. An interview schedule carries more validity in studies of the black population than self-administered questionnaires. This is particularly relevant in light of recent findings that of 23 million ineffective Americans who were deficient in reading skills, the weakest performances were by black males.

Among the other pertinent issues to consider in research on the black male are attitudes toward family planning and concepts of masculinity. For too long, birth control has been regarded as belonging solely in the female domain. Even black females who have been willing to assume that responsibility alone have been discouraged from doing so by their male partners.

Again, a central focus should be on the young black male, since the largest number of unwanted and unplanned births occur to teenage black females. The source and content of sex education of young black males should be examined and their attitudes toward the use of male contraception (condoms and vasectomy) assessed. Within this context it would also be useful to examine their attitudes toward women.

Among adult black males one would explore a number of factors. A large number of black males, for example, remain unmarried to a later age than their white counterparts. One would investigate the lifestyles of these men; why they are single, how they cope with celibacy, whether they are carrying out father-surrogate roles in a single-parent family, and so on. Actually, recent trends indicate that a majority of black males may fall into the category of the "unattached." Hence, we need to know what kind of relationships, if any, they are forming with black women or females from other races. A neglected group is the increasing number of households headed by black males. How do the strictures of race affect their functioning?

Finally, a paramount issue to deal with in studying black men is their mortality rate. While it is obvious that biogenic factors play a large role in black male mortality, it is equally true that a larger percentage of black men are dying prematurely because of environmental forces. This is a matter of serious concern because the fragility of the black male's existence in this country is such that his life-expectancy rate is actually declining while that of other sex-race groups is on the increase. To assess the etiology of black male mortality, one needs to look at his overall lifestyle, to pay attention to his concentration in hazardous occupations, to examine income factors, availability of health care, education, diet, personal hygiene and related considerations.

However, the major causes of death among black males (homicide, suicide, hypertension, heart disease) are related to socio-psychological factors. Since the death rate among black females is considerably lower, we need to consider stress situations peculiarly related to black masculinity and its expression or lack of expression in American life. Along with the low sex ratio of black births, the high mortality rate of black males serves to create a male shortage in the black community that will cause a number of problems in that group. Among these difficulties will be the mere lack of opportunity for many black women to form a monogamous family, the kinds of tension and conflict produced by the intense competition for the available males, and the ego expansion among the black males who find themselves in short supply.

These are among some of the major issues to be considered in any study of black males. It is, by no means, an exhaustive list. Other issues not mentioned here are the liaisons between black men and white women, how the inclusion of women in Affirmative Action programs and the use of black women as a double minority affects the black male's occupation mobility, how the Women's Liberation Movement ideology has affected black women in their relationship with black men, whether the changing definitions of masculinity (the unisex phenomena) has made any impact on black men, and so on. With the shortage of reliable research on black men, there is a vast void to be filled by study of this neglected topic.

part six

THE NEW MAN: INNOVATIVE PATTERNS

This wire must go here

If we both lift together

Dad, I didn't know work can be fun

THE NEW MAN: INNOVATIVE PATTERNS

You've got the hang of it now

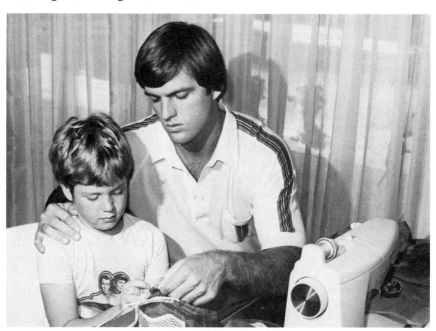

Some of the resources for change discussed in the previous section have already produced new kinds of men and some innovative patterns of masculintiy. This closing section of the book illustrates some of the new types of men which are appearing, particularly in the United States and Western Europe, as a positive response to Women's Liberation and to the destructiveness of sexist attitudes in society at large.

Daloz in the first article "Shared Parenting" describes how he quit his full-time job, to the disbelief of many friends, and with his wife shares part-time work roles so that both of them have more time to share the parenting of their first child. Although he many deny it, Daloz is a role model of a new type of nurturing male who finds that caring for a new child can be a very fulfilling experience in life, even though it may be difficult to fit earning and nurturing into a busy life.

Vittitow describes some innovative styles of masculinity which are displayed by men who are reexamining for themselves the strangling hold of the "myth of manhood" by demanding less perfection in themselves and others, exploring and experiencing a spectrum of feelings, and learning to enhance their growth and intimacy with themselves. According to Vittitow, it is through experiencing our own *aloneness* that men can be opened up to deeper relationships and stronger human bonds. Another kind of new man, therefore, is a man who through exploring his aloneness experiences a lasting "intimacy with himself."

Overton also is optimistic in believing that some men can create situations where self and others can be freed from the restrictions of traditional male roles. Overton relates his own rich experiences with men at his work setting (a mental hospital), in his own therapy group, in consciousness-raising workshops which he has led, and in a commune. He concludes that the greatest changes in men occur where men are willing to risk changes in themselves, as are, for example, the mentally ill, who give their need to be in control, and where men, such as those in groups, risk caring for others, showing affection and expressing grief.

Lastly, Bell suggests that new male roles will continue to form, since the means for real change lie in societal and economic changes which have already come about. According to Bell, we have experienced historically the transition from an industrial society to a late industrial or postindustrial society, where social roles are less tied to one's sex. Men are overcoming much that is negative in the traditional model of patriarchy, not, however, without role strains and psychological tension. In line with this analysis, then, male dominance and sexism are current "historical lags." In summary, less destructive roles for men lie in societal changes which have already occurred.

This book ends, therefore, on the optimistic note that the discovery and dissemination of new knowledge and the greater allowance for individual fulfillment currently enable women to seek more instrumental pursuits and men more expressive ones. Whether a man is awakened to the need for change in his own life and is willing to seek unfamiliar but humanitarian goals will, however, be ultimately determined by each man and his willingness to bear the costs of egalitarian relationships.

Shared Parenting:
The Male Perspective

LARRY DALOZ

I am not sure when the idea first struck me. I know that Judy and I had dreamed for several years of sharing part-time work to allow us each more time for other interests. When it turned out that we were to have a child, it became apparent that those interests would include shared parenting as well. The reasoning was logical enough: When one of us worked, the other would care for our child, and vice-versa. At first anyway, shared parenting seemed a natural consequence of shared work. In fact, I think it is the other way around.

For any reasonably sensitive man who has read and been moved by feminist literature in recent years, the idea of sharing the raising of a child has great romance about it. It does not take much to see how our own options in life have been restricted by sexual stereotypes just as surely, if not as brutally, as those of our sisters. In trying to unlearn some of the lessons we have been taught—I remember my own father announcing that babies are smelly, dirty and most appropriately born at the age of seven— we are drawn to the idea of taking major responsibility for the nurturing of our children.

Shared parenthood poses different problems for men than for women. For a woman, difficulties often lie in adjusting to the world of work.

Unless her upbringing was out of the ordinary, she was conditioned to think of herself as a mother some day. Men, on the other hand, assume that they will become the breadwinners; their adjustment must come in learning to share the responsibility for the direct care of their children.

While there is a growing number of models of women who work outside the home, there are precious few examples of nurturing men. The prevailing male model, that of a productive, assertive, disciplinarian father who may guide, but rarely nurture his children, is deeply ingrained. The two do not go well together, and much of the old must be eliminated to make way for the new.

When I first began to let the world know that I would be quitting my full-time job, everyone's first question was, of course, "What are you going to *do*?" For a long time, my only response was silence. It was not that I did not know *why* I was quitting. That part was easy. I felt I had accomplished what I had set out to do and now wanted to explore some new areas for growth and meet some fresh challenges. Although there were many things I wanted to do, none carried the same sense of complete absorption that I had felt with my former job. Eventually I replied that I planned to do a little consulting, some writing and perhaps a bit of physical labor.

In time I began to realize that I had been answering the wrong question. What I kept hearing was "How are you going to earn money?" After all, that is the question I had been asked from the time I was old enough to talk. I had learned my lesson well: Good fathers bring home lots of bacon for the wife and kids. That is the primary responsibility of a man just as surely as changing diapers is the primary responsibility for a woman. Yet what I really wanted to do was take care of my daughter, Kate. Rarely did that answer come out first.

To my surprise, when I finally began trying out the real answer on people, the response was generally positive: "Oh really? How nice." This would be followed by a brief sermon about the importance of changing sex stereotypes, punctuated by a resounding, "How courageous!" I glowed. I even felt courageous. Noble. Virtuous. Sacrificing. Sacrificing? I should have known then and there that something was fishy.

I think I began to realize that something was really going to happen when Judy and I found ourselves sorting through a pile of hand-me-down baby clothes one afternoon. Miniature sweaters, weeny undershirts, minute socks, tiny mittens—each thundered its message against my determined righteousness. Yet deep down there must have been a response, a dawning awareness that something more substantial than ideas about changing sex stereotypes would be in order during the coming months, something more sustaining than nobility, more realistic than sacrifice.

During the final weeks of Judy's pregnancy, the warnings, admonitions and advice rained upon us in a growing storm.

"Your life will never be the same again!"

"Enjoy your last full night of sleep."

"Go out together for an evening; you'll never have another chance."

"Prepare, prepare, prepare for the First Coming!"

What can you do with all this? What can you do but try to nod and duck your head at the same time?

Since Judy and I had decided to have our baby by "prepared childbirth," we had read a number of books about it. The trouble was that many of those books seemed to assume that the birth itself is all there is to it—the climax of all that waiting and hoping and planning and preparing. Not so. The birth is *only* the beginning. At most, it lasts a few days. Babies last for years. Sometimes, we romantics forget that. I did. So I felt a good deal of frustration in the final days because even though I was going to be present during the Great Moment, I knew, deep down, that it was not my show. I am sure that is one of the reasons fathers have kept out of the mothering business for as long as they have. No matter how much we try to get involved with the birth by discussing at length the pro's and con's of an episiotomy, breast feeding, or dorsal delivery positions, the show still belongs to Mom. The fundamental relationship is mother and child, and it will remain that way for some time after the performance. The father's role is to support that pair. But he cannot make it a trio.

So I spent a good deal of time shouting my frustrations at absent doctors. It helped me a lot. I am not so sure about Judy.

Then Kate arrived. As I held her for the first time, and felt the earthshaking ticking of this tiny, delicate, miraculous mechanism against my stomach, I discovered something. I did not need to invade the intimacy of Judy and Kate. That was their thing. Kate and I had our own thing.

Kate's presence spoke to a whole new part of me. I knew what it was like to be a boy. I had been one for a while and part of me still was. But a girl! That was quite new. That was why I had left my job. It was a strange but compelling feeling, for I knew that part of my new search was for the female in myself. Kate could be my guide. I could learn a lot from her. Then I remembered that all along I had felt she would be a girl. "Men's intuition," I had quipped at the time. I was still a romantic.

It always annoys me to hear people say, "You can't know it until you have experienced it." Yet there is no way on earth I could have known what it would be like to hold Kate in my arms and feel her smile radiate every bone in my body. Nor could I have anticipated the frustration of trying to sit down to write during Kate's nap only to be derailed again and again by her waking cries.[1]

For me, the moral of the story is that you cannot expect to live the

---

[1]Supposedly, someone once asked Gloria Steinem whether she would be able to have a child and keep up with her writing. Her answer was quick: She would just write while Baby slept. You're a better man than I am, Gloria.

same life with a child that you lived before. You cannot expect to remain the same productive, aggressive, goal-directed male. Not if you want to learn what your Kate has to teach you. The truth is, there are better things to do with your time. Like cuddle her. And change her. And play hide-the-ball. And nourish her.

So I am left with a few questions that any noble, sacrificing, prospective father would be wise to ask before he jumps. I have not answered them all, but I like to think I am working on them.

Are You Ready?

Beware the quick answer. The current research on adult development warns that young males in their twenties have a good deal on their minds besides caring for children. Now is the time to gather experiences, to make their way into the world where productivity—where outwardness, not inwardness—is rewarded. Those well-learned lessons about finding a job and making money are not easily shunted aside, and they do not go well with the demands of childrearing. You cannot get into this business by believing that you are "giving up" something or that it will demand a "sacrifice." That can only end in resentment.

Can You Shift Roles?

Do you enjoy homemaking so that after feeding and changing baby all day you can also cook supper when your wife comes home from work? There's more to the shift than just cooking. If you plan to share the full responsibility, it also means planning and buying food for the family. It means developing a whole new consciousness about *nurturing* the family and caring for them. There is more to it than having your wife tell you which button to push on the radar range.

Can You Get into Being Instead of Doing?

Although I have been somewhat surprised and relieved to discover that I am not ridiculed for "giving up a career" to care for Kate, the question is always there in people's faces. "Doesn't he work for a living?" "His wife supports him?" "Oh."

Perhaps more difficult is the lack of genuine, understanding support from others. Few understand in the bone-deep way one learns from direct experience what it means to care for a child all day. They may admire, but they do not understand. Admiration is cold comfort when you have just discovered the light of your life has been sitting on a mess through lunch that has soaked its way down to her left shoe . . . and you are out of clean pants . . . and she kicks over the water bowl while you are trying to change her. All with a beatific smile. For most men, caring for a child is like the Amazon: a great place to visit but only women ought to live there.

I have only felt genuine support once when a friend called from his office. I had been bouncing off the walls that day with Kate. "At least you are doing something worthwhile," he said. "I've been sitting at this desk all day and feel I've accomplished nothing." Rare words.

The fact is, caring for a child can be enormously fulfilling. We men must learn to recognize it as an end in itself, as having its own value. The hardest thing for most of us is not learning how to change diapers or mix a formula or comfort a crying baby. That is technical stuff. The hardest thing is unlearning all those lessons of our past about doing "important" things in the world like bringing home the paycheck. This is not to say paychecks are unnecessary—only that they have their place. Perhaps what has to happen is that men must learn that there is a time to be and a time to do, a time to nurture and a time to earn. Whether you choose to spend a few years out in the world and then turn inward, or the reverse, depends on your own style and the circumstances of your life. Trying to mix the two at once is tough. Believe me.

With You I Begin

With you I begin
to find my body again.
Senses come slowly alive
sphincters soften
turtle head rises
inch by inch
out of shell.
I remember the most basic pattern—
sense the warm pulse,
move closer
beat by beat.

Pray for safety
for open arms.
Test every step twice,
remember the possibility
so often impossible,
reach shaky fingertips
out into the blackness,
wanting you to be real,
wanting to trust the touch of you,
finding finally
fingers that are not mine
also reaching
also afraid
also beginning to believe
again.

DAVID STEINBERG

Changing Men and Their Movement Toward Intimacy

DICK VITTITOW

Manhood is a myth and like many myths, involves men in an unending quest. Manhood represents a task for men from which they can seldom gain a genuine sense of fulfillment despite all their efforts, toil and momentary accomplishments. Men, as often defined, are seldom men.

The myth comes about in the way we create our "ideal man." This mythical man in the American culture is thought of as a man who is capable of overcoming his human frailties, especially his emotions, which he must continually deny. The promise is that by conquering his own nature, mythical man frees himself of the laws that bind and limit others. Mythical man possesses only strengths.

It is not clear why our demands for men are so harsh. Perhaps Lewis Mumford in his work *The Pentagon of Power* provides a clue. He describes how historically and culturally men have been dissatisfied with their own limitations and have searched for models outside themselves. The machine has precision, strength, dependability, efficiency and numerous other traits that we humans so often lack. We depict the ideal man as being cool,

A special thanks to Marie Wells for her helpful editing comments.

controlled, durable, firm, functional, reliable, productive, progressive—a man with machine-like characteristics.

In the 1960's Robert S. McNamara was often described as a man with such qualities. As Secretary of Defense he seemed to epitomize all the values that we felt a real man should possess. He was efficient, crisp, firm, concise, brusque and impatient with ineptness. He was never emotional, nor personally needy. He got up early and went to bed late. He worked hard and, when time permitted, he played hard. With an overwhelming grasp of statistics, he could persuade President, Senators, and the American public what it required in tons, pounds and units of manpower and materials to win a war, and how long it would take.

We did not know, and perhaps did not care to know, Robert McNamara as a man with limitations, frustrations, hurts and fears. We did not know, nor care to explore, at what price such a man becomes so commanding and so efficient. Now we kow that he was wrong about Vietnam. Now we know he was incapable of understanding the human factor—the ability of the North Vietnamese not to be overwhelmed by statistics.

No individual man, not even Robert McNamara, can ever become the "ideal man" he constructs for himself. Yet many men drive themselves to emotional and physical sickness in trying to become the mythical man, continually dissatisfied with who they are, always wanting more—more money, more power, and more recognition.

They are in a double-bind: They are not satisfied with their successes and they are acutely aware of their failures. Failure debilitates and depresses. Failure is the greatest taboo in the quest for manhood. President Nixon serves as another example of a man who failed. For him his failure came not in what he did, but in being discovered.

Failure, though, is not the greatest loss that a man incurs in his pursuit of manhood. The greatest loss comes from never knowing, or seldom experiencing, his real self. In trying to meet the demands of a role, a man gives up his connection with his unique self and thereby neglects the growth and nourishment of the person he really is.

Women have known for a long time how painful it is to live in a culture that considers them inferior because they are not men. Paradoxically, men too are continually belittled and belittle themselves because they do not measure up to the standards of ideal manhood. It does not matter that the demands are unrealistic; men still experience themselves as falling short.

Boys are exposed to this process of measuring up quite early. The measurement for being a boy is not based on being a person, but on how well the boy is learning to become a man. If, in his growth, his play and his interests, a boy gives evidence that he is learning what it means to be a man, then he is judged as doing well. He is rewarded and admired for having the "manly qualities": being strong in body and mind, silent when in pain, rational and pragmatic, not too ethical or moral, open to taking orders and advice from his elders, appreciative of authority and possessing a demonstrated ability to wait for his rewards.

Fun, play, and fantasy are tucked away forever at the ages of 13 and 14, and as boys' voices change they begin to assume their preordained roles as men. They put aside the boy things of tag, cowboy, and occasional abandon. In their place they take on the role of manhood which for some mean alcohol, fast cars, and a growing sense of anomie. They give up boyhood for a role. In so doing at this traumatic time, they also give up life and a connection with themselves they will never have or enjoy again.

Many men feel betrayed because, as boys, they were misled into believing the Myth of Manhood. Many feel a strong sense of anger at their own culpability for accepting the myth and giving up so much for so little. Their anger at present is helping them break through the web of the myth.

The process of giving up the myth is not easy, and it generally involves considerable pain and uncertainty. Without the myth, men are faced with the insecurity of not knowing how to evaluate themselves and their actions. Career, power, affluence—which they accepted as so important and spent so much of their life energies working for—now seem neither as important, nor as contributory to growth and development. Changing men are now investing their energies into finding out what living is about and developing ways of guiding and contributing to their own growth and development as the unique persons they are.

THE COMMANDMENTS OF MANHOOD

The Myth of Manhood is based on a set of commandments that men learn to follow. These commandments are as harsh and as limiting as anything Moses brought down from the mountain. While not written on a tablet, and seldom conscious, they are nonetheless engraved on the spirit of American men. Some of the most evident commandments of manhood are

1. Thou shalt not be weak, nor have weak god before thee.

2. Thou shalt not fail thyself, nor "fail" as thy father before thee.

3. Thou shalt not keep holy any day that denies thy work.

4. Thou shalt not love in ways that are intimate and sharing.

5. Thou shalt not cry, complain or feel lonely.

6. Thou shalt not commit public anger.

7. Thou shalt not be uncertain or ambivalent.

8. Thou shalt not be dependent.

9. Thou shalt not acknowledge thy death or thy limitations.

10. Thou *shalt* do unto other men before they do unto you.[1]

Commandments, once we have them, are terribly difficult to get rid of. Even though Moses threw his tablets to the ground and broke them in his anger, somehow they got back together. As we have since learned, even if we do not obey the commandments, or profess to believe in them, they still have a way of hanging around as a continuing criteria by which to judge our conduct and our actions.

Yet, some men, despite the difficulties, are overcoming the demands of their internal commandments of manhood. In anger, they are rejecting their set of commandments and are refusing any code of manhood that comes from outside themselves.

In destroying the traditional commandments, these men are doing what it is said men do not do. They are learning to cry. They are expressing their anger openly and directly. They are exploring their own feelings, ideas, and sexuality; they are beginning to relate differently with women and are beginning to find themselves less threatened by homosexuality, whether their own or that of others. They are demanding less perfection of themselves and others. They are learning to search out ways to satisfy their personal needs and to enhance their growth.

Movement toward Intimacy

The changing man is moving toward increased intimacy by a continuing progression of seeing, exploring and experiencing. He is seeing by *acknowledging* his situation, acknowledging the Myth of Manhood and the investment he has had in it. In the second stage, he is *exploring*, increasing his awareness of how living and acting on this myth and its commandments affects his life. And in the third, he is *experiencing* an intimacy with himself, encountering who he really is. As this intimacy with self increases, so does his capacity to genuinely and intimately experience others.

I believe that the main obstacle to intimacy with ourselves, or with others, is our fear of coming to know our own aloneness. Rather than experience our aloneness in the world, and therefore, fully experiencing

---

[1] I wrote the first draft of this paper in 1974. It is meaningful that Warren Farrell in *The Liberated Man* (Bantam, 1975) also developed the "Ten Commandments of Masculinity." It reinforces this notion men feel of having internal roles which dictate their behavior.

our own living and dying, men elect to accept the Myth of Manhood. If we accept the idealized, machine-like man, we may not have to deal with our own mortality, except, perhaps, in dreams.

My own first in-depth experience with my aloneness came in a personal growth workshop conducted by John and Joyce Weir for the National Training Laboratories. We were in the fifth or sixth day of a ten-day workshop, and our group was involved in an experience of dancing, each person moving spontaneously around the room. I forget now the specifics of the assignment, but as I danced I began to get in touch with a sense of loneliness that I had never experienced before. It involved experiencing my own uniqueness and my separateness from others. It was more a sense of aloneness than loneliness.

A deep sense of pity for myself and my aloneness began to emerge within me. I was not lamenting my shortcomings or feeling sorry for myself because of what others had or had not done for me. Nor was I feeling regret for what I did not have. Rather, it was a pity for the sense of aloneness about me that only I could know. Like a flower that may have bloomed in the desert unnoticed and unexperienced, I felt there was no way of my ever communicating my real existence.

There was a core self which only I could know, which only I could truly experience, and for which only I could pity. I felt nurturing and caring toward that core self, and that was the nature of my pity.

At first I denied my feelings of pity, saying to myself that they were inappropriate. One should not feel pity for oneself. That is narcissistic and selfish. Then I recognized that such a prohibition was a commandment. I gave into my pity, my caring, and I experienced me. I went over to the side of the room and wept for myself. I wept very deeply and strongly.

After my crying, I still was working with my feelings of aloneness. I thought unexpectedly about the shark. The shark is biologically designed so that he breathes through forward, continuous movement in the water. If he stops, or is stopped, he dies. From birth until death the shark must always move forward. It seemed to me that in my life and in my aloneness I was experiencing many of the dilemmas and restrictions of a shark.

While I was dancing, I too had felt the need to move forward. I was not sure why, I just knew that I had to. That has been true throughout my life. Many times, I have reached certain levels of thought and awareness and have felt that I knew enough, that I wanted to rest. I remember, as a child, thinking how great it would be to be an adult. When I got to be 30 or so, I would know what the world was about and what my place was in it. I would no longer have to struggle and worry about all the petty things that children involve themselves with. Now I know one never reaches the end of growth and learning. I become weary, but, like the shark, I have to move forward.

I feel that my experience with loneliness and the analogy of the shark is similar to experiences that many changing men are having in their movement toward intimacy. The changing man does not really have a choice; he must move toward intimacy. The changing man does not really have a choice; he must move toward intimate contact with himself and his own development. Once a man has made the decision to move into himself, he can no longer return to the past. He cannot stay with the Myth of Manhood and its commandments. Like the shark, which suffocates if pulled backward, the changing man cannot return to the safety of past myths. He must risk the movement forward, not always knowing where he is going, only knowing he must move onward.

The fear that we must live with and experience is our aloneness and our death. Yet, ironically, it is in living with our aloneness and our death that we experience life. Clark Moustakas describes this process and its effects for him:

The sudden recognition and depth of my own loneliness was a revelation which changed the nature of my life. . . . I learned that I could thrive in lonely silence. This recognition and meaningful awareness of myself as an utterly lonely person opened the way to deeper human bonds and associations and to a fuller valuing of all aspects of life and nature. I realized that man's inevitable and infinite loneliness is not solely an awful condition of human existence but that it is also the instrument through which man experiences new compassion and new beauty. It is this terror in loneliness which evokes new senses and makes possible the experiencing of deep companionship and radiant beauty. [2]

A More Intimate Relationship with the World

An increasing number of creative and innovative men are involved in the movement toward intimacy. Whether they represent a cutting edge movement for the man of the future, or whether they are the last of an emerging and dying breed, is not altogether clear. They are, however, clearly in conflict with the present order.

Often, as I see how destructive and incompetent our present leaders are, and how thoroughly they and our culture are committed to the Myth of Manhood, I feel discouraged and pessimistic. Our leaders of government and enterprise, who most need the skills and abilities to innovate, adopt and change are the people most committed to the status quo and the myth.

We can influence and support changing men in a number of ways. As individuals, we can examine the ways we each have bought into and promote the Myth of Manhood. We can allow changing men the space to

[2]Clark E. Moustakas, *Loneliness* (Englewood Cliffs, N.J.: Prentice-Hall, 1961).

experiment with new behavior, to make mistakes, to regress and to express themselves and their emotions.

As fathers and mothers we can understand more clearly how we have instilled the Myth in our children. As families we can examine how we have expected our fathers and husbands to obey the commandments and to perform as heroes in the Myth. As persons working in organizations, we can understand and identify how our entire economic system has been built upon the furtherance and maintenance of the Myth of Manhood.

As citizens we can change the kinds of demands we are presently making on our leaders. We demand that our leaders, as persons, give up too much. We ask them to give up their families in the interest of their work; we ask them to give up their emotions in the name of strength; we ask them to deny their own personhood in the interest of portraying an image that we want to see. As citizens, we need to understand that our expectations can be met only by the most closed of personalities, mythical men who can withstand and accept the demands and pressures of present public life.

Women need to continue their support in a number of ways. They have paved the way toward liberation. In the past, women looked to men for models; now it is men looking toward women. This is a new direction, and requires a different relationship. Women, in their urgent quest for liberation, can be helpful by differentiating between those men who are changing and those who are locked into the masculinist shackles: Some men will need encouragement, others need to be denied.

Older men, who themselves have worked through the Myth of Manhood to their independence, can also support younger men. They can serve as models and encourage younger men to risk new and different behavior. Publicly and privately, they can use their influence to make it legitimate for each man to respond to his own nature.

Men can be supportive to one another by making themselves available to listen to other men and to share with them as intimately as possible what is taking place in their own lives. Men have had little experience in this process of sharing and need to develop support systems which allow them to develop the necessary skills and abilities.

Perhaps the single most important thing each of us can do is elect to spend more time and energy with our aloneness, trying to see, to explore and to experience our own selves in more full and complete ways.

Ballad for the Isolated Man

You say you're disillusioned and you don't know how to live,
You say you've given all you can and you've nothing left to give,
Your energy lies liquified in a bottle on the shelf,
And you look around the room and you cannot find yourself,

You cannot find yourself.

You say you've tried the singles' bar and you've been to the Friday dance,
You walked around in circles and everyone was in a trance,
No one seemed to understand, no one seemed to care,
And you wonder what's the reason for the fact that you were there,

For the fact that you were there.

You say you've had your women, you say you've tried men too,
and now you're left with no one and you don't know what you'll do,
You've taken out the telephone, stopped answering the door,
The walls are moving in but you've known it all before,

You've known it all before.

You disconnect your body and you live life in your mind,
You've cut off all your feelings and your heart's so hard to find,
You want someone to love you, to meet your every need,
Well, first you need to love yourself if ever you'll succeed,

If ever you'll succeed.

The Men
in My Life

THOMAS OVERTON

I am going to share with you the men I know and how they respond to their difficult times. Because I am the man I know best, I expect this paper will be a compilation of personal observations from my own experience. I want to share what seems true to me with the hope that my experiences will touch part of yours.

My experience is mostly of Middle America. My social and economic status has always been middle, and my values for most of my life were "middle-of-the-road." My family always seemed fairly average to me; we fit into the community. I escaped all but the usual childhood traumata; I was married and finished with college before I realized life ever *could* be any different than what I had been experiencing. Then, one fine morning as I was job hunting, I realized I had absolutely no idea what I wanted from life. I went a little haywire after that. I spent the next few years systematically rejecting everything that seemed tinged with anyone else's seal of approval. I took a low-paying job in a VD clinic that did not require my college degree. I successfully practiced to change my Southern accent. I divorced my wife and told my parents how awful they were. I quit my job—I had advanced to supervisor and that was *too* All-American for me. I gave away my stereo and sold my car—too many material things. And I joined a local commune. In my reactive flurry I also espoused every anti-Middle American philosophy I ran into. This is how I first arrived on the women's and men's liberation scene, as an armchair radical philosopher. In the two years that have passed since that kind of insane revolution, I have assimilated some of my Middle American self, toned down my philosophical ravings, and begun to be personally involved in liberating myself while supporting liberation for other men.

There are four groups of men important to me now. The first I will discuss are the men I experience through counseling. These are men under psychiatric treatment in a private hospital where I am a counselor. Second, I will tell you about men with whom I share my own therapy in a group run by pastoral counselors. Third, I will share some of my experience with men in consciousness-raising groups and weekend encounters I have led. Finally, I will be telling you about the men I live with communally. Part of what I hope to share in some measure about these men is (a) how they respond to changing attitudes about work, competition, and success; (b) how they respond to women and women's rights; (c) how they relate to other men; and (d) how they are emotionally literate.

Counseling

The most difficult group, by far, for me to deal with is the group of men hospitalized for psychiatric treatment, for they are the most tied to traditional values. Since one of these values is that men take care of their own problems, especially emotional ones, the number of men in this voluntary and private setting is small. Two characteristics of these men and most "patients" in this setting are that they have become very outwardly emotional and, therefore, a worry to others, and secondly, that they are dependent and externally controlled. Men are supposed to be neither outwardly emotional or outwardly controlled, so to be both is something few men, I believe, will allow themselves. The interesting fact is the more their control seems necessary to them, the more likely men are to end up on a ward like ours. Most of the men I have worked with here are those who have temporarily "lost control" and "had to" come into the hospital.

One man I have counseled beautifully exhibits some of the most self-destructive symptoms I find in my psychiatric patients. He is a 50-year-old to whom work is everything. He claims to have been spending up to 20 hours a day working, before his fuses blew; and he could no longer deal with the world except destructively. His relationship with his wife is one of considerable tension, in which he thinks he should be the one who has "hold of himself" so that she can be as emotional as she likes. He has no hobbies and no interests except work. At work he even has to control himself to keep from being upset with his boss over "little things" which he denies are important but from which he feels the burden of suppressed anger. So he looks out over his life each day and takes stock of how well he has control. This is his only measure of manliness, and it is all-pervasive. One day, he loses his "cool" and begins raving and breaking things. I see him about four days into his hospitalization. From the sound of his deep, well-modulated welcome and slight smile, I know already the story I am going to get. "Yes, I'm fine, back in control now, just needed a bit of rest and relaxation." I am warm and friendly in return, and I let him know that from what he is saying about his blow-up, he let anger build up under a facade of control until he had to explode. "Well, yes of course," he is saying, but he is not really listening. He isn't ready yet. He has himself under control again and feels good. He wants to be out of the hospital and back to work.

I am firmly convinced that most people who come for psychiatric treatment will do nearly anything in therapy except give up their symptoms. Change comes very slowly and necessitates a lot of convincing, demonstration, or discovery that "what I do causes me to feel so bad." The average man I see, though, is only interested in regaining control and believing he can keep better control next time under stress. Then he can go home and perhaps get ulcers, a much less worrisome condition than "mental illness." This is OK for many of the (always male) psychiatrists, too, for they are just as invested in helping men to keep cool, calm and in control.

So what is there to do? I admit my personal frustration over dealing with these men; many times I want to shake them to their senses (*my* senses, actually). Most of the time I give them their right to be as rigid as they want, in an effort not to be so rigid myself. Along with acceptance, I include using myself as a model and, therefore, a powerful way of inducing change. With a man who obviously does not want to change, I show him myself. I disclose personal information without getting him to be my therapist. I tell him about how I play when I am not working or studying. I show him a somewhat less serious attitude toward "career" than perhaps he has encountered. Around the counseling unit, I show him the respect I feel for the women who are patients there, voicing humorous but firm protests against sexism I see him or other people engaging in.

Group Therapy

Another way a man can deal with difficulty is to go to counseling outside a hospital, not when he is at the point of no choice, but when he wants to take responsibility to work on himself. I put myself in this category. When I first went for personal counseling a year ago, I remember being extremely nervous and self-doubting. I was writing in a note pad as I awaited my first appointment: "I'm . . . wondering if I'm crazy to be thinking of seeking out services here . . . I seem to hear a mocking voice in the back of my head saying I'm weak, that I want to be dependent, that I can't solve my own problems . . . ah, the stinky, sweaty armpits of anxiety. . . ." Filled with anxiety over living, faced with barely recognized anger directed toward my parents, the world of work, and women, I wanted someone with whom I could work through my ambivalence. I did not want "help"—I was telling myself I'd be doing all the work—my counselor would just be there. I would not admit until months later that I was getting help.

After three months of individual counsel, I joined a group in which I have been participating ever since. I suspect the lack of men in group therapy indicates our unwillingness to use helpers. The group has been comprised of seven to eight women with only one other man in attendance. I certainly had to rationalize my way into therapy.

The one man who has been part of this group is J. Now, I am a man with a history of being afraid of men, especially from more traditional molds. At first glance, J seemed to fit the traditional role perfectly. Short-haired, conservatively and neatly dressed in comparison to my shaggy locks, beard and duds, J looked like someone I thought I might have difficulties with. Then he opened his mouth and with his country accent, which I immediately contrasted to my well-learned, more urbane tongue, began pouring forth his grief over his impending separation from his wife. I was touched by his ability to grieve and noted to myself that he had been more real in his first night, less self-controlled, than I had been in the weeks before his arrival in the group. And he was the one who I supposed to be so traditional! I have learned a great deal about support and gentleness from J in the months which have passed since we met. He is always there with a kind word for someone who is suffering, and he always lets his support be known. J is a great appreciator, too; often I've felt boosted by his appreciation of my freeness or my ability to say what's on my mind at certain times. He is a most unusual man, a caring, sensitive, emotional person. These are qualities usually eschewed by men, and in J I love them. Occasionally I suspect he has forgotten how to be angry or nasty, and most of the time I just think he is a deep-down good.

My own therapy progresses slowly. I am very interested in my ongoing process and focus on myself very hard while in the group. Still, I have at times fooled myself with intellecutal lies: "Oh, I just take a long time to get to know people," instead of "I am scared to death of *you.*" Realizing slowly how some of this thinking clouds my awareness and experience is helping me to be with my anger, my anxiety, my joy, and to allow myself more expression of these feelings. For a man who wants to be less destructively traditional, being more spontaneous and emotionally expressive is a first step, and one which has continued to support other personal changes.

Consciousness-Raising Groups and Workshops

Changes can take place in a group specifically set aside to deal with difficulties in life that are due to our male identities. During the past several years, I have involved myself in a continuing effort to bring together men interested in exploring new approaches to "brotherhood." I have done this mainly through Virginia Commonwealth University's Awareness Series, a program of personal development in human relations for the university. The one-and-a-half-day weekend workshop I convene is called "On Being a Man: Is Brotherhood Possible?" It is advertised as an "experiential workshop (revolving) around definitions of manhood, how and where we learned the definitions we have, and how to share new perspectives ... generally groups have focused on the male as competitor, aggressor and provider; emotional expression; brotherhood among men; male as partner; male as parent; women's and men's liberation movements, how they affect and don't affect us; father/son relationships; and other topics."

I have just completed the last of these workshops I will experience for, unfortunately, they have been cancelled due to lack of interest shown by men. Ironically, the workshop filled this semester, and I consider it one of the best I have attended. The problem still remains, or so it seems, of getting men to risk a consciousness-raising experience. A similar workshop for women fills to the overflow level twice per semester while the male workshop usually fills once per year. In my experience with gathering men for either weekend or ongoing consciousness-raising experiences, I find strong initial interest which is usually not sustained. There is always something more important happening. Perhaps when issues become more personally important, more men will take action.

Men who are willing at least to look at alternatives to old roles are among those who came to this last workshop. A 12-person group which was similar to other men's groups I have worked with contained all-white and middle-class men mostly early to mid-twenties, a few married, a few openly gay. As in other workshops there was one man who was very invested in his "male role." The rest of the group seemed willing to explore new ways of being, or finding support for, the less-than-traditional ways they already were.

The workshop itself was designed to allow progressively more freedom of movement and choice, from heavy experimentation with self-disclosure to more low-risk activities. Friday night was a get-to-know-you session consisting of introductions in pairs, small groups and finally the large group. We worked with how we got our ideas of what a man is through a one-half-hour developmental fantasy. Finally, we set objectives for the weekend. Saturday morning was structured to help us explore each other and ourselves in the here and now through non-verbal exercises emphasizing contact and cooperation. Saturday afternoon the group split and discussed a number of male issues. The range of subjects was wide, so the risk involved was to come to consensus on an activity. Getting personal feedback on behavior during the weekend has been the most popular activity for this period; sometimes it takes the entire three hours.

The focus is almost always on two areas: how we are relating to each other as men and our emotional expressiveness. The exercises are designed to allow participants the freedom to disclose at whatever level seems to fit the circumstances. I've found that a little structure and freedom from me as leader, plus trying to establish trust from everyone, is enough to encourage high levels of personal disclosure. Many men report being able to talk with other men for the first time about difficult and embarrassing topics such as negative feelings about their bodies, impotence, fear of other men (homophobia) and crying. Through such workshops I do experience new willingness to change, yet they are special situations and somewhat hard to extrapolate to outside situations.

Commune

The most amazing collection of people I know are those I live with. I have lived here for nearly two years and seen our number fluctuate from 23 to 12, seen the male-female ratio loaded heavily male and seen it more even. We are in many ways a transient community, though the dream of a few of us has kept the group together since 1972. The men who live here are an unusual mixture of strong, silent, and crazy; professional, artistic, and blue collar; gay and straight; gourmet chef and gourmand eater; poor and broke; emotional and intellectual; traveler and homebody. We are a "rag-tag bag of city hippy gypsies" and also a group of middle-class gentlemen. We are currently nine men out of sixteen people, much different and preferable to me over the two-to-one majority we used to experience.

In part, the impetus for us to live together has been, from the beginning, a desire to share our lives, to truly become brothers and sisters. We even call ourselves "family." What that means to us is as varied as the people who individually make their home here. Some practices have organically emerged which define us. The one I most surprisingly noticed at first was that it really *is* OK to touch other people here. We do this as an expression of our caring for each other, not as an expression of lust. I have become so accustomed to being hugged by one of my "brothers" or standing with one of them, arm around shoulder, that I forget at times what a shock this may be to others outside the family.

The way we men of the group express affection for each other is a metaphor for our emotional expressiveness in general. Joy seems the easiest for most of us to express. The men in this group, as much as anyone else here, laugh easily and profusely. To watch A and S become excited over a movie they have seen, or a little trinket of some sort, is to see child-like merriment at its best. One of my biggest problems has always been my inability to express, or occasionally even feel, joy or excitement. To be around a number of men for whom this ability comes easily has given me permission to try new behavior.

Another area of emotion I experience difficulty with is grief. Crying has never come easily to me, and even in some of my most grievous times I have not always been in touch with feelings of grief. Since living with this group I have heard men talk about times they cry and have been amazed at the depth of feeling and expression I have seen. In the two years I have lived here, I have twice allowed myself public tears—once out of a very painful loneliness, and once when I was feeling very unimportant to someone else who was very important to me. Twice in two years is more than I have cried in the ten years before.

Sexual pleasure and related feelings men also have traditionally kept quiet about. During my brief marriage I remember never being very expressive in this area. In the past few years I have become gradually more and more noisy when making love. The more expressive my partner, the more I get into noises. I am certainly encouraged in this at home by midnight sounds of sexuality and discussions over breakfast the next morning. As a group we have a real dedication to supporting sexual pleasures, and we value their expression.

The one emotion men and women alike in our group seem to fear somewhat is anger. There are very few times I remember since living here that anyone has really blown up. Most frequently I hear resentments brought up at our weekly meetings and expressed sometime after the event which has caused the resentment. At the times when I have heard someone close to exploding, someone else inevitably asks for an explanation. I believe we are partly reacting to the rough-and tough male behavior anger can elicit. In part, too, many of us are people for whom anger has some fearful past associations. I personally have difficulty believing anger will not damage my relationships. Yet I know this to be untrue, since my feelings know otherwise. So, this is an area I am currently working with for myself.

The men in the group deal with work in very different ways. On one extreme is S, who is an artist, and who occasionally works to pay his bills or take a trip once in awhile. He seems to be a true free spirit with no desire to establish himself in the traditional male rat-race. He won't go to an art school to be spoiled by the competition there. On the other end of the spectrum is G, who is our oldest member and well-established in his career as a school administrator. His work occupies most of his days, many of his evenings, and a fair number of his weekends. He "can't" take a vacation in the summer, or his summer program will not get done. Most of the rest of us are somewhere in-between. I am, with my 40-hour work week, weekend classes and occasional workshops, one of the most career oriented. Most of us are not totally committed to a career and toy with everything from small business enterprise to teaching, to professional dancing, to real estate, or to counseling. Most of us are in our mid-twenties and might be expected to have made a firm career choice. Being in a group helps us be in less of a hurry to climb any traditional ladder, and all of us intend to work in ways that will be personally fulfilling.

The men of the group have long been focusing on our attitudes toward women and women's liberation. Espousing liberal views on women's issues is easy enough, but living our values and encountering our own sexism is the real test of our sincerity. The way the group conducts the business of living together exemplifies the values we individually hold. Women in the group are always heard as equals in the decision-making process; we value and support each person's assertive behavior. Some very powerful women have lived with us, and more than once the opinion of a woman has changed all of our minds. When a woman wants to try on a task men have traditionally performed, we always make a point of saying OK unless the task and the individual are obviously inappropriate. Individual sexism is individually dealt with. I have occasionally felt hurt by comments made by radical lesbian feminists I have lived with and I am not always understanding. I am even resentful at times. Experiencing and expressing these feelings is difficult but very important to me.

In summary, my experience with men is now rich and varied. I really do feel a sense of discovery and excitement through viewing men with new awareness. For years men were obstacles to me; they either laughed at my shy, unaggressive manner or rated me in some way. Very few men in my life showed me gentleness and caring, and I in return offered them little of myself. I lived for years believing that men were devoid of emotions—I never saw beyond the surface toughness. I now feel good about myself as a sometimes shy, bookish, gentle-man with what seem to some outlandish ideas about life. More importantly, I am beginning to experience that emotionally-blocked, mean, aggressive, analytical part of me which has been so threatening as I perceived it in other men. In gently accepting my darker side, I find myself accepting other men; to me, this seems the solution most growth producing for all of us. Men are usually resistant to change, and we cannot be forced to change. The most promising possibility for growth, as I see it, is for men who care about men's lives to go about creating situations in which others can feel acceptance free of the restrictions of male roles. Only in a place of genuine caring can significant changes be made. I believe that we may only grow through mutual togetherness.

Up from Patriarchy: The Male Role in Historical Perspective

DONALD H. BELL

Some writers have argued that male supremacy appears to be a prevalent condition in all societies, and that *patriarchy*, a hierarchical relationship in which men dominate women, has been a fundamental means of dividing power throughout human history.[1] The structure of the *biological family*, the basic unit of man-woman-child, has often been linked with patriarchal patterns. Women in this view have been restricted to caring for the young within the setting of the family, while men have been free to organize production and society.[2] Other writers claim that men share a pattern of bonding with other men, either biologically determined or founded on a sociological basis.[3] Such biological male bonding, or

[1]See, for example, Heidi Hartmann, "Capitalism, Patriarchy, and Job Segregation by Sex," in Martha Blaxall and Barbara Reagan, *Women and the Workplace* (Chicago: University of Chicago Press, 1976), pp. 137–169.

[2]See Shulamith Firestone, *The Dialectic of Sex* (New York: Bantam, 1970); Eli Zaretsky, *Capitalism, the Family, and Personal Life* (New York: Harper & Row, 1976), p. 15.

[3]See, for example, Lionel Tiger, *Men in Groups* (New York: Vintage, 1969); Jean Lipman-Blumen, "Toward a Homosocial Theory of Sex Roles: An Explanation

homosociality, its social variant, supposedly lays at the root of men joining together "to derive satisfaction for their intellectual, physical, political, economic, occupational, social, power, and status needs."[4] Homosociality, in this view, results in the creation of self-sufficient male societies which, by their very nature, tend to exclude women. Still other writers note that patriarchy has been closely linked with the division of labor in society and has historically resulted in job segregation by sex, especially in a capitalist economic environment.[5] Such writings make it clear that male dominance and patriarchy have been important features of our social life. Patriarchical relationships, however, have not always and universally been the same. Such relationships have altered as society has changed and especially as changes have occurred in the productive processes of society. Levels of male dominance and the sharing of work roles between men and women have varied in the past, and present-day trends introduce the possibility of further change.

In this essay we shall look at three eras of Western life which have differed in terms of economic relationships, work situations, and the kinds of behavior required of both men and women. The first is the *preindustrial period,* a time which we might generally identify as comprising the seventeenth and eighteenth centuries. The second is the *industrial age,* encompassing the nineteenth century and roughly the first half of the twentieth. The third period might be called the *late industrial or post-industrial era,* a phase recently entered by several Western nations and which increasingly defines economic and social life in "advanced" societies. Each of these eras has been characterized by specific kinds of work and by specific roles assigned according to sex.

"Work defines who we are," in the succinct phrase of a recent group of feminist authors,[6] and throughout recorded history, male work has been a fundamental determinant of the male role and of the way in which men have thought, behaved and identified themselves in the world. This essay contends that the preindustrial era saw a greater degree of sharing of work and emotional roles by men and women than the industrial era which followed. Work, family life, production and emotional nurturance were typically less segregated by sex in the preindustrial world than in the

of the Sex Segregation of Social Institutions," in Blaxall and Reagan, *Women and the Workplace,* pp. 15–31.

[4]Lipman-Blumen, "Homosocial Theory of Sex Roles," p. 16.

[5]See, for example, Hartmann, "Capitalism, Patriarchy, and Job Segregation."

[6]Rosalyn Baxandall, Linda Gordon, and Susan Reverby, *America's Working Women: A Documentary History—1600 to the Present* (New York: Vintage, 1976), p. xiii.

industrial one; however, power relationships within the family were generally organized along sex-based lines. The rise of factory industry at the end of the eighteenth century and an increasing specialization of work helped to bring about the striking division of labor between men and women which, until recently, was thought to be "natural." Such a clear assignment of roles both inside and outside the home prevailed until about the middle of the twentieth century, at which time a number of changes involved in the coming of "postindustrial" society helped to promote the restructuring of sex roles in which men principally worked outside the home and women within it. Societies entering the most recent stage have seen the beginnings of a pattern of integrated roles in which both men and women share work responsibilities outside the home, and family responsibilities in it. We shall see that the segregation of roles which prevailed during the industrial era was anything but "natural," and that a greater sharing of male and female responsibilities characterized the period both before and after the beginnings of factory industry (though the way in which roles were shared differed greatly in each of these eras).

I. PREINDUSTRIAL SOCIETY

In around the year 1730, an unknown English poet wrote the following verses describing a dinnertime conversation between a master weaver and the members of his household:

Quoth Maister—"Lads, work hard, I pray,
Cloth mun [must] be pearked [readied] next Market day.
"And Tom mun go to-morn [tomorrow] to t'spinners,
"And Will mun seek about for t'swingers [combs]
"And Jack to-morn, by time be rising,
"And go t'sizing house for sizing [dressing with size: a ground for dye]
"And get you web, in warping, done
"That ye may get it into t'loom.
"Joe—go give my horse some corn
"For I design for t'Wolds [Yorkshire district] to-morn;
"So mind and clean my boots and shoon, [shoes]
"For I'll be up it 'morn right soon!
"Mary—there's wool—tak thee and dye it
"It's that 'at ligs [lies] i th'clouted [mended] sheet!

Mistress: "So thou's setting me my wark, [work]
"I think I'd more need mend thy sark, [shirt]
"Prithie, who mun sit at' bobbin wheel?
"And ne'er a cake at top o' the creel! [spinning frame holding bobbins]
"And we to bake, and swing [comb] and blend,
"And milk, and barns [children] to school to send,

"And dumplins for the lads to mak,
"And yeast to seek, and 'syk as that'! ['fetch me that!']
"And washing up, morn, noon and neet, [night]
"And bowls to scald, and milk to fleet, [skim]
"And barns [children] to fetch again at neet! [night]"[7]

Despite its archaic forms of speech and the peculiarities of northern English dialect, the poem has been quoted at length because it provides a striking view of the personal relationships and daily work roles which prevailed before the coming of factory industry. Work in preindustrial society was carried on within the household, whether in urban craft shops or on rural farms. One can imagine the master in this poem seated at the head of the table, the evening meal eaten, the fire burning low. The work day, extending from "five at morn till eight at *neet,*" has been completed, and the master is assigning tasks for the next day to the members of his household—Tom, Will, Jack, Joe, and Mary. We do not know the age or relationship of these household members; however, it is likely that some of them were the master's own children, but probably not more than two or three, since due to a high infant mortality, not many more survived in a typical laboring family. Others would be apprentices, those children taken into the house from other families to receive training in the master's trade and a rudimentary education in reading, writing, and the principles of religion. Whether in urban workshops or on rural farms, the pattern was the same: Children would circulate as apprentices or servants from household to household, living with a master and his family and learning a trade. Scholars have recently found that families in Western Europe and America were typically not structured in an extended manner (that is, with three or more generations living under the same roof), but for the most part resembled the modern two-generation nuclear family (restricted to parents and children). They differed from the modern nuclear family, however, in the fact that they were typically embedded in a large household, numbering often between seven and ten individuals and averaging in representative communities about 4.75 persons apiece.[8]

The household in the poem quoted was engaged in the weaving of cloth, one of the chief manufacturing occupations before the coming of factory industry. The society in which this household lived was basically agricultural, however, and around the cottage lay a small plot of land on which was grown some necessary foodstuffs not purchased in the market, and on which a few head of cattle might be grazed. As the poem indicates,

[7]E. P. Thompson, *The Making of the English Working Class* (New York: Vintage, 1965), p. 272.

[8]Peter Laslett, *Household and Family in Past Time* (Cambridge: Cambridge University Press, 1972), p. 69.

a division of labor between men and women prevailed within the household. The master and his apprentices were responsible for working yarn into cloth to be sold in the market. The mistress, and presumably her daughters and female servants, were responsible for other functions: spinning yarn, preparing meals, milking the cows, making butter and cheese, maintaining the house. In more agrarian settings where household industry was less important, men were assigned the task of ploughing and harvesting; women were engaged in tending the small garden plots in addition to their other tasks.

In the society which we are describing, a mode of social organization prevailed which might in theory be called that of patriarchy. In the sphere of work, men typically assigned and monitored tasks within the family economy, and in the wider social realm the premodern world was basically organized, in the words of historian Peter Laslett, "as an association between [the] heads of such families."[9] Men, and especially literate and property-holding men who headed productive households, collectively made up the nation, and they largely acted to make decisions affecting the lives of others. We should not, however, allow this to obscure a simple fact: While preindustrial society was theoretically organized in a patriarchal fashion, in practice there was much sharing of work, of emotional roles, and of childrearing by men and women. Work and family life were not separate spheres, but continually overlapped; and roles, though sometimes formally segregated along sexual lines, were often shared by members of both sexes.

In practice the work of men and the work of women was often interchangeable. Depending upon geographical location and customary usage, either sex would be found primarily in trades such as the weaving of textiles. The poem is drawn from the north of England and in that location men tended to dominate the trade. In other areas, for example in the Swiss highlands above Zurich, both men and women worked in such cottage industry; while in other zones, cottage industry was primarily women's work. Edith Abott, in her classic study of women's labor, noted that in colonial America, "such manufactures that were carried on . . . were chiefly household industries, and the work was necessarily done mainly by women. Indeed, 'during the colonial period, agriculture was in the hands of men, and manufacturing, for the most part, in the hands of women.' "[10] Although men dominated craft manufacture in urban workshops during the prefactory era, many trades were open to women, and female masters were found belonging to the various guilds which regulated manufacturing in premodern cities.

[9]Peter Laslett, *The World We Have Lost* (New York: Scribner's, 1965), p. 19.

[10]Edith Abott, *Women in Industry* (New York:), p. 11.

Other opportunities, as well, were open to women. Wives shared with their husbands in keeping inns or public houses and at times ran them alone. Some women headed middle-class mercantile houses engaged in international trade and were involved in finance,[11] though they were less numerous than those women engaged in independent craft manufacture. Traditions of patriarchy were more pervasive in purely agricultural zones than in areas of mixed farming or domestic manufacture and in urban artisan shops. Although the division of labor was rather sharply drawn in farming, with the men and boys usually working in the fields while the women worked in the houses and barns, the busy seasons of the year required shared and cooperative labor:

At harvest time, from June to October, every hand was occupied and every back was bent. These were the decisive months for the whole population in our damp northern climate with its one harvest in a season and reliance on one or two standard crops. [12]

In England (from which the example is drawn) both men and women were hired as rural wage labor at these crucial times of the year, with the wages of men generally higher than those of women. In some European zones, however, male and female wage levels seem to have been similar.[13] The premodern world was one of great diversity in which local customs and a myriad of differing social usages prevailed.

If labor during the prefactory era was a collective household enterprise, so too were other functions of life. The rearing of children, for example, was not rigid and took place in the home/workshop setting under the guidance of both men and women. Not much is known about the specific manner in which children were raised; however, most learning was carried out in the home environment as part of mastering a trade and earning a livelihood. The practice of taking apprentices and servants into the craft household meant that beginning at about age seven children moved about between families and that they were exposed to the care and training of a number of adults in addition to their biological parents. In general, men were responsible for inculcating the essentials of a trade to the children in their care, and women for teaching the rudiments of letters

[11]See Elise Boulding, "Familial Constraints on Women's Work Roles," in Blaxall and Reagan, *Women and the Workplace,* p. 106.

[12]Laslett, *The World We Have Lost,* p. 13; also see Ivy Pinchbeck, *Women Workers and the Industrial Revolution, 1750–1850* (London: Frank Cass, 1930, reprinted, 1969), p. 53.

[13]Pinchbeck, *Women Workers,* p. 56; Rudolf Braun, "The Impact of Cottage Industry on an Agricultural Population," in David S. Landes (ed.), *The Rise of Capitalism* (New York: Macmillan, 1966), pp. 53–64.

and religion. The men provided instruction in all vital areas of life, and children, therefore, learned about the life and work by observing both men and women in the daily household setting. In contrast to a later day, men were not removed from child-care functions, and children were constantly exposed to the examples and training provided by adult males.[14] The contemporary poem quoted earlier indicates as much; and although apprenticeship training could be difficult, it often led to lasting bonds of affection. The preindustrial era was a time in which childhood was a very different experience than in our own day. Children, in general, were considered to be little adults and were expected to learn from examples acquired during the experience of daily living.[15] The coming of the industrial age marks a radical shift in the nature of childhood and in the relationship of men, women, and children.

In the prefatory era emotional relationships were played out within the setting of the household. In theory, men were dominant within the family, and religious teachings often supported the "subjection" of the wife to her husband. Yet, in practice, men and women (especially in England and America) seem to have provided each other with emotional support and to have made important household decisions in a joint and mutual manner. In the words of John Demos, a historian who has studied the seventeenth century Plymouth Colony, "This does *not* seem to have been a society characterized by a really pervasive, and operational, norm of male dominance. There is no evidence at all of habitual patterns of deference in the relations between the sexes."[16]

Preindustrial society, in short, was a society of primary and personal relationships. Although marriage was a bond which grew out of economic necessity and which created new households as productive units, such households could and did provide a shared experience of love and affection.[17] Edmund Morgan has found in studying the Puritan family that

---

[14]Boulding, "Familial Constraints on Women's Work Roles," p. 106; Laslett, *The World We Have Lost,* p. 104. In addition, when children in preindustrial society were sent to school (usually before their apprenticeship began), they were often in the care of male schoolmasters. See John Demos, *A Little Commonwealth* (New York: Oxford University Press, 1970), p. 143; Joseph E. Illick, "Child-Rearing in Seventeenth Century England and America," in Lloyd de Mause (ed.), *The History of Childhood* (New York: Harper, 1974), p. 329.

[15]Demos, *A Little Commonwealth,* pp. 116–117, 182.

[16]Ibid., pp. 95, 181.

[17]Edmund Morgan has found in studying the Puritan family that bonds of love played a central role in the relationship between husbands and wives, and indeed a central duty of those beginning a marriage lay in creating such bonds. The Puritan conception of love, however, focused more on the rational rather than the

bonds of love played a central role in the relationships between husbands and wives, and indeed a central duty of those beginning a marriage lay in creating such bonds. Even where conflict arose, it probably arose mainly as a result of the cramped quarters in which people lived and the intense face-to-face relationships which they experienced throughout their lives. In places where preindustrial families have been closely studied, there is little evidence to suggest that strong emotional conflict often erupted within the household environment. People seem to have been carefully taught to manage their anger from the time that they were children, although such anger seems to have been directed more toward other persons in the community. The large volume of property litigation between neighbors in Plymouth Colony seemingly attests to this phenomenon.[18]

In pre–factory society, to quote Peter Laslett, "everyone belonged in a group, a family group. Everyone had his circle of affection: every [personal] relationship could be seen as a love relationship."[19] In theory, male dominance and patriarchy were central aspects of this society. In practice, however, patriarchy was mitigated by a sharing of personal and productive life by men, women, and children. The preindustrial world should not be mistaken for a utopia or a lost paradise. It was a time in which economic survival was procured with great difficulty and in which demographic crisis was a recurring aspect of life. In many ways, however, the world before the coming of factory industry was the scene of a greater social integration of men and women than the industrial world which followed.

II. INDUSTRIAL SOCIETY

The hallmark of industrial society was the factory; and with the rise of the factory, beginning roughly in the mid-eighteenth century, came a decline in the preindustrial household economy and an increase in the division of labor between men and women. In addition, the factory era saw a strengthening of traditional forms of patriarchy and male dominance and consequently the emergence of new modes of male supremacy. The pre-factory household which had united economic production, emotional nurturance and a sharing of relationships between men, women, and children gave way to the industrial family in which role responsibility was carefully divided: Men worked outside the home and played a lesser part

"romantic" aspects of affection. See Edmund Morgan, *The Puritan Family* (Boston, 1956), pp. 12, 18.

[18]See Demos, *A Little Commonwealth,* pp. 48–50.

[19]Laslett, *The World We Have Lost,* p. 5.

in family life, while women continued to work within the household and assumed almost total responsibility for both child care and the family's emotional support. In a sense, the division of labor within the household paralleled the growing division of labor outside the home. From this apportionment of labor energy stems the male role of the industrial era—with its "instrumental" and production-oriented focus, its devaluation of feeling, and its reliance on the emotional support of women combined with a resentful proclamation of male superiority. Such an outline of male identity has prevailed for over two centuries and has often been viewed as belonging to the "natural" order of things. How did it evolve in response to industrial society, and what have been the main features of the male role in the industrial era?

The first stage in the rise of factory industry was one of transition from the pre-industrial household economy which was based on craft manufacture and domestic cottage industry. By the mid-eighteenth century such an economy had come to depend upon capitalist merchants who distributed raw materials (such as wool and yarn) to cottage households, which worked these into finished products. The merchants found that in order to simplify distribution and to increase production, they needed to control the process of manufacture more carefully and to standardize both the labor and the work patterns of domestic workers. Thus, the merchants grouped cottage laborers into central workshops, or factories, first in spinning and later in weaving; and such factories progressively became mechanized in order to increase production.

In this first phase, capitalist factory entrepreneurs seem to have recruited whole families for factory labor. Men continued to head such units, apportioning the work to their wives and children or hiring assistants (often local children) on a subcontract basis.[20] In effect, the household economy had been translated into the factory. Eventually, however, such a transitional phase came to an end as factory managers began to hire independent workers who were free from the bonds of earlier household manufacture and were thus more easily regimented. Men, women, and children were recruited separately, and at the same time previous modes of family relationship underwent change. The labor of women and children became central to certain trades such as textile manufacture, since industrialists sought to benefit from traditions of female and child labor in the domestic industry. Factory industrialization removed work from the home and thus removed the mitigating features of the home environment with its sharing of labor and personal roles. In so

[20]See Neil J. Smelser, *Social Change in the Industrial Revolution* (London: Routledge and Kegan Paul, 1969), Chs. 9–11; also, Michael Anderson, *Family Structure in Nineteenth Century Lancashire* (Cambridge: Cambridge University Press, 1971), pp. 114ff.

doing, it reinforced patterns of male dominance and raised the relative level of patriarchy in society.

Eventually, the proportion of women and children in industry began to decline, and work outside the home increasingly became a male province.[21] How this occurred is the subject of much debate, but we can cite several leading features of this shift to a male-dominated work force and the growing division of economic and emotional roles between men and women. Basically, the process was two-fold: First, women were reduced as a percentage of the industrial labor force by several developments which pushed them out of the factory; second, they were pulled into the home or remained in the household as a result of new conceptions of family and emotional life and the rise of new ideologies justifying the careful separation of male and female roles.

Some trades, such as mining, transport, and metallurgy, had been male preserves since their inception; and as these industries grew in importance with expanding industrial economies, the number of jobs open to men increased. In addition, trades such as textile manufacture became progressively mechanized, and factory managers claimed that the introduction of heavier and more rapid machinery required greater physical strength. Thus, the U.S. census for 1900 stated that "the number of places in which women can profitably be employed in a cotton mill in preference to men or on an equality with them, steadily decreased as the speed of the machinery increases, and as the requirement that one hand shall tend a greater number of machines is extended."[22]

Male workers seem also to have organized themselves in order to resist female participation in the labor market. During the early years of industrialization, male trade unions often called for the elimination of child and female labor and the limitation of the available work to men. In England an alliance of male trade unionists and Victorian social reformers joined together to restrict the labor of women and children on humanitarian grounds, but with the added effect of preserving industrial jobs for men. Trade unions in American industry also acted to restrict female unemployment. Male unionists in the U.S. printing trades resisted the hiring of women and passed resolutions at national conventions, "to oppose any recognition of the employment of females."[23] With the introduction of the

---

[21]Between 1850 and 1890, for example, the percentage of women employed in all American industries declined from 24 to 19 percent, and in cotton manufacture it declined from 64 to 49 percent, while between 1870 and 1900, the percentage of children employed in industry declined from 5 to 3 percent (Abbott, *Women in Industry*, pp. 358–359).

[22]Quoted in Ibid., p. 108.

[23]Ibid., pp. 256–257.

linotype late in the nineteenth century, the unions succeeded through stringent apprentice regulations in effectively preserving the trade for men. Protective factory legislation was also urged by American male trade unionists in an attempt to keep women out of such professions as cigar-making, typography, and shoe manufacture.

It is possible, in addition, that the representation of women in the industrial labor force was reduced owing to the reaction of factory entre-preneurs against the radicalism of female workers. Feminist historians are today rediscovering the outline of factory agitation and organization among women and are presenting a new picture of a long-submerged history. There are indications, for example, that female workers struck repeatedly in early textile mills, and that they provided impressive num-bers of militants and organizers.[24] In the view of some researchers, factory managers seized upon arguments concerning the need to preserve men's work and the family and made use of these reformist claims in reducing the number of potentially radical female operatives that they employed.[25] A view of labor history is now emerging which accords a greater place to the organization and action of women. In time, such a view will play a central role in our understanding of the industrial past.

While the world of work outside the home increasingly became a male preserve, the home itself became a feminine province. Women were pulled from the labor market (or induced not to enter it) by means of a new conception of proper social behavior in the home setting. Women now came to view themselves as essentially responsible for homemaking and child care; therefore, there arose in the mid-nineteenth century a cult of motherhood and a celebration of domesticity.

The view that motherhood and housecare were the proper areas of feminine activity originally arose not among the working class but among the middle classes. Some years ago, the French historian, Phillipe Aries, demonstrated in his classic book *Centuries of Childhood* that beginning in the seventeenth and eighteenth centuries, childhood came to be perceived as a definite period of life, and that children came to be regarded as needing special care not available through the round of adult activity in which the young had previously been raising. This view first took root among the bourgeoisie, and by the late eighteenth and early nineteenth centuries had begun to make its way through the popular classes in society.[26] Mothers were encouraged to breastfeed their infants rather than

[24]See Baxandall et al, *America's Working Women*, esp. pp. 41–68.

[25]Personal communication, Gisela Bok.

[26]Phillipe Aries, *Centuries of Childhood* (New York: Vintage, 1962); Edward Shorter, *The Making of the Modern Family* (New York: Basic Books, 1975), pp. 170ff.

put them out to wet nurses, to worry over the care of their children, and to sacrifice their own interests for those of their offspring. Children became essentially a mother's concern and took a decreasing part in the lives of men who increasingly preoccupied themselves with salary or wage labor. At the same time, the modern nuclear family arose around the bond between mother and child and around a growing conception of the importance of domestic life. Family units increasingly sealed themselves off from previous community activity and, while surrounding themselves with walls of privacy, pursued the goal of a personal life divorced from that of society at large. Women became primarily responsible for child care and for maintaining the emotional and psychological well-being of this enclosed family unit; men concerned themselves with work outside the home and viewed the family as a refuge from the competitive world of industrial society.

The cult of motherhood and of domesticity grew out of the general world-view of Victorianism, a set of beliefs and attitudes which came to permeate industrial society. Victorianism arose as an ideology to reinforce and justify the sexual division of labor and the segregation of roles. The division of society into economic classes and the conflict between them were a new and disturbing feature of the industrial world. Victorianism, in positing a natural divergence of interest and attitude between men and women, sought to mask the conflict of classes and to draw energy away from such class rivalry. In the words of one modern writer, Victorianism

was an effort to retain the . . . goal of domesticity by continuing the belief that society's fundamental social divisions were the "natural" ones of sex, rather than the "pernicious" ones of class.[27]

In practice, Victorian ideology imposed a differing code of behavior on men and women. Men were viewed as creatures of sexual passions and aggressive impulse, and in the words of one contemporary manual of domestic instructions, they were compelled "by that fierce conflict of worldly interests, in which [they] are so deeply occupied, to stifle their best feelings."[28] A series of handbooks and treatises counseled men in becoming "self-made" individuals who were able by hard work to triumph in the deadly jungle of competition which lay outside the home. Family life was viewed as the proper sphere for male sexual relationships with women, and men were enjoined to restrain their impulses and as much as possible to avoid ejaculation, either through immoderate intercourse or by masturbation. In the view of this materialistic culture, male sperm was the

[27]Kathryn Kish Sklar and Catherine Beecher, *A Study in American Domesticity* (New Haven: Yale University Press, 1973), pp. 212–213.

[28]Quoted in Eli Zaretsky, *Capitalism, The Family, and Personal Life,* p. 52.

source of masculine energy and thus had to be harbored carefully. Contemporary medical writers and social moralizers urged a strict regime of self-government and a turning of energies toward work.[29] If the male passions became ungovernable, however, prostitutes were readily available in Victorian society, there being in most cities a large number of "fallen" women, mainly from working class backgrounds, who plied that trade. Prostitution represented the underside of Victorian morality and was part of the price which nineteenth century industrial society paid for the repression of natural impulses and for adherence to a code which arbitrarily assigned spheres of "proper" behavior to men and to women.

While men were expected to dedicate themselves to hard work and moderate behavior, women, at least those who lived by the code, were encouraged to pursue an ideal known as the "true womanhood." Such a model of feminine comportment was presented by means of women's literature and Sunday sermons. It urged a combination of attitudes which could be defined as piety, purity, submissiveness, and domesticity.[30] Women were expected to lead virtuous and religious lives, dedicating themselves to acts of pious missionary zeal if they belonged to the middle class, and to regular church attendance if they were from a working-class background. It was supposed that, conversely from men, women were endowed with a weak sexual drive and had at all times to moderate whatever sexual feelings they possessed. Men, it was thought, would tend to strive for sexual release; but women, being stronger and more pure, were expected, in the words of one contemporary writer, not to allow men "to take liberties incompatible with (female) delicacy." Women were also expected to follow the direction of men and to show "a spirit of obedience and submission, pliability of temper, and humility of mind."[31] Women, in other words, were presented with a set of ideological beliefs which counseled passivity and non-engagement in the world of work outside the home. That this conception of correct behavior was fully adhered to only in a middle-class setting should not obscure the fact that it had a pervasive influence on all parts of industrial society.

Such idealized behavior, and the sexual division of roles and identities, continued to play an important part in industrial society until well into the twentieth century. Indeed, such attitudes have only recently begun to change in a meaningful way, and the source of this change is a

[29]See Ben Barker-Benfield, "The Spermatic Economy: A Nineteenth Century View of Sexuality," in Michael Gordon (ed.), *The American Family in Social-Historical Perspective* (New York: St. Martin's Press, 1973), p. 344.

[30]Barbara Welter, "The Cult of True Womanhood: 1820–1860, "in Gordon, *The American Family,* pp. 225ff.

[31]Ibid., pp. 227, 231.

phenomenon which we shall examine in the concluding portions of this paper.

III. POSTINDUSTRIAL SOCIETY

A major theme of this paper is that alterations in the social and economic environment have historically conditioned sex-role behavior and traditional conceptions of masculine identity and male dominance. Today we are living through another period of change, one which is connected with the transition from an industrial society to one which might be called late industrial or postindustrial.[32] Such a transition raises the possibility of social roles less segregated along sexual lines and which demand a high degree of sharing between men and women. Such a time of transition is not an easy one, but it promises identities which are more flexible and less stringently defined for both men and women alike.

Although the integration of roles emerging in today's society might seemingly hark back to the sharing between men and women which was evident in preindustrial life, the outlines which characterize our world are very different from those which defined the pre–factory environment. History is not a process of linear and progressive change, and our probable future will carry us in directions very different from those followed by previous societies. Let us now look at some of those directions and their sources.

Beginning approximately with the end of World War II, and accelerating thereafter, the Western world, and most especially the United States, entered into a new phase of historical development. Industrial production began to occupy a less central place than consumer-oriented activities, and the industrial sector of economy began to be less dominant than the sector concerned with services.[33] Such a service-oriented economy is perhaps the key defining feature of recent Western society, but

[32]The concepts of *late industrial and post–industrial* society have been assigned a differing range of meanings by their formulators. The point to be made here is, in fact, that many commentators have come to see the current historical phase as qualitatively different from that of "industrial" society. See, for example, Ernest Mandel, *Late Capitalism* (London: NLB, 1975); Daniel Bell, *The Coming of Post-Industrial Society* (New York: Basic Books, 1973).

[33]Thus, in 1947 the goods-producing sector of the U.S. economy accounted for 51 percent of total employment, while the services sector accounted for 49 percent. By 1968 services accounted for 64.1 percent while manufacturing accounted for only 35.9 percent; and a year later, in 1969, services made up 60.4 percent of the Gross National Product, a far greater figure than ever before, and far more than half of U.S. economic output. Projections to 1980 see the service-producing

such a society exhibits other important characteristics as well. Within the service sector, professional and technical occupations become more important, and the training of skilled managers and technicians becomes a central activity. Education takes on a more vital role, and new elites based on educational background emerge to challenge old elites which derive their power from industrial or familial sources. "Post-industrial society," in the words of one leading commentator, "is organized around knowledge . . . and this in turn gives rise to new social relationships and new structures."[34]

The rise of education as a component of social change has caused several important developments. In the first place, over the last several decades, greater numbers of individuals than ever before have attended colleges and universities and have gone on for advanced degrees. Women have comprised a large percentage of such a college-trained population, and in growing numbers they have not been content to occupy traditional roles as housewives and mothers. Since 1960, women have played an increasing part in the job market, and especially in the technical and professional fields which are the central occupations of the modern economy. Out of such training, in turn, has emerged the contemporary women's movement, originally the concern of college-educated and middle-class women who reacted against sex-based roles at variance with their training and aspirations. It should be noted that women have traditionally occupied a large proportion of service-sector jobs, but that the jobs available to educated female personnel are increasingly those which require a level of technical expertise and training. At the same time, discrimination continues to exist against women in the labor force, both in service and professional occupations and in industrial employment.[35] Such discrimination is largely the result of traditional male conceptions of a woman's "proper place" and the ideology of male dominance and

---

sector accounting for 68.4 of total U.S. employment, and the goods producing sector declining to a level of 31.7 percent.

Western Europe, while moving toward a new stage of economic development more slowly than the United States, has essentially followed a similar course. In 1969, for example, 51.0 percent of Britain's GNP was produced in the service sector, while industry accounted for only 45.7 percent (the rest being supplied by agriculture); and Sweden's service economy accounted for 48.9 percent of GNP, while the industrial sector produced 45.2 percent. The figures for countries such as France and Germany show industrial production still outrunning that of services, but they also indicate that the gap is closing between the two sectors, and that a service-based economy is in the offing. (See Bell, *Post-Industrial Society,* pp. 17, 132–135).

[34]Ibid., p. 20.

[35]Ibid., pp. 220ff.

supremacy which characterized the industrial era. A leading task of the present and future is to end such discrimination and to dispel such anachronistic notions. The shift from one state of economic and social development to another is often accompanied by a lag in the rate at which ideas and attitudes change. The continuation of beliefs supporting male dominance (although at present they are eroding) represents just such a historical lag.

Increased education has had an important effect in another way. Such learning, both formally and among contemporary peer groups, has focused upon the dissemination of new cultural values. Men and women have come to be more centrally concerned with personal development and individual fulfillment. Similar attitudes were not altogether alien to industrial society, but the dominant ethos of that society stressed self-sacrifice and achievement measured in terms of wealth and power, rather than attainment of inner development and individual fulfillment. New values which stress personal satisfaction have been labeled as narcissistic and excessively self-centered,[36] and there is little doubt that extreme proclamations of an inalienable right to personal "growth" can be seen in that light. The new stress on individual fulfillment, however, has begun to have a marked effect on everyone's behavior, raising for women the possibility of attaining greater satisfaction through work and for men the opportunity of defining themselves in less "instrumental" and job-oriented ways and, importantly, of increasing their range of "expressive" and nurturant behaviors. Recent research indicates that male attitudes are presently in the process of a marked change and that men have begun to take part in activities and careers that previously would have been thought to be feminine: child care, social work, elementary-school teaching and the sharing of housework within the family setting.[37] The outlines of a new male role are currently emerging, appropriate not to the requirements of an essentially industrial environment, but caused by the shift to new types of social and economic structures. While of increasing importance, the development of such a male identity (and the parallel shift to a greater integration of male and female roles) is still in its inception. Many problems and limitations stemming from earlier forms of social organization

[36]See, for example, Richard Sennett, *The Fall of Public Man* (New York: Basic Books, 1976); Christopher Lasch, *Haven in a Heartless World* (New York: Basic Books, 1977).

[37]See Mirra Komarovsky, *Dilemmas of Masculinity: A Study of College Youth* (New York: W. W. Norton & Co., Inc., 1976); Jessie Bernard, "Historical and Structural Barriers to Occupational Desegregation," in Blaxall and Reagan, *Women and the Workplace*, pp. 92–93; "A Nursery School Has Men to Look Up To," in the *New York Times*, Feb. 28, 1977.

must be overcome if men are to define themselves in new ways, to share with women, and to give up ideas of inherent superiority.

One major question concerning the current shift in male behavior might be called that of ideational and institutional lag. We have seen that beliefs and attitudes often change more slowly than the social and economic circumstances in which they are embedded. Thus, conceptions of male dominance and patriarchy continue to play an important role in contemporary society at a time of change in the sexual division of labor which provided the underpinning for such ideas. Leadership positions in government, industry, and education continue to be dominated by males; and competitive male sports, the rise of which paralleled the spread of Victorian ideology, continue to play an important role in our society.[38] Present-day research has indicated that conceptions of inherent superiority are beginning to change among younger men, but that such change is often accompanied by a certain ambivalence. Men have increasingly begun to express a belief in sexual equality, but such belief is often coupled with adherence to earlier stereotypes of the self-sufficient and unemotional male.

Institutional structures which favor traditional male employment roles have also impeded change. Many employers assume that a man's primary responsibility is to his work and that the home continues to be a place for recuperation from job-induced stress, rather than a place in which men have a responsibility for sharing and for providing emotional support. Such limitations to role change can be overcome by a combination of institutional policies which favor dual male and female careers, shared part-time work for men and women, flexible work hours, egalitarian rules regarding hiring and promotion, and institutional support for family-related circumstances (for example, paid leave for childbirth and child care). Indeed, evidence from institutions which have introduced some of these reforms indicates that, despite the fear of employers, productivity has risen following adoption of policies favoring shared and egalitarian work roles.[39]

Another problem stemming from the adoption of new male roles concerns the degree of stress entailed in such change. It is clear that changes in roles and expectations involve a certain degree of psychological

[38]See Frederic L. Paxon, "The Rise of Sport," in George H. Sage (ed.), *Sport and American Society* (Reading, Mass.: Addison-Wesley, 1974), pp. 80–103; Paul Hoch, *Rip Off the Big Game: The Exploitation of Sports by the Power Elite* (Garden City, N.Y.: Doubleday, 1972).

[39]See, for example, Carol S. Greenwald, "Part-time Workers Can Bring Higher Productivity," *Harvard Business Review,* Sept.-Oct. 1975; "The Family and the Firm," *Wall Street Journal,* Sept. 24, 1974; *New York Times,* April 12, 1977.

strain and tension. Shifting from a perspective which rewarded instrumental male behavior to one which promotes expressive activity creates a degree of conflict and confusion within individuals and a sense of difficulty in fulfilling role expectations. In a recent study, Mirra Komarovsky has analyzed such role strain and has concluded that a high proportion of her young male research subjects exhibited a wide range of confusion about role expectations and that they experienced "difficulties in fulfilling what they conceived to be the normatively expected masculine roles in intellectual, sexual, and emotional relationships with women." In addition, Komarovsky writes that few of her subjects recognized or understood the social origins of their confusion and frustration.[40]

In a time of transition, men are experiencing difficulty in overcoming the traditional model of male identity handed down from industrial society and reinforced by institutions and family patterns of socialization. That men are beginning to overcome the traditional model is a conclusion that can be drawn from an examination of contemporary life. That transcending such a model will entail much conflict and stress is an additional conclusion. Historically, men have possessed power within society, and the development of a new male identity requires yielding some of that power. Those holding power have never relinquished it easily, but in the case of contemporary men the possible benefits are great. In the words of Joseph Pleck, an important writer in the field of men's studies, the evolution of a new male role will allow men

deeper emotional contact with other men and with children, less exclusive channeling of their emotional needs to relationships with women, and less dependance of their self-esteem on work.[41]

Such goals are ultimately worth the difficulties encountered in achieving them.

[40]Komarovsky, *Dilemmas of Masculinity*, pp. 226ff, 248–249.

[41]Joseph H. Pleck, "The Male Sex Role: Definitions, Problems, and Sources of Change," *Journal of Social Issues*, Vol. 32, No. 3, 1976, p. 160.

A Spirit In Me Waits To Be Born

A spirit in me awaits to be born
expectant
watching
listening for the right time.
I wait with the spirit
wondering what is birthing.
Nothing perhaps,
yet I feel a kicking.
The spirit asks permisison
and waits for reply.
We wait together
silent and still
letting the world outside turn to fog.
We wait and contemplate being born.
Nothing else matters.

DAVID STEINBERG
Copyright © 1979 by David Steinberg

Index